Spaces in European Cinema

Edited by
Myrto Konstantarakos

intellect™
EXETER, ENGLAND
PORTLAND, OR, USA

intellect – European Studies Series
General Editor – Keith Cameron

Humour and History	Keith Cameron (ed)
The Nation: Myth or Reality?	Keith Cameron (ed)
Regionalism in Europe	Peter Wagstaff (ed)
Women in European Theatre	Elizabeth Woodrough (ed)
Children and Propaganda	Judith Proud
The New Russia	Michael Pursglove (ed)
English Language in Europe	Reinhard Hartmann (ed)
Food in European Literature	John Wilkins (ed)
Theatre and Europe	Christopher McCullough
European Identity in Cinema	Wendy Everett (ed)
Television in Europe	James A. Coleman & Brigitte Rollet (eds)
Language, Community and the State	Dennis Ager
Women Voice Men	Maya Slater (ed)
National Identity	Keith Cameron (ed)
Policing in Europe	Bill Tupman & Alison Tupman
Regionalism in the European Union	Peter Wagstaff (ed)
Spaces in European Cinema	Myrto Konstantarakos (ed)

First Published in Paperback in 2000 by
Intellect Books, FAE, Earl Richards Road North, Exeter EX2 6AS, UK

First Published in USA in 2000 by
Intellect Books, ISBS, 5804 N.E. Hassalo St, Portland, Oregon 97213-3644, USA

A catalogue record for this book is available from the British Library

ISBN 1-84150-004-6

Cover Photographs:	*La ricotta* – © Archivio Fondo Pier Paolo Pasolini
	Metropolis – © Films Sans Frontières
	Les Enfants du paradis – © Pathé Films

Series Editor:	Keith Cameron
Cover Design:	Bettina Newman
Copy Editor:	Lucy Kind

Printed and bound in Great Britain by The Cromwell Press, Trowbridge, Wiltshire

Contents

Introduction

1. Space

There has been a recent shift from history to geography in social science. New historicists, such as Steve Mullaney, are tending to lean towards geography in their work.[1] There has been an increasing interest in the study of location, of space, in the constrast between landscape and cityscape, the country and the city, the psychological mapping and the mythology (in Roland Barthes' sense of the term) of the city.

This new perspective is also starting to influence literary and cinematic studies. Space is not merely the setting of stories but actually generates the narrative both in prose and films, assuming the status of a character and becoming the fabric of the narrative itself. Cinema may appear to be more successful than other art forms in conveying the dynamics of space but the usual analysis of film does not devote much attention to this. However, space can be seen to contribute to the dynamics of the narrative and can be shown to play an important part in the development of a variety of considerations, both ideological and artistic. Space is not only recorded as a background stage – its very organisation implies a handling of space, revealing the ideology of the time.[2] Moreover, as with maps, cinema acquires a power of control by fixing in place conflicting ideas about the constitution of social space.

2. Europe

Whereas most recent studies on space in film concentrate on North American and British cinema, our aim is to promote an understanding of what makes the specificity of European Cinema.

Film-going is healthy in Europe: there was an increase of almost 10 per cent at the box office in 1997 in France, whereas before there had been a decrease of 2.3 per cent each year. Also, France used to be the European country where most films were made, thanks to State subsidies of around 110 per year. Now Italy, Britain and Spain are catching up. More and more European nations are eager to fight the cultural domination of Hollywood products on their screens. Through financial aids from the European Community for production, the concept of European Cinema is being consolidated and has taken on a new institutional form. This assistance has developed lately for distribution and exhibition through the Media 2 programme, and the International Trade agreements opposing Europe to the USA.

But is there such a thing as European Cinema? Can we talk about European Cinema when so many identities and languages are concerned? And, if we assume there is such a thing, what constitutes its specificity when compared to other types of cinema? What is different about it? Is it the mode of production, distribution and exhibition, its treatment of genre, treatment of gender, its star system and/or its representation of space? This book will attempt to address and explore a number of these issues.

1

3. Definition

What do we mean by space?

Without disregarding the main theorists of space – Gaston Bachelard, Raymond Williams, Noël Burch, Henri Lefebvre and Walter Benjamin – a number of papers in this volume rely in particular on the work of André Gardies, who sets out to establish the value of space in narrative, both in literature and cinema, which he sees as of equal value with the characters. Without distinguishing between film and literature, he considers narrative in its own right. In his attempt to define *l'espace*, he is unsatisfied with the following: 'a three dimensional environment in which objects take their place' ('un milieu à trois dimensions où s'ordonnent les objets', p. 70) because it does not differentiate space, *l'espace*, in relation to place, *le lieu*. In order to do so, Gardies borrows Saussure's distinction between *langue* and *parole* by making *place* 'the textual manifestation of a latent order which is that of space' ('la manifestation textuelle d'un ordre latent qui est celui de l'espace', p. 71) Gardies posits the superiority of space over time arguing for instance that Proust's so-called temporal quest is in fact a spatial one and emphasises the importance of space in narrative. However, this is not the point of view we will adopt. Although our subject is space in European Cinema, space is in fact indissociable from time, as is argued by Mikhaïl Bakhtin in the development of his most effective concept of chronotope.

Bakhtin is one of the most challenging intellectuals of our time. He lived through the difficult circumstances of the Bolshevik Revolution, two World Wars, internal exile and illness, which made the writing and the publishing of his works often difficult and sometimes impossible. He was discovered by the West in the 1960s, first in France thanks mainly to Julia Kristeva and Tzvetan Todorov, and in the 1970s by scholars all around the world. But, if Bakhtin's concepts have been applied to cinema, what does Bakhtin have to say about the mode of expression itself? There is only one sentence in his Dostoevsky essay: 'As far as whirlwind movement is concerned, the most banal contemporary film-movance can outdo Dostoevsky.'[3] His silence is all the more surprising because some of Bakhtin's peers such as Lotman were writing about the new medium whose possibilities were so successfully explored by Russian film-makers. Bakhtin's reticence on the subject of cinema may have been because films were so much controlled and discussed by the Communist Party, of which he did not approve. Or was he suspicious of the medium for the same reasons he disliked drama in that he was critical of performance, believing vocalisation implied monology, as opposed to the symphony of the silent reading of the novel?[4] He had a profound mistrust of loud intonation which monologises discourse and does not give enough space to the other voice within this discourse. One might argue, however, that because of the *recorded* nature of film, cinema is far more a form of writing than a performance.

Although Bakhtin has not actually written on film, the concepts identified by him have been applied to cinema by Gérard Genette and Julia Kristeva, then by Robert Stam, who have concentrated mainly on dialogism and carnival. During the carnival, the marginalised and the oppressed take the centre stage and contrast their vital values with those of the official culture. Bakhtin analyses the subversion of Medieval carnival as portrayed by Rabelais. *Rabelais and His World*, Bakhtin's dissertation, was written in 1940, but only examined in 1947 because of the war; the degree was awarded in 1951 and the book published in 1965.[5] He celebrates the vitality of the world turned upside down, hence the dislocation of space developed in particular in David Berry's study of the *métro* in French cinema in this collection.

While such Bakhtinian notions as 'carnivalisation' or 'dialogism' have been extensively debated, the concept of 'chronotope' has to date not received nearly as much attention. This is evident from the fact that while those other concepts have successfully been applied to texts other than those studied by Bakhtin himself, there appear to be fewer attempts at identifying chronotopes not described by Bakhtin. As 'chronotope' is a term that Bakhtin leaves more open and less defined than his other concepts, it lends itself to further applications and interpretations. 'Chronotope' literally means *time-space* in Greek and indicates the way time and space is represented in narrative. While acknowledging that Emmanuel Kant was right to define 'space and time' as indispensable forms of any cognition, Bakhtin goes on to say he differs from Kant in taking them not as transcendental, but as forms of the most immediate reality. The crucial difference from Kant is that Bakhtin perceives that we live not in an abstract time and an abstract space but in specific 'different time' and 'different space'. Bakhtin wrote 'Forms of Time and of the Chronotope in the Novel' (hereafter FTCN) in 1937-1938, but the essay was not published until 1974, when he added some concluding remarks. 'Epic in the Novel' (1941, then in *The Dialogic Imagination*) is also a fruitful essay for the understanding of this Bakhtinian category. Some very interesting remarks on the chronotope are also to be found when he reads Dante or Rabelais, for he reckons that the former, unlike the latter, did not merge time and space.

Unlike other terms, which he 'invents', this time Bakhtin borrows a term he had heard at a biology lecture given by Uxtomsky in 1925 and had found in Einstein's mathematical theory of relativity because it expresses the inseparability of space with time.[6] Bakhtin defines chronotope as 'the intrinsic connectedness of temporal and spatial relationships that are artistically expressed in literature,' (FTCN, p. 84) and later in the essay. 'The chronotope is the place where the knots of narrative are tied and untied.' (FTCN, p. 250).[7] Time and space are the major organising factors of fiction and chronotope constitutes a spatio-temporal matrix shaping any narrative text. Bakhtin considers the chronotope as a characteristic of the novel, but it can be useful in our appreciation of film, as this *is* by its very essence time and space. This concept permeates the rationale of this whole collection (more explicitly so in the pieces on Wim Wenders, Alain Tanner and Pier Paolo Pasolini) for space cannot be separated from time.

4. Space in European Cinema

Is there therefore a chronotope specific to European cinema?

Having established the topicality of space and its representation both in literature and cinema, can we then go on to associate specific representations to specific cultures, to specific national cinemas? Is there a depiction of space that is particular to American, Indian, African or Australian cinema? If there is, what can one then say of the influence of American cinema in this respect on that of Europe, for example on the projection of the town in Spanish film noir or of the Paris métro? This collective volume aims to open the debate. What the following contributions seem to suggest is that European Cinema is articulated around spatial oppositions – that of centre and periphery in the cases of Alain Tanner and Pier Paolo Pasolini; of gendered interior and exterior for Léos Carax, Agnès Varda and the Turkish cinema of Germany; East and West in Russian Cinema and in the representation of Berlin; and town and country in Finnish film. While the vertical contrasts with the horizontal in the Paris métro, the opposition of public and private is identified in British documentary and movement/immobility in the work of Pasolini and Varda. The recurrent theme is that of centrality and marginality and, more precisely, of exclusion and inclusion - a *leitmotif* one does not find in the film making of other cultures with quite the same obsession.

Spaces in European Cinema looks at the representation of the city versus the countryside; private and public places; movement and means of transport; gendered, racial and social mappings of the city, both in natural surroundings and in studio sets in the cinema of France, Italy, Spain, Germany, Switzerland, Russia and Great Britain. There is no imposed time span: for most countries, films analysed will range from the 1920s to the 1990s. The majority are feature films, but newsreels are also considered. We have not edited the book on the basis of nations but on the basis of a variety of perspectives and insights into the subject. A wide mix of national representation has only been considered with this in mind, and if articles based on work originating in some nations that have clearly made a very important contribution to European Cinema are not present here, there should be no interpretation placed on this beyond the overall aim of the book as stated.

5. Individual Chapters

Paris occupies a central position not only in French but in European cinema as a whole. Susan Hayward looks at the real and the imagined Paris, portrayed as a female body. A body mainly identified by its lower bodily functions in the case of the Paris métro studied by David Berry. The anal, the sexual - not dissimilar to the sewage system of *Les Misérables* – evokes other non-European dream cities, the New York of Luc Besson's *Subway* for instance. Also via *Subway*, Keith Reader proposes a re-reading of the role of the set-designer Alexandre Trauner as part-auteur of his, and others', remarkable evocation of the *métro*. As an imagined city from abroad also, as shown by Graham Roberts, Paris represents a gendered West in Eastern cinema. Yuri Mamin's *A Window to Paris* contrasts the closure and confinement of the East with the spaciousness, openness and freedom of the West. Paris' centrality in Europe permates Benjamin's view of Berlin, which is said to have heavily influenced Wim Wenders' films on this city: only through Paris did Berlin reveal its true nature. However Martin Jesinghausen argues that Wenders is more closely linked to Doeblin than to Benjamin.

Trauner's sets recreate the *zone* outside the city's frontiers. Raynalle Udris looks at marginal spaces in French cinema, articulated around a gendered inside/outside opposition in Agnès Varda's *Sans toit ni loi* and Léos Carax' *Les Amants du Pont-Neuf*. Carol Diethe argues that the same gendered axis structures Expressionist cinema, where the fear of the outside is tantamount to that of 'loose women'. Inside is also the space traditionally assigned to migrants, and in particular to Turkish women, in German cinema, both by German and Turkish film-makers. However Deniz Göktürk astutely takes account of a reversal and subversion of the voyeurist ethnographic gaze in the last decade: these films have been shifting from 'subnational' to 'transnational' as borders (particularly visible in cities like Berlin), identity and difference are no longer so firmly fixed. It is also the contrasts of the inside and outside of the city, the periphery and the margins that Lieve Spaas sees as the determinant factor in Alain Tanner's representation of space, as I do in that of Pier Paolo Pasolini. Jukka Sihvonen makes some very similar comments about the in-between spaces in Finnish cinema, what he calls 'connectors' that link the country to the city, i.e. rivers, rapids, lakes, seas, forests, roads, streets and railways. In a Romantic and Rousseauist vision – not far from Pasolini's own – the countryside is tantamount to childhood and the absence of language, hence rural images, which in turn are opposed to the urban culture of adulthood. The recurrent movements from forest to village have in this context to be interpreted as itineraries, rites of passage, between childhood and adulthood.

Leonardo Ciacci's piece witnesses the creation of the 'Rome of Mussolini' through newsreels where the *Duce* is presented as being in control and at the very centre of a clean and organised capital city. Only from there can the new periphery develop. The film-makers looked at in the Italian section choose to challenge this very representation of the periphery. Italian neorealism gave to the representation of the city a place it had not had for a long time and Pierre Sorlin showed how in films in the 1960s the city begins to be seen in a negative light.[8] Antonioni and Pasolini put the representation of urban space firmly amongst their prime concerns by setting its narratives in locations of urban liminality and dereliction. However, Antonioni's periphery is strangely geometrical, whereas Pasolini is still identified with shanty towns and deprived locations at the outskirts of cities. David Forgacs takes the theories of Lotman, Kazanskij and Burch further in order to re-assess Antonioni's use of space, in which the role of sexuality and the body of the woman has been hitherto neglected. Alberto Mira illustrates that Spanish attempts at film noir, though strongly influenced by neorealism, were rendered void by the impossibility of representing corruption and a police force that was anything less that most effective during Franco's regime. It is therefore only in the 1980s and 1990s that this genre could develop new visions of the city in Spain with some highly interesting results.

This review of European cinema looks at truly European film-makers, who have worked in other European countries. These include Pasolini and Antonioni in England; Tanner in Ireland, France and Spain; Wenders in Portugal and Trauner, who was born in Budapest and worked in France then in England during the war. They may have filmed other continents, like Tanner and Pasolini did in India and Africa (or even in America, like Wenders), but Pierre Sorlin showed how the representation of space, and in particular towns, in European film 'contributes to estranging European movies from Hollywood' (1991, p. 112). There is a specificity to the European representation of space, which clearly characterises it and makes it unique, even in such American genres as the *film noir*.

Like urban planning, film acquires the power to change and re-map space. Inspired by Benjamin, Michael Sheringham compares film to maps in as much as 'it reproduces diagrams that fix in place conflicting ideas about the construction of social space'.[9] The reflection, real or artificial, of space in film is highly ideological. It is not by chance that the majority of contributions are centred on cities, urban space, but also political space – from the Greek *polis*. The production of urban space is a conflictual operation, whether real or represented: it is the locus where conflicts and power-struggles are played out. As Gustave-Nicolas Fischer argues, by challenging it one challenges the power structure.[10] We have here a few examples of spatial challenges to class, gender and ethnic exclusion, which occur often by representing forbidden movements across frontiers.

By means of conclusion, is space just the latest fashionable frame of reference in the academic world, just as gender or race may have been just a few years ago? Or is it what founds the film's identity? The following essays seem to suggest the latter.

Notes

1 Mullaney, S., *The Place of the Stage: Licence, Play, and Power in Renaissance England*, Chicago, University of Chicago Press, 1988.

2 Gardies, A., *L'Espace au cinéma*, Paris, Meridiens Klincksieck, 1993, p. 161.

3 Bakhtin, M., *Problems of Dostoevsky's Poetics*, Emerson, C. (ed. & trans.), Manchester, Manchester University Press, 1984, p. 15. Subsequent page numbers for this essay will be given in the text and the title of the essay will be abbreviated to PDP. 'Film-movance' does not seem to exist in English, but it is the one used in the translation: what mostly impressed Bakhtin in film was movement, revolution in the etymological sense (from *volvere*, to turn).

4 Let me give a few quotations to make Bakhtin's position clearer: 'Pure drama strives toward a unitary language, one that is individualised merely through dramatic personae who speak it.' ('Discourse in the novel', in *The Dialogic Imagination*, hereafter DN, p. 405) 'The internal dialogism of authentic prose discourse, which grows organically out of a stratified and heteroglot language, cannot fundamentally be dramatised or dramatically resolved.' (DN, p. 326) 'Drama is by its very nature alien to genuine polyphony.' (PDP, p. 34) Although it could be argued that drama, by its very nature written in dialogue, presents the spectator with more than one voice, Bakhtin maintains that: 'Dramatic dialogue or a dramaticised dialogue [...] is not a clash of two ultimate semantic authorities, but rather an objectified (plotted) clash of two represented positions, subordinated wholly to the higher, ultimate authority of the author. The monologic context, under these circumstances, is neither broken nor weakened.' (PDP, p. 188) '[T]he very kind of development quasi-direct discourse has undergone is bound up with the transposition of the larger prose genres into a silent register, i.e., for silent reading. Only this "silencing" of prose could have made possible the multi-leveledness and voice-defying complexity of intonational structures that are so characteristic for modern literature.' (Bakhtin, M. & Voloshinov, V., *Marxism and Philosophy of the Language*, translation by L. Matejka and I.R. Titunik, Cambridge, Mass. – London, Harvard University Press, 1973, hereafter MLP, p. 156) '[Double-voiced] discourse is difficult to speak [...] aloud, for loud and living intonation excessively monologises discourse and cannot do justice to the other person's voice in it.' (PDP, p. 198)

5 Bakhtin, M., *Rabelais and His World*, translation by Helene Iswolsky Indiana, Indiana University Press, 1984.

6

6   See Dentith: Bakhtin 'is profuse in coining new terms, but "chronotope" is actually not one of his coinages.' (p. 52) For Michael Holquist, chronotope 'is a useful term not only because it brings together time, space, and value, but because it insists on their simultaneity and inseparability.' (*Dialogism: Bakhtin and his World*, London – New York, Routledge, 1990, p. 155)

7   'Thus the chronotope, functioning as the primary means for materialising time in space, emerges as a center for concretising representation, as a force giving body to the entire novel. All the novel's abstract elements – philosophical and social generalisations, ideas, analyses of cause and effect – gravitate toward the chronotope and through it take flesh and blood, permitting the imaging power of art to do its work. Such is the representational significance of the chronotope.' (FTCN, p. 250)

8   Sorlin, P., *European Societies European Cinemas*, London – New York, Routledge, 1991.

9   Sheringham, M., *Parisian Fields*, London, Reaktion, 1996, p. 73.

10 Fischer, G.N., *La Psychanalyse de l'espace*, Paris, PUF, 1981, p. 57.

Underground Cinema:
French Visions of the Metro

David Berry

Beneath the surface of the Paris city-scape; way below its architectural splendours, glittering new shopping malls, high-rise apartments; the monuments to culture, glass pyramids, triumphal arches and *très grands bâtiments* to the new millenium; under the riverside motorways and the *grands boulevards* radiating in all directions; deep in the belly of the monstrous, tentacular metropolis – 'cette ruche bourdonnant' ('this humming bee-hive'), as Balzac calls it in *Le père Goriot* – lurks a vast network of subterranean tunnels, corridors and passage-ways. This is the Métro, aka internationally the underground, the subway, the tube, the U-bahn. The métro has featured in a multiplicity of French films, from *Ali au Pays des Mirages* (Rachedi,1979) and *Les Amants du Pont-Neuf* (Carax,1991), via *Masculin Féminin* (Godard,1966) and *Peur sur la Ville* (Verneuil,1974), to *Le Voyou* (Lelouch,1970) and *Zazie dans le Métro* (Malle,1960); and from *Métropolitain* (Cam,1938) to *Louise (Take two)* (Siegfried, 1998). A list from the audiovisual department of the métro gives some 65 films but contains some notable omissions: *Porte des Lilas* (Clair,1957), *Marche à l'Ombre* (Blanc,1984) and *Violette Nozière* (Chabrol,1978). And of course, in this discussion, we are concerned mainly with the underground section of the métro, not with what is known as the 'métro aérien', the overground section, which even Zazie herself makes quite clear is not the real métro.

In the métro we discover the amalgamation of two topographical inventions, the collision of two disturbing phenomenological creations: the tunnel and the maze. The maze is normally a complex network of pathways above the surface and often open to the skies, like the maze at Hampton Court. Enclosed and enveloped by the tunnel and buried underground, the maze is transformed into the labyrinth, a topos of mental confusion, oneiric terror and claustrophobia. The métro thus becomes the modern manifestation of the legendary labyrinth. What latterday Minotaurs prowl in its passageways, what Thesean heroes brave its dangers, what modern Ariadnes lead their bewildered cavaliers through its complexities? The fantastical nature of the métro is visibly heralded by the strange, organic convolutions of its art nouveau entrances by Hector Guimard, a few of which still survive. In this respect, and in a wider critical context, the métro, with its intestinal and visceral characteristics, can be seen as a modern metaphor for what M.M. Bakhtin, in his study of Rabelais, put forward in his interpretations of the images of the grotesque human body and their relationship, in folk culture, to the underworld: 'The mighty thrust downward into the bowels of the earth, into the depths of the human body (...) animates all his images (...). Rabelais' world in its entirety (...) is directed towards the underworld, both earthly and bodily'.[1] Some of the films discussed here are not without certain Bakhtinian associations, which help to throw light on their significance in a wider tradition of sexual and mythological imagery, together with their impact, at certain moments, upon the collective unconscious of the spectators. On the one hand, the métro, as a dark subterranean space, suggests associations of entombment, encapsulation, the horrors of sewers and catacombs or speleological engulfment, evoking thoughts of Poe's *The Premature Burial* and recalling Hugo's expressive exploitation of multiple metaphors involving 'égouts', 'labyrinthes' and 'dédales'.[2] On the other hand, paradoxically, this tomb can become a womb; it can then represent a place of safety and protection, as during the Second World War, when it functioned as a vast air-raid shelter; it becomes a refuge and a means to freedom, an area where pursuers can be thrown off the scent. And, in this respect, it is naturally connected with speed and dynamic movement, with rapidly moving trains and doors that frequently close too fast, as with the London Underground in the film, *Sliding Doors* (Howitt,1997).

With regard to this topic, two films immediately spring to mind – Malle's *Zazie dans le Métro* (1960) and Truffaut's *Le Dernier Métro* (1980). The eponymous references would seem to promise a good source of material but we would be disappointed. In *Zazie dans le Métro* the allusion is ironic: the young heroine's ambition, at the beginning of the film, to ride in the métro is thwarted; there is a strike, the métro is closed,[3] and, peering through the shuttered gates, she is forced to remain not in it but frustratingly out of it, almost to the very end, when we have a brief glimpse of her on an overground section as she returns to the railway station. *Le Dernier Métro* contains a few brief visual and verbal references. The title is explained in the commentary to the documentary-style introduction: 'En zone occupée le couvrefeu vide les rues après onze heures du soir et pour les Parisiens il est terriblement important de ne pas rater le dernier métro' ('Because of the curfew, streets in Paris are deserted after 11pm. No-one must miss the last métro'); and we see documentary footage of people hurrying through white-tiled corridors. Subsequently, the last métro, meaning the last train, plays a temporal role, indicating the passing of another day and marking divisions in time, the dividing line between freedom and imprisonment, between diurnal activity and nocturnal isolation. After the last métro, when everbody has gone home, Catherine Deneuve can visit her husband in his underground hide-out in the cellars of the theatre. At one point a shot of Deneuve spreading her fur coat on the bed is immediately followed by one of the métro rushing by, signalling the end of another day's drama.[4] In a way the references promised by the title are as superficial and anecdotal as the rest of the film, which has been variously described as 'une oeuvre sans mystère', in which 'the depiction of the (...) Occupation (...) is entirely personal and from which history has apparently been evacuated'.[5]

Let us begin with a brief look at the visual impact of the tunnel. In Renoir's *La Bête Humaine* (1938), there are several powerful images of tunnels. At the very beginning of the film, we plunge headlong and violently into a tunnel, a dark narrow space is penetrated with mechanical brutality and the symbolic presence of the 'human beast' is immediately established. The image suggests an impression of sexual invasion, even of rape. Later, the tunnel is the place in which a murder on a train is committed, hidden by darkness and noise. The tunnel becomes, therefore, a setting in which violent drama is often enacted. As we shall see, such dramatic action frequently occurs in the tunnels and corridors of the métro, as, for example, in *Les Amants du Pont-Neuf* (1991). Further interesting examples of the cinematic exploitation of the métro can be found in the following selection of films.

Le Samouraï (1967) by Jean-Pierre Melville stars Alain Delon as a fastidious hitman on a job that goes seriously wrong (Melville has been highly influential on the work of such contemporary action directors as John Woo and Walter Hill, who borrowed this plot for *The Driver* and whose recent *Last Man Standing* was a reworking of Akira Kurosawa's *The Seven Samurai*). This stylish existential gangster film features a brilliant chase sequence in the métro, filmed by cameraman, Henri Decae.[6] Alain Delon, at the height of his career, is perfectly cast as the gaunt and oppressed hired killer stalking the mean streets and seedy hotels of Paris, on the run from both the police and other criminals. His character, self-contained, ascetic, single-minded and ruthless looks forward to other portraits of the contract killer as in Zinneman's *The Day of the Jackal* and Besson's *Léon*. In spite of the fact that very little happens in the film and that there is almost an absence of plot, there is nonetheless a powerful atmosphere of tension, betrayal and fatality. The epigraph at the beginning of the film establishes the tone: 'Il n'y a pas de plus profonde solitude que celle du samouraï, si ce n'est celle d'un tigre dans le jungle peut-être' [Le Bushido – Le Livre des Samouraï]; ('There is no greater solitude than the samourai's, unless it perhaps be that of the tiger in the jungle'). Like the elite, dedicated ancient Japanese warrior, this modern metropolitan professional killer, the tigerish Jef Costello, is cold, calculating, meticulous and normally in control. 'Je ne perds jamais, jamais vraiment', he says at one point ('I never lose, not ever'). He lives in a bare, darkened room with a caged finch, from whose twittering and general behaviour he is able to discern if his room has been visited by intruders, such as police agents who plant a bugging device, which Jef, thanks to the bird, discovers. This ingenious ornithological warning device reveals the hitman's clever mind and links up with the devious way he prepares his alibi, a dual arrangement with both his mendacious girlfriend and with the gangland card players. In this respect the importance of time is essential. Various images in the film underline the importance of the chronology and the synchronisation of events: the time and the day are indicated visually at various critical points, and at another moment there is a close-up of the dial of the hitman's watch, accentuating the role of his carefully timed programme. The nature of Jef's alibi is discussed in detail by the gangsters who have hired him and who have admired his qualities of a lone wolf: 'Il a manigancé son alibi d'une façon fantastique; il est en deux temps, en deux parties distinctes' ('he set himself up a terrific alibi, it's in two parts, each one entirely separate'); and they go on to describe how he operates alone: 'il est suprêmement fort, c'est bien pour ça que nous sommes adressés à lui pour tuer Martey sans laisser aucun indice, aucune trace, c'est un loup solitaire' ('he is supremely strong; that's why we hired him, to kill Martey without leaving any trace, he's a lone wolf'). However, since his interview with the police, the gangsters believe he has become the main suspect and is now a danger to them. Thus, they have tried to kill him but have only managed to wound him, so that now he has become 'un loup blessé et maintenant il a laissé les traces' ('a wounded wolf who now is leaving tracks').

Within the framework of this relatively actionless film, dependent less on exciting events than on the creation of brooding atmosphere and on the lovingly detailed presentation of the haunted, anti-heroic star, portrayed here as a fascinating tarnished idol, the two métro sequences become highly significant and in a way provide the film with its raison d'être. The first sequence takes place about halfway through the film (45–49 mins), when Jef uses the métro to throw the police off his trail and to keep his appointment, far from the centre of the city, with the criminal who is to pay him for his contract. He travels on the Vincennes-Champs Elysées line, changes direction at Palais Royal, emerges at the Porte d'Ivry and crosses over the street to the main railway line, marked Orléans, where he is to keep his fateful rendez-vous with his would-be assassin. His utilisation of the métro network as a tool of his trade once again shows his devious cast of mind. The métro becomes a vital escape route for confusing his enemies and throwing them off his tracks. It becomes a visual symbol of his mind, of his complex psychological processes, distinguished by elaborate complications and intentionally disorientating arrangements, just like the construction of his alibi. The métro becomes a reflection of his psyche. His mental methods are not straightforward but tortuous; his physical journeys are not direct but circuitous. With this we can also compare his use of stolen cars, when he twice stares with cold concentration through the windscreen whilst searching digitally through his vast selection of car-keys; and his frequent visits to the provider of new number plates, false registration papers and illegal revolvers. His essential personality is deep, dark and introverted; his whole life is dedicated to anonymity, deception and evasion.

The second métro sequence takes place almost at the end of the film and is incorporated into the dramatic climax. All the elements of the first sequence are reinforced and developed in this much more lengthy section, lasting about eight minutes. The police chief himself recognises the killer's knowledge of the métro. At the start of the chase he announces 'Il connaît le métro comme sa poche' ('He knows the métro like the back of his hand'). Having slipped through the fingers of both the police and the gangsters, Jef is once again seen at home in the twisting corridors of this subterranean and twilight space, a symbol of 'la pègre', the criminal's underworld. His essential elusiveness and shadowiness are thus cinematographically contextualised. His environment at this point in the film consecrates his being. He is in fact, through another twist in the plot, heading towards the target of his final contract and, of course, in this existential doom-laden film, an appointment with destiny and death. The suspense is developed by the intercutting between the métro and the police chief's office where we see an illuminated map of the métro, showing the progress of the disguised police pursuers as they track their quarry. He gets on at Télégraph, travels on the Lilas-Châtelet line in the Châtelet direction, gets off at Jourdain, becomes suspicious, goes through the barrier and doubles back in the Lilas direction to Place des Fêtes, changes lines and travels to Châtelet where he leaps over the barrier of the moving walkway and escapes into the street, eventually shaking off his pursuers and outwitting the police, in spite of all the blocks which they have set up at other stations – Botzaris, Pré Saint Gervais, Place des Fêtes. The labyrinthine structure of the métro is exploited to overcome the forces of order. All in vain, however. In the final showdown in the nightclub, he is shot by the police whilst drawing a gun on his final intended victim, the woman who has both saved and betrayed him. Ironically, we discover that he merely meant to frighten her and had earlier removed the bullets from the chamber of the gun. We are left looking into six miniature tunnels which are not without subliminal reminiscence of the tunnels of the métro but here are emblematic of emptiness and annihilation. In this film the deep-seated convolutions of the hero's mental existence find their cinematic paradigm in the Paris underground.

In 1979 the métro, or more specifically its RER extension, features as the setting for the prologue of Bertrand Blier's bleak, black comedy, *Buffet Froid*. The station La Défense becomes part of the nightmare scenario in which one of the first retorts is 'Mais puisque je vous dis que c'est un cauchemar' ('But since I tell you it's a nightmare'). It is all very reminiscent of Beckett, Ionesco and the theatre of the absurd.[7] The metaphor of the nightmare reflects the discomforting atmosphere of the film, full of narrative ellipses and disconcerting illogicalities. Blier's intention, as he has made clear in various interviews, is to disorientate and unsettle the spectator, forcing him to move out of his conventional rut: 'Ce qui m'amuse, c'est de piéger le spectateur, de l'amener sur des fausses pistes, dans des labyrinthes.'('What amuses me is to trick the spectator, to send him along false tracks, into labyrinths').[8] This journey into a mental labyrinth begins appropriately in the métro at La Défense. This setting, a triumph of modernism, ultra hygenic and brilliantly lit, is curiously devoid of people, a vast dehumanised space of neon and concrete. Within minutes of the film's opening, an anonymous accountant, having been last seen boarding a train, is, in the next shot, mysteriously stabbed to death in one of the dark corridors. Was the killer Gérard Depardieu or not? The station La Défense, where, as Russell S.King says, 'there is no *defence* for innocent victims',[9] thus provides a fitting introduction to Blier's vision of dystopia and an immediate visual metaphor for the film's themes of alienation and violence.

Diva, directed by Jean-Jacques Beineix in 1981, is a post-modern, neo-nouvelle vague exercise in style. It represents the apotheosis of the visual, a cinema of image and surface meant to fascinate the eye rather than stimulate the brain, a brilliant example of what has been called the 'cinéma publicitaire' and the 'cinéma du look'.[10] It is filled with material objects and concerns from advertising and the media – designer labels, fashion trends, interior decor, smart cars, tape-recordings, innovations in lighting, a whole series of settings which depict what the hero describes as the 'désastre de luxe', from his own weird and opulently distressed apartment to the extravagant converted loft of his subsequent accomplice, who is obsessed by waves and water and has a second home in a reconditioned lighthouse. The film is also a farrago of cinematographic influences, notably from film noir and gangster movies, and intertextual references to several Hollywood iconographic stereotypes, the most obvious being the allusion to Marilyn Monroe as she walks over the ventilation shaft in *The Seven Year Itch*. However, in spite of the trendy, glossy visual appearance of the film, the scenario deals with various deeper cultural issues connected with art, particularly the reproduction and conservation of the operatic voice. The voice of the black diva, Cynthia Hawkins, will not last forever, yet, much to her manager's chagrin, she refuses to record her performances and he urges her to commit herself to a recording, thus rescuing her sublime talent from death. However, the plot has earlier revealed that her voice has already been recorded clandestinely by a young postman, himself the innocent recipient of a similarly inflammatory tape containing the confession of a murdered prostitute implicating a police chief as the leader of a ring of white slave traffickers. His own recording is also the target for two Taiwanese record pirates. The two tapes thus provide a striking contrast between the divine voice of the singer with the sordid earthly revelations of the prostitute, the orphic with the underworld. The stolen voice of the goddess is a treasure from the gods for which the hero is prepared to run wild risks and undergo frightening ordeals. His megalomania has pushed him to extremes: at one point he gets a black prostitute to put on a dress which he has also stolen from Cynthia Hawkins in an attempt to make love vicariously to his diva. The prostitute thinks he is a bit crazy whilst he believes he is consummating his passion for a myth. It has been said that to cast the hero in the role of a postman-courier is ironic, given that the film is at the outer limits of communicative cinema and is devoid of clear social messages.[11] This is not entirely true: his role is symbolic rather than ironic and his function as a conveyor of aesthetic messages comes over quite clearly at the end of the film when he is finally united with the singer of such rapturous songs. We know his name is Jules, given to him by a traditionalist father, and thus associated with love and the romantic past. Art has allowed him to undergo a transcendental experience and his secret recording of the diva's performance, which she sees as both an act of theft and of rape (vol/viol), is justified by his conviction that life-enhancing artistic moments must be perpetuated. For him art is shown as a means of creative and ecstatic experience. On the other hand, pirate recordings are only concerned with exploiting the commercial value of art. The title of the film itself points to the divine nature of art and, if reversed, curiously gives us 'Avid', synonymously emphasising the greed of the art pirates.

The métro sequence lies almost at the centre of the film and lasts about four minutes.[12] It can be seen to fulfil three functions: it is a further episode in the exploration of metropolitan space and reinforces the element of claustration in a film that plays upon the contrast between open and closed spaces, a decor of lift shafts and underground parking lots juxtaposed with spacious lofts, empty stages and wide open vistas. Secondly, it contributes to the dramatic suspense and to the dynamic and frequently humorous action; and thirdly it provides a symbolic, mythological dimension as this latterday Orpheus descends briefly into the underworld, to the accompaniment of other-worldy tinkling bells. A chase sequence, with the hero on his motor-bike, takes us through Paris transmogrified into a glittering 'ville de lumières', intensified by rain-damp surfaces, and then propels us into the métro. This underground space is invaded by an alien presence, since Jules is still on his bike, and is reminiscent of Peter Collinson's *The Italian Job* (1969) where Mini cars drive through shopping arcades and over the roof tops of factories in Turin, the penetration of the usual by the unusual. His identity as an alien has already been underlined whimsically by another character who says that his crash helmet makes him look like an alien from outer space, an image of him which has been presented at the very start of the film. The pursuit takes us down the usual lavatorial white-tiled corridors, adorned with advertising posters, down stairways, escalators and moving walkways. The hero drives his bike on to the train. There is a moment of comedy. A pursuing policeman, who has jumped on to the back of the train and is anxious to be let in, brandishes his identity card at a passenger through the window of the emergency door only to see that the passenger, an ex-service man, waves his own identity card back at him. The hero emerges significantly at the station 'Opéra', when the mystical music stops. The sequence can be seen to fuse the two main strands of the story, the criminal and the artistic, with the figure of the policeman and the topos of the Opéra. In a way the métro, with its maze of corridors, becomes a metonymic structure for the convolutions of the plot, which itself, once the rite of passage through the underworld has taken place, begins to resolve and unravel itself. The métro once again becomes a paradigm, this time of the film's convoluted narrative structure,[13] yet also providing a ludic space where *Diva*'s humorous, puzzling elements can be momentarily played out.

Luc Besson's *Subway* (1985) takes place almost entirely in the métro, filmed partly on location, partly in sets designed by Alexandre Trauner.[14] As Besson has indicated in an interview with *Film Français*, the germinating nucleus of the film was his fixation with the métro, an urban space symbolic of the city as a whole and a powerfully evocative setting which took hold of his imagination.[15] His preoccupation with this setting, at once hostile, alienating yet compelling, eventually spawned the diegetic treatment and also produced the stylised visualisation of what for him was its special atmosphere, that of a rather clinical and timeless world. In *Subway* the métro, in Trauner's constructions of latterday poetic realism, and in keeping with Besson's expressed intentions, becomes a sort of underground space-station, with the emphasis on colour and form rather than on graphic realism and thus prefiguring some of the images of space-craft interiors which appear in *The Fifth Element* (1997). The film opens with a maniac chase sequence at the end of which the hero, Fred, played by Christophe Lambert, with yellow blond hair and in a dinner suit, sends his car crashing down an entrance to the métro, from which he will never emerge. The métro, which during the film offers him the means of evasion, refuge and romantic fantasy, will ultimately become his mausoleum. Another orphic figure who has strayed into the underworld,[16] Fred dies with a song on his lips, as we see in the last shot. He expires in ecstasy, with the métro once again establishing itself as a locus of music and murder, rapture and death.

Subway attracted excellent reviews from the British press: 'Full of dazzling sequences that are a treat to watch' (Shaun Usher, *The Daily Mail*); 'Stunning...held me enraptured throughout' (Geoff Andrew, *Time Out*); 'A beautifully inventive and original fantasy thriller' (*The Guardian*); 'enthusiasm and a passion for the cinema shine from every frame' (anonymous blurb on video cover). Such praise would lead you to expect a great deal but the film often disappoints and irritates. Whilst Besson undeniably mixes humour and action with consummate ease, particularly in several breathtaking chase sequences both in cars and on roller-skates, many passages remain, it must be said, jejune, pretentious and desperately striving for effect. They are full of deliberately contrived incongruities which are intended to dazzle but which are frequently silly – Lambert in his dinner suit, Isabelle Adjani in diamonds and evening dress, champagne dinners on a concourse of the métro at midnight, and several lacklustre interviews between Adjani and the police inspector. It is very definitely a curate's egg. However, the role of the métro is quite clearly to provide a setting for a bizarre assortment of underworld fugitives. The roller-skating purse snatcher echoes words we have already heard in *Le Samouraï*: 'Je connais les couloirs comme ma poche' ('I know the way like the back of my hand'): in his flights of evasion, he leaps from platform to platform and ski-jumps down escalator slopes. The double-dealing flower-seller is both a police informant and and an accomplice in armed robbery; the black muscleman, 'Gros Bill', is a benevolent minotaur who can pull handcuffs apart. Even the métro police, the plodding representatives of conventional law and order, are frequently thwarted by this perplexing environment. As the inspector himself says: 'C'est grand ici; nous-même, on s'y perd des fois' ('It's a huge place; even we get lost sometimes'). The métro provides an almost magical alienation from the conventional world: below the surface of the city, ensconced in their subterranean hideouts, we discover a weird and wonderful collection of endearing and eccentric members of an enchantingly alternative society. A travelling shot (34″), with the camera mounted on the front of the train, emphasises the contrast between the working hours of the métro, with platforms full of passengers, and the closed métro when the platforms become stages for wonderful nocturnal revels. In this underground, subversive world, below the chic apartments, there is a corresponding reversal of values, as though Paris is turned in on itself, characterised by an unexpected and incongruous glamour; a flight from reality into a realm of fantasy. In this respect the Bakhtinian configuration of the banquet, the body and the underworld is clearly apparent in *Subway*. Susan Hayward, in her book, 'Luc Besson', draws attention to the significant role of food and drink in the film, seeing them as substitutes for lost values: 'they also signify a nostalgia for an aestheticism (...) that has disappeared'.[17] There are various manifestations in the film of a collective carnival; the dinner party on the platform becomes a popular feast, an aspiration to a new universal spirit expressed in the hyperbolic, frequently grotesque behaviour of the revellers; the carefree habitation of this underworld shows a group of rebels who have come to terms with the forces of darkness and have conquered their fears of a repressive social hierarchy; the downward movement is subversive yet creative; the authoritarian, material world on the surface has been penetrated and undermined by the irreverent invasions of the underground; these 20th-century troglodytes, in their festive pursuits involving music and collaborative schemes, are looking forward to a utopian future. In *Subway*, as in Rabelais's novel, 'The downward movements, scattered throughout the forms and images of popular merriment and grotesque realism, are reassembled (...); they are understood anew and merged into one single movement directed into the depths of the earth, the depths of the body, in which the treasures and the most wonderful things lie hidden.'[18]

The progress of the hero himself through this underworld is like a rite of passage in which his identity is transformed and through which he seems to be increasingly imbued with magic powers. He becomes able to perform several vanishing tricks and to practise the art of escapology: at the beginning he escapes his pursuers by jumping under the wheels of the train and crawling along the tracks of the métro; he begins a science-fiction style journey down a series of corridors, armed with a tubular glass light, as if both a sword and a wand, like the famous laser weapon in *Star Wars*; he falls through a grill in the floor and, unharmed, dangles in space; much later he disappears mysteriously from inside a lift. He begins to feel at home and remarks to his fellow troglodytes 'Sympa chez vous' ('Not a bad place you have'). When Gros Bill rips off his handcuffs, the last vestige of social restriction is removed. An underground birthday party reveals to him the existence of a hidden world full of possibilities for fun and fantasy; at times even the sunlight comes in through a disused window. In *Subway* the whole métro becomes a vast cabinet of Dr Caligari, a gigantic box of tricks.

The heroine, Héléna, played petulantly and provocatively by Isabelle Adjani, becomes a Cinderella in reverse, turning from an expensively kept princess into a subterranean gipsy, changing out of her finery into designer rags, with a gun as her new magic wand. Just as she changes her clothes, so too does she alter her attitudes, as she gradually falls for the renegade hero, drinks champagne on empty platforms, smokes dope with her new friends, and, as fireworks light up the darkness, surrenders to the alluring atmosphere of the métro. Comparing Cocteau's *Orphée* to *Subway*, Phil Powrie makes the point that 'both Death in *Orphée* and Héléna in *Subway* are cold women who will gradually fall in love with Orphée and Fred, and both (...) will find their lost voices'.[19] She has discovered new values and, in a subsequent confrontation with her husband, whom she calls 'Mr Moneybags', tells him that she is sick of his money, is being crushed by his wealth and possessiveness, and has found her real element not on the streets but beneath the streets. Through the transforming chambers of the métro, she will be able to enter into the realm of myth. She will henceforth play Eurydice to her underground Orpheus, take on the role of Persephone, queen of Hades, opposite her prince of darkness with his bottle-blond halo, the king of a world turned inside out and upside down.

The desire to gain access to a foreign, exotic environment, to an exciting state of other worldliness is implicit from the very title of the film. The word 'subway' immediately evokes the New World, the glamour of New York. The métro has become 'Americanised'. This strong aspiration to Americanisation is quite plainly apparent in many features of the film, often expressed humorously. The epigraph at the beginning signals this obsession: 'To be is to do – Socrates; to do is to be – Sartre; Do be do be do – Sinatra'. The meaningless refrain of the crooner triumphs over the maxims of philosophers and the American singer's rap is finally mouthed by the dying hero. The police inspector refers to his deputies in English as 'Batman and Robin', who are 'les meilleurs' ('the best'); one of the deputies has a habit of swearing in Anglo-American. Anything culturally French is, it seems, eschewed: the champagne dinner party takes place as an American song is played in the background. Later, another song with English words is sung by a black singer, functioning as a diatribe against television, 'which takes our strength away', and preferring life as 'a mystery and I like it', a sentiment which the hero himself has discovered underground. The heroine, with new-found freedom, flouts convention by going to a bourgeois dinner party sporting an alarming coiffure which she describes as 'Iroquois'; at the same time she behaves oddly, pretends to speak and gesture like a Red Indian, and ultimately insults the hostess: 'Votre dîner est nul, votre baraque est nulle' ('Your dinner stinks and so does your house'). The final concert in the film is one in which classical music is replaced by another American-style rock song, once again emphasising the interplay between high and low culture. It is an event organised by the hero in his role as an Orphic impresario, whose mission is to spread happiness and unity.

Besson's attraction to the lower depths continues in *Le Grand Bleu*, where this time he pursues his explorations far beneath the surface of the sea and where ultimately his ascetic, obsessive hero goes not in search of Atlantis, or the company of dolphins, but of total self-immersion, self-annihilation and nothingness.

In 1991 the métro featured in the most expensive French film of all time, that monumental folly, *Les Amants du Pont-Neuf*, directed by Léos Carax, a banal and bizarre Chaplinesque love story of Michèle, a young artist with a degenerative eye-disease, which helps to explain the ghastly pictures she has painted, and Alex, a self-mutilating fire-eating homeless punk, with an ending lifted straight out of Vigo's *L'Atalante* (remember the underwater photography). In a preposterously melodramatic finale, the repellent pair, having fallen off the Pont-Neuf, emerge reborn, as it were, from the waters of the Seine – cured, cleansed and chastened – to clamber aboard a passing barge from which they triumphantly bid 'adieu' to what they now describe as a rotten city. Within the framework of what Guy Austin describes generously as the successful coexistence of neo-realism and fantasy,[20] and what Jacques Siclier dismisses as a spineless, artificial scenario, full of hallucinatory vision,[21] the métro provides several nightmare images. Early on in the film, Alex follows Michèle along the moving pavement, before continuing to chase her through the corridors; she in her turn is searching for a busking cellist whose music is heard on the sound-track. The cellist has been threatened by Alex and has run away; thus adding to the heroine's confusion when she fails to discover the source of the music which she has been moving towards. She manages to elude her tormentor by jumping on to a train. Her nightmare journey continues when she appears to be trapped in an empty train running out of control. Thus, the métro becomes a symbolic feature of her psychological confusion and of his mental obsession; its corridors become obstacles to his fulfillment, providing an appropriate décor for psychotic disturbance, just as, much later, in a surrealistic dream sequence, they become the setting for a violent conflagration. So that Michèle will not be found and he can keep her to himself, Alex, the love-sick arsonist, sets fire to dozens of Missing Persons posters which line the walls of the corridor and which show the face of the missing heroine. The hero's pyromania and pyrophagia are also consummated in a fantastic pyrotechnic fusion of water and fire as they all go water-skiing down the Seine, streaming with cascades of fireworks from the bicentennial celebrations. Some viewers squealed with delight and the producers had a heart-attack.

A variation on this métro theme occurs in *Delicatessen* (1991), Jeunet and Caro's extravagant and visceral exercise in *grand guignol* and a bizarre allegory of the

Occupation. In the near future, society is on the brink of collapse. Nowhere could be more apparent than the Bakhtinian collision of exaggerated comic images of strange exhibitions of eating, sexual exploits and misadventures, with concomitant forays into the underworld. In a run-down city, a butcher and landlord prospers by killing his tenants and selling their flesh as meat to their hungry neighbour. Right from the start the camera penetrates the intestines of the architecture, plunging down ventilation shafts and down water-pipes, through which intimate sounds also travel to distant eavesdroppers. However, it is nothing quite so nauseating as in *Trainspotting* (Boyle, 1995). The forces of resistance to this oppressive and terrifying dystopia are found in a movement shown in the headlines of a newspaper: 'Troglodisme: une organisation souterraine' ('Troglodism: an underground organisation'). We enter a manhole and journey into the sewers, where we encounter the troglodyte outlaws who are ready to ambush spies from above the ground, people from the surface who distort the truth and spread deceit; the troglodytes, symbols of the resistance, describe themselves as live game for the meat-eating predators who live above in this delicatessen for human flesh. The underworld of the sewers thus becomes a brave new world for freedom from oppression.

A similarly utopian dimension can be found in the Argentinian *Moebius* (Universidad del Cine, 1995). It offers us a fascinating example of the use of the underground as a metaphorical space and provides a striking Latin-American reference with which to conclude this chapter. This supernatural mystery film, made by students from the Universidad del Cine, under the general direction of Gustavo Mosquera, and filmed almost entirely on location in the Buenos Aires métro, exploits the underground system as a multiple metaphor. The whole film is dedicated to the underground and uses this topographical space to express and explore various themes – urban alienation, the flight from the forces of ignorance, human disappearance under oppressive political regimes, the search for inner values, the mystery of the fourth dimension, and the cryptic workings of fate. All these themes are enmeshed and symbolically represented within the spatial complexities of the métro. At the beginning a voice-over from the hero prefaces the story, subtitled as follows: 'Subways are undoubtedly a symbol of current times. A labyrinth where we silently walk past our own kind, never knowing them or their ways. Hundreds of platforms where we analyse situations, not really trying to catch a train but rather a change in life, a strange game we plunge into through endless tunnels, unaware that with every change of train we definitively change our fate. I found subways to be life's greatest observational apparatus but I never imagined what was in store for me.' The film's hero, significantly an expert in surface topography, attempts to solve the mystery of a train with more than 30 passengers which has vanished on a recently opened section of the system. His investigations lead him towards the phenomenon of the Moebius band, already shown in an image in the title-sequence: the outside edges of the band, twisted and joined to form a figure of eight, criss-cross each other to infinity, just like the new section of the railway which has apparently catapulted the train into the fourth dimension, with its passengers caught in a time warp. The hero's solution to this puzzle is inspired by watching the cars on a roller-coaster, another kind of intertwining track-system. There are several thrilling rides at high speed through a nightmarish intestinal landscape, with red warning signals mysteriously flashing on and off, automatic points constantly changing for no apparent reason, and rushing winds unexpectedly occurring as the invisible train hurtles along the tracks. The authorities, showing at once fear and indifference, try to suppress information about the disappearance. When faced with a possible explanation, they refuse to accept it, with the hero becoming increasingly alienated and frustrated. In a startling climax, he himself is eventually caught in the trap of this gigantic Moebius band and enters the fourth dimension. Here he discovers his old teacher, a sort of latterday Prospero and perpetrator of the riddle, who tells him that nobody can confront infinity without feeling vertigo, that nobody can experience it without feeling deeply puzzled, thus confirming both the hero's existentialist angst and his physical malaise. This alternative time-traveller stresses the need for self-knowledge and the importance of seeking our inner reality. 'Neither man nor time can disappear without leaving traces; they stick to our souls', our hero is told, before he disappears on yet another vanished train, leaving behind a notebook containing thoughts which link up with those of the initial voice-over: 'I never imagined what was in store for me when I got the 86 train and met my old teacher, tired of repeating always the same story, tired of fighting and being ignored. I felt he was entrusting me with his time. It's easy to understand why I choose to follow his steps instead of uselessly trying to explain to a bunch of fools something they won't understand. Anyway, the old man was right. We live in a world where nobody listens.' By means of the underground metaphor, *Moebius* brilliantly evokes an inspiring variety of alternative ideological and social dimensions.

The métro can thus be seen as instrumental in creating dramatic supense, particularly in chase sequences where it has a significance on the level of action, as in *Diva*. It fulfils a function, in certain cases, as a reflection or signifier of a psychological space, as in *Le Samouraï*; in others, it takes on a symbolic, almost mythical value, and its images have an impact on our imagination and on our collective unconscious, as in *Subway*. In our descent into the underground, towards the bowels of the earth, we are confronted by symbols of darkness, of the lower depths, of the domain of the dead, which provoke vertigo and inner anxieties. But at the same time we can experience a Bakhtinian sense of discovery and liberation. The métro is therefore shown to have become the underworld of Paris, a focus of reversed values, both social and moral, paradoxically a new source of creativity in films like *Diva* and *Subway* which revel in the subversive aspects of the postmodern city, characterised by its juxtaposition of disparate elements and where a formerly utopian coherent surface has been displaced underground. The métro represents a place of both recurrent myth and revitalised postmodern reality, at once emblematic of 'la pègre' and of Hades, a labyrinth of dream, fantasy and nightmare. It is the perfect space to be explored by our imaginations from the darkened recesses of the cinema.

Notes

1   Bakhtin, M. M., *Rabelais and his world*, trans. Iswolsky, H., Indiana University Press, 1984, cited in *The Bakhtin Reader*, Morris, P. (ed.), London, Edward Arnold, 1994, p. 238. Compare also p. 234: 'the artistic

logic of the grotesque image ignores the closed, smooth and impenetrable surface of the body and retains only its excrescences and orifices, only that which leads beyond the body's limited space or into the body's depths. Mountains and abysses, such is the relief of the grotesque body; or speaking in architectural terms, towers and subterranean passages.' In Bakhtin's interpretation the dominant image is that of the grotesque, devouring mouth, constantly open to the world, swallowing it and ceaselessly reproducing it, in a huge and carnivalesque banquet of life, which symbolically attempts to defeat time and death. The entrance to the métro is in a way a huge mouth which swallows us up and spits us out on our diverse visits to the underworld.

2   See Victor Hugo, *Les Contemplations*: 'Quel Zorobabel formidable / Quel Dédale vertigineux, / Cieux! a bâti dans l'insondable / Tout ce noir chaos lumineux?' ('Magnitudo Parvi'); 'O châtiment! dédale aux spirales funèbres! / Construction d'en bas qui cherche les ténèbres, / Plonge au-dessous du monde et descend dans la nuit, / Et, Babel renversée, au fond de l'ombre fuit! / (...) / Ce gouffre, c'est l'égout du mal universel.' ('Ce que dit la Bouche d'Ombre'). ('O punishment! labyrinth with funereal spirals! / an underground construction seeking out the darkness, / Plunging below the world and descending into the night, / And, a tower of Babel turned upside down, receding into the depths of the shadows! / (...) / This chasm is the sewer of universal evil'). These metaphors are often developed into a more complex network of associations involving references to Piranesi and his *Imaginary Prisons*. The subterranean quality of these pictorial visions by Piranesi has been strikingly described by Peter Ackroyd in his novel, *The House Of Doctor Dee*, (London, Hamish Hamilton, 1993, pp. 43-44): 'Only a few yards away, on a stall by Red Lion Passage, I had first come across the work of Piranesi. It was a book with many of his etchings reproduced; its title was *Imaginary Prisons*, but as far as I was concerned there was nothing imaginary about them at all. I recognised this world at once; I knew that it was my city. (...) Piranesi's world was one of endlessly ruined masonry, of labyrinthine passages and barred windows; here were blocks of stone, massive, dark, their textures swamped in shadow, here were giant recesses of brick, huge banners of tattered cloth, ropes, pulleys, and wooden cranes that towered up to broken balconies of stone. The artist often used the framing device of a ruined arch or gateway, so that I was drawn into the scene and knew myself to be part of it; I was in prison, too. (...) I (...) looked down at the etching again, only to see another flight of steps that seemed to lead down into an abyss of stone. It occurred to me that this was really a city under the ground. It was the eternal city for those who are trapped in time.'

3   One shot is taken from inside the métro, looking back up the empty stairway towards the barred entrance.

4   Other references include plot developments: a stage hand has caused consternation at the theatre by arriving late; he has taken the métro and a power-cut has delayed has delayed him between stations; and also a reference to the métro's use as a shelter when there is an air-raid alert. The Gestapo have asked why the actors have not been using the cellars of the theatre for this purpose. Deneuve quickly puts them off the scent by saying that the cellars have been declared unfit and they have been using the métro.

5   See Siclier, J., *Le Cinéma Français*, vol.2, Paris, Editions Ramsay, 1993, p. 132; and Forbes, J., *The Cinema in France*, London, Macmillan, 1992, p. 105. As Jean-Michel Frodon shows, the underground title is more appropriate to one of the main locations of the film, the cellar beneath the theatre: 'Un film au fond du trou, à la cave, sous terre (...), un film gigogne, situé dans une grotte où niche une caverne où se cache une crypte.' ('A film at the bottom of a hole, in the cellar, below ground (...), a hideaway film, situated in a cave, in which there is a cavern, in which there is a crypt'). (*L'Age Moderne du Cinéma Français, De la Nouvelle Vague à nos jours*, Paris, Flammarion, 1995, p. 545)

6   Jill Forbes draws attention to the significance of this illustrative and atmospheric *polar*, which includes 'a

superbly orchestrated chase sequence in the Paris métro and a psychological study of some subtlety. Costello's emotional austerity, his repression and his adherence to an anachronistic code of honour which has ceased to be a necessity rooted in a social context and has become almost entirely abstract and formal, are all matched by the austerity of the *mise en scène* and by locations, such as the tunnels of the métro, which emphasise a geometric formalism.' (pp. 54-55) She later makes the important point that 'the virtue of the American *film noir* (...) was that it posited an organic relationship between the individual and an urban rather than rural setting, suggesting how the city affected the behaviour and the emotions of those who lived in it'. (p. 75). For a discussion of the charismatic presence, at once seductive and dangerous, of Alain Delon in this film, see Jean-Michel Frodon, p.181.

7   The sequence of incongruities and the director's playful subversion of the conventional by means of humour and unexpected confrontations are fully analysed in King, R. S., 'Help yourselves at Bertrand Blier's *Buffet Froid'*, in *Nottingham French Studies*, Vol.32, No.1, Spring 1993, pp. 99-108. See also Forbes, J., pp. 175-76.

8   Interview with Blier, *Buffet Froid*, *Avant-Scène du Cinéma*, March 1980, p. 7.

9   See Hayward, S., *French National Cinema*, London, Routledge, 1993, p. 247, for an incisive definition of the 'cinéma du look', which, among other things, is seen as 'a sort of BCBG on celluloid'. For an interesting and perceptive analysis of the combination of old and new elements in *Diva* itself, see Powrie, P., '*Diva*'s Deluxe Disasters', in *Nottingham French Studies*, Vol.32, No.1, Spring 1993, pp.109-20.

10 'Que le héros du film soit un postier est ici parfaitement ironique tant le film est aux antipodes du cinéma message, prenant existence par la pure présence esthétique de l'apparence visuelle.' ('The fact that the hero of the film is a courier is perfectly ironic here since the film is at the antipodes of message-cinema, owing its existence to the sheer esthetic presence of visual appearance.') (Frodon, J.-M. p. 575)

11 Guy Austin has recently noted the importance of the métro as a key setting for the 'cinéma du look'. (*Contemporary French Cinema, an Introduction*, Manchester, Manchester University Press, 1996, p.121.)

12 The significance of the labyrinthine structure of *Diva* is discussed by Powrie: '*Diva* is a traditional narrative of initiation, a rite of passage through a variety of labyrinths, as Beineix himself has suggested: "C'est un film labyrinthe, un fil qui se répond, un film de correspondance et de connotations qui se déplacent; c'est comme un puzzle". The labyrinth is signalled here by the obsessive repetition of confusing double- talk and double image.'

    My translation of Beineix: 'It's a labyrinth film, a thread which intertwines with itself, a film full of shifting correspondences and connotations; it's like a puzzle' (p. 118).

13 Jacques Siclier stresses the fantasmagorical climate of the film: 'Aventure singulière dans le dédale du métro et du RER, jeu de cache-cache dans les décors fantasmagoriques d'Alexandre Trauner.' ('A strange adventure in the labyrinth of the métro, a game of hide-and-seek in Alexandre Trauner's fantastic sets.') (in *Le Cinéma Français*, Vol.2, Paris, Editions Ramsay, 1993, p.259) *Subway*'s affiliation to certain aspects of traditional French cinema is discussed by Jean-Michel Frodon: '*Subway* tente une greffe des apparences contemporaines sur le vieux tronc du cinéma français traditionnel (...) où règnent la réplique sentencieuse, la gouaille mémorable des seconds rôles, le réalisme poétique.' ('*Subway* attempts to graft new contemporary appearances on to the old stock of the traditional French cinema (...), typified by sentencious retorts, notably cheeky supporting roles and poetic realism.') (p. 689).

14 *Film Français*, no.2029, March 85, p. 8: 'j'avais une idée forte: le métro. Mais je n'arrivais pas à trouver une histoire aussi forte que ce décor.' ('I had a strong idea: the métro but I couldn't find a story as strong as this setting.').

15 Susan Hayward refers to the myth of Orpheus in relation to the narrative of *Subway*, linking it to an

earlier up-dating of the myth by Cocteau in his film *Orphée* (1949) (1993, p. 233). This theme is developed more extensively in her recent study of the director Luc Besson: 'this film can be read as a counter-Orpheus narrative because it is Héléna (...) who goes down into the labyrinthine underground to find Fred.' (*Luc Besson*, Manchester, Manchester University Press, 1998, p. 35).

16 Bakhtin, M. M., p. 239. Compare also the following lines which are of significance for *Subway*: 'In the Rabelaisian system of images the underworld is the junction where the main lines of this system cross each other: carnivals, banquets, fights, beatings, abuses and curses. (...) If the Christian hell devalued earth and drew men away from it, the carnivalesque hell affirmed earth and its lower stratum as the fertile womb, where death meets birth and a new life springs forth. (...) The image of the netherworld in folk tradition becomes the image of the defeat of fear by laughter.' (pp. 241-42).

17 'Un scénario invertébré, des dialogues réduits à leur plus simple expression, des personnages sans aucune épaisseur: voilà pour le refus du cinéma traditionnel! Chez Carax, la mise en scène est, avant tout, choc esthétique, poésie de l'artifice engendrant des visions hallucinatoires, (...) l'expression suprême du narcissisme de Léos Carax.' ('A spineless scenario, dialogue reduced to its simplest expression, characters without any depth: so much for the rejection of traditional cinema! With Carax, direction is maily esthetic shocks, the poetry of tricks, giving rise to hallucinatory visions,(...) the supreme expression of Carax's narcissism.') (Siclier, J., *Le Cinéma Français*, Vol.2, Paris, Editions Ramsay, 1993, p. 306) Compare also Susan Hayward: 'the visual virtuosity of *Les Amants du Pont-Neuf* is not enough to sustain a fundamentally flawed narrative or even counter-narrative.' (1993, p. 253).

The City as Narrative: Corporeal Paris in Contemporary French Cinema (1950s-1990s)

Susan Hayward

Introduction

The second part of the title of this essay, 'corporeal Paris', suggests that there is a body in Paris which may *or* may not be real (corp/*or*/real in one word), so possibly an imagined, metaphoric body. Conversely this part of the title suggests that there is a Paris that is real ('real') as opposed to the imagined body ('corps'). This suggests then that 'corporeal' can be deconstructed as having two distinct and opposing meanings: first, 'corps'/the imagined body-Paris; second, 'real'/the real-Paris. The whole title proposes that cinema represents Paris as a system of shifting signs, of 'narratives' that reveal *both* the imagined city and the real city. In this essay, I shall tell a tale of these two cities and their ineluctable co-presence in cinema, even though as we shall see there is an over-investment in the former, that is, Paris as the imagined body – in the form of an overexposed, too visibilised cinematic city – at the expense of the latter (the real-Paris) which remains for the greater part an invisibilised entity – an underexposed cinematic city. This is not to say, however, that the imagined body-Paris is always an ideal body. As we shall see, in its *imaging*, this cinematic Paris reveals as many paradoxes and inconsistencies as it may seek to deny – but it does so unconsciously. When, however, the repressed invisibilised Paris does appear, it opens up the cracks the imagined city attempts to conceal and shows us a very different city from the one we typically/visually feel familiar with.

What I am saying therefore is that there are two cities: there is, first, a city of our imaginings including a *repressed* city of our imaginings that is a certain type of body – a corporeality that is linked to our psyche ('it's in there in our minds and it's real'); and, second, there is an invisibilised city of our *suppressed* imaginings, another type of 'body'– a corporeality that is linked to a fragmented social existentiality ('it's out there in the world and it's real').

A Tale of Two Cities Part I: the body-Paris – the one of our visibilised imaginings

This body that is Paris, this metaphoric imagined body begins with the major typification of Paris as female – an imagined body which we can trace back to Revolutionary Paris at least, but certainly to 19th-century literature when Paris began to change radically under the impact of modernisation through Haussmann. This 19th-century Paris was one of paradox, the modern 'clean' Paris that allowed women of all classes onto the streets and into the glass-enclosed arcades and then, later, department stores. Women emerged out of the privacy of the home or the brothels where they had formerly lain hidden. The hidden Paris was still there, of course: the East side of Paris, the Latin quarter and the Montmartre/Pigalle area, for example, were to remain largely untouched. It was primarily this hidden Paris that was Baudelaire's mistress and that of many other writers and painters. This vision of Paris as the muse, the cocotte, the ideal mistress of male imaginings was however a deeply nostalgic vision of femininity and Paris itself – a nostalgia that can be seen as a resistance to the modernisation of Paris (Weiss, 1995, p. 25). But the parading female of modern Paris, the unprivatising of her sexuality was also part of this Paris that Baudelaire loved and celebrated in his poetry. This vision of Paris, which he helped to consecrate – Paris as the private and public female body, is one that does not go away: only recently a photo-supplement of *Le Monde* (29 November 1997) was entitled 'Paris ville de femmes'. Predictably, the images were of the chic, the beautiful and the famous out and about in the streets of Paris.

Why female? A first obvious answer is that the imagining serves to keep in place the erotic myth that is Paris (city of pleasure and frisson), the city of freedom, sexual freedom/anonymous promiscuity, to which my response would be – freedom for whom? To keep one myth in place is to disguise the other that 'we' do not want to see. And this practice begins (in this context) with 19th-century anxieties about modernity and industrialisation. For, as Walter Benjamin (1997) reminds us, although Paris was Baudelaire's mistress he also expressed his ambivalence towards the new Paris in terms of attraction and fear. Nor did all authors of that period perceive Paris in the light of an ideal mistress, or in terms of ambivalence (as pleasure/unpleasure). For example Zola's Parisian women are not pleasurable metaphors for sexual freedom at all, but are redolent with danger and instruments of death. Why, one might ask, is his representation of women (particularly Nana, of which some eleven of films have been made) one of female sexuality as uncontrolled disorder? Why, to take the example of Nana again, is her body the medium for unsafe speculation (both in terms of looking and money)? Zola's city is the city of mad extravagance, the Haussmannisation of Paris under the Second Empire, the destruction of history, culture and personal memory: in other words a modern city that he hated – a mad rush of capital speculation that instead of revitalising the capital-city would, according to Zola, kill it.

The *why* of 'why female?' in the above sets of questions and answers allows us to uncover a deep ambivalence towards the idea and concept of the city. To perceive it as female and then project onto that representation of the city one's love or hatred of it tells us that the female body/the feminine was constructed as the site/sight where the contradictions of modernity got played out. The female figure becomes the symbol of both the danger and the promise of the modern age. She comes to represent the city of pleasure and excess (both sexual and political). As the *erotic* public woman, she is prostitute (Nana) – the site where capitalism and sex unite. Literally, the public and private spheres come together in that intercourse; she is a conduit of pleasure but also of filth. She is the potentially diseased body, the underbelly of Paris – the sewers and excrescence of the city. Conversely, maybe, as the *political* public woman – the promise of the new age – she is Marianne, the revolutionary bare-breasted (so still erotic, hence the 'maybe') heroine. But as Elizabeth Wilson points out (1992, p. 7) not all revolutionary bodies are good bodies. And when the revolutionary body becomes a threat, it becomes known as 'the mob in the city' and as such becomes invested with female characterisations such as 'hysterical', 'flood' etc. The undesired revolutionary body therefore becomes typified as an unruly and blood-excreting female body.

What we are witnessing here in all these discourses is a feminisation of a distinctly masculine space. The city of Paris of the 19th century was after all one that was designed by male architects – and this continues to be predominantly the case for the Paris of the 20th century. Capital and therefore power was and still is vested in men and was, and still is, visible within the public sphere, the private sphere being more readily the province of the woman. And the question is: 'why this displacement and containment of the male city as female?' A second obvious answer to our questions of 'why female' is that it is easier to blame the failings of the city through displacement onto an 'other'. But displacement also occurs because of fear. Thus a third reason for the feminisation of Paris becomes apparent: quite simply the fear of the modern city itself. This fear is the stuff of science fiction and sci-fi movies and it is worth remembering that Fritz Lang's film *Metropolis* (1926) – meaning 'mother-city' – still stands as *the* archetypal science-fiction futuristic movie of the city as dystopia, and it is even more worth remembering that the major menace to that society is embodied by the female robot Marie. This fear of the city is deeply sexualised – as women have become more visible and moved into the public, capital sphere; as they have become more part of the spectacle of the city, so too they have come to embody female freedom, escape from the authority of the family (the father and the husband). In short, they constitute a threat to patriarchy. Thus man's fear of the metropolis has much to do with his fear of female freedom within that space – a freedom which must be surveilled and policed (just one example of which, in the context of Paris, is the obligatory official registration of all prostitutes [a law dating from the 19th century]). The private, once it becomes public, must be controlled.

Finally, the need to feminise the ultimately male-modernist city stems from the deep-rooted psychological need of the male, first noted by Freud, for the female presence to affirm the male's sense of self. She is the 'other' to his 'self'. The city then in this context affirms male subjectivity/identity. It confirms, therefore, his at-homeness, he experiences a sense of the familiar (what Freud terms *heimlich*). But the relationship is a fraught one, since it is one of dependency on the other. If we think of the representations of the city in *film noir* thrillers – with the dark, dimly lit, *wet*, often dirty city streets; or indeed of the expressionist city in the Weimar cinema of Lang, Weine or Murnau, with its steep, uncanny angles, fiercely contrastive lighting and its sets of deranged people groping along walls, we can easily see how cinema, with these threatening images (the familiar rendered unfamiliar: *unheimlich*, as Freud puts it) reflects the deep-felt anxieties of the male unconscious within the city. The familiar becomes strange and uncanny, and the drive is to penetrate the appearance (the masquerade of the city as a female body) and get to the essence of things (in this case the wholeness of the [male] body). So the city is probed, investigated. The image of the all-seeing, observing *flâneur* comes to mind – close in genesis to the private-eye-voyeur of the *film noir* thriller. In film, this is precisely what the male gaze does – it probes and investigates the female body-parts (as city), and this is also exactly what the camera does. The camera is technology's *flâneur*-voyeur *par excellence*.

It will not surprise you, therefore, if I say that film fetishises the city – that it reduces it to less than the sum of its parts so as to contain and make it safe (the city becomes corporeal so that its threat can be contained through fetishism). The city, in this case Paris, becomes in turn a playground, a series of monuments, a set of familiar sites/sights (the Eiffel Tower and Notre Dame – as seen in, for example, *Les 400 coups*, [1958], or *A bout de souffle*, [1959]); it becomes the 'good-breasted' maternal body or, conversely 'the bad-breasted one' – the maternal body that rejects and must be punished, therefore. In *Touchez pas au grisbi* [1954], Mme Bouche is the good mother, and Josie, like any other drug-dependent prostitute, is the bad-breasted mother.

Clearly, to typify Paris as a woman, as a female body, helps keep out other bodies (such as the queer body, the dying/ailing body, the raced body and so on). That is, to reduce them to bodies that do not matter. It allows for two things: on the one hand, to construct the apparently safe and containable female as signifier of male identity and, on the other, to perceive it as the *only* body that can act as a threat to the social (patriarchal) order of things. *This* is the utility of the misrecognition of Paris as female. As Rita Felski (1995, p. 19) and Andrea Weiss (1995, p. 25) make clear, gendering the city points to the inescapable presence and power of gender symbolism. Furthermore this first effect of gender symbolism – that is, establishing the city as a primary binary opposition of male/female – sets in motion a whole chain of binary oppositions that allows the city to be contained as safe. These oppositions, as we have already seen, are (amongst others): Self/other; public sphere/private sphere; familiar/unfamiliar; presence/absence.

To speak of Paris as a body implies mastery over that body. That the body enters into discourses of power and control, that it is disciplined and regulated. To control that body implies, furthermore, that that body is potentially deviant and that it must be policed. In today's city, CCTV is the ideal tool for detection and identification; it watches the circulation of bodies and goods. The city is in the eye of the camera or the 'I' of male technology; for just as the city is a creation of male technology and controlled by men, so too is the technological apparatus of the camera. Virginia Woolf (in a 1926 essay entitled 'The Cinema') saw the moving camera and cinema as potentially the most appropriate modernist form of expressing the complexity of the city and its modernity (James Donald, 1997, p. 191). But one wonders if she had women in mind. The woman in Paris of French cinema (and here I speak of the younger woman) has in great part fallen into two sets of representations. She finds herself as the 'deviant' (temptress, whore, fallen woman, liar, cheat, murderer), even in comedies (neglectful mother, for example) – *or* she is represented as in distress (suicidal

– possibly mad – so still deviant really), or confused either by being in the city or in mortal danger. Rarely is she represented as heroic. Rarely does she express her own subjectivity. The price of *embodying* the city then is that the woman *within* the city is without an authenticated voice, without agency, therefore effectively silenced. Think, for example, of the neglectful mother in *Trois hommes et un couffin* (1985), and again of the confused yet supposedly independent young woman in *Les Nuits de la pleine lune* (1984). Rarely, does the woman occupy a voiced position, does she become in a sense a truly female modernist *flâneur* with power to walk through the city on her own terms (much as the male *flâneur* did before her). Only two films of woman as female modernist *flâneur* spring immediately to mind: Cléo walking through Paris as she faces death in Agnès Varda's *Cléo de 5 à 7* (1961), and Florence roving the streets of Paris at night searching for her lover in Louis Malle's *Ascenseur pour l'échafaud* (1957). In both instances it is their subjectivities and subjective experience of the city that we are privy to.

This then is the imagined corporeal Paris. A symbolically gendered Paris that 'overlooks' the way in which race, ethnicity, class, age, ability and sexual preference are also issues of gender; that imagines those issues away; that absences and silences these many 'others' that are the Metropolis. Metropolis, again to give its original meaning, means 'mother' (*meter*) and 'city' (*polis*) – mother city. But *polis* means also the body politic, democracy. Thus, mother and democracy; metropolis: mother of democracy. It means also 'mother-nation' (and *la métropole* is still used today by the French to refer to France). What is this cinema that colludes with a corporealisation of Paris that denies otherness, that consigns perceived metropolarities to the margins, to an exopolis, to a city 'without' – outside the 'polis', outside democracy, outside the nation-state? To deny and repress the real, the undesired is to make it both a structuring absence (it confirms our presence) and a territorialised, geographically pathologised elsewhere, a spectre (an unpleasant and menacing image) which the (imaginary) city walls (the maternal city, the body boundaries) keep at bay. Clearly there is more to the city than the (female) body, than its gendered symbolism. Indeed, discourses and technologies of power through the very force of their reiteration finally expose their own contradictions and it is through these gaps that the 'real' suppressed city seeps into view and the spectogram comes onto the cinema screens.

A Tale of Two Cities Part II: the real city – the one of our suppressed imaginings

I said earlier that Virginia Woolf saw cinema as the most appropriate tool for representing the modernist city in all its complexities; Siegfried Kracauer (writing in 1924), for his part, saw cinema as singularly suited to capture a disintegrating world without substance (Hansen, 1995, p. 369). What do we make of these views in our tale of two cities? Simply this:

- that cinema was virtually contemporaneous with the modernist city (late 19th century)
- that it is a machine that produces narratives, and could potentially produce as many narratives as there are cities within a city (thus it is a fiction-machine much as

architecture is itself fictional in that it imagines how people will use the spaces it has invented)
- that cinema is about memory and destruction just as is the city itself.

Let's now develop these ideas.

Cinema has a complex relationship with the real since it realises reality on to the screen – it puts real architecture on screen and it also recreates architecture in studios in the form of studio sets (a form of hyper-real, if you will). The real cinema offers, or 'images', a form of detached unsubstantial real – it isn't really there. But as I shall suggest in a moment, the city itself has a complex relationship with the real. Walter Benjamin (1997) was another of the early cultural theorists to perceive a correlation between the city and cinema: as he points out, it records the human eye/'I' experience of the city, registers the shifts in our sense perception and, just as the city itself is an organisation of time and space, so too is cinema – it edits footage (i.e. time) into a narrative (product, i.e. space) and in so doing it gives, for the most part, a temporal-spatial coherence to the city. The modernist (Fordist) city was a way of regulating time through space. By centralising industry and the workforce into one place, efficient (undelayed) productivity was guaranteed. The city organised and routinised people around work, sleep and leisure. This practice continued into the new urbanisms of the 1950s and 1960s which strove to improve the physical mobility of people and goods but which made people an impersonalised part of the captital flow. The French famously epithetised this routinisation as: *métro-boulot-dodo* (which Faraldo hilariously satirises in *Themroc*, 1972).

This urbanisation of space has given way now, as Paul Virilio explains, to an urbanisation of real-time, an abstract telecommunciations city that annihilates space with time (as opposed to the modernist/Fordist city that sought to annihilate time with space). Email is a kind of *pneumatique invisible* and the system of telecommunications already allows for the city of capital to be no more: the 'ether-real' city is not far away – the Internet and the website are poised to replace the polis. But who or what will occupy the barren city? Barren because there is no more meter/mother in the metropolis and the city no longer flows with capital, will it be filled by replicants and robots? The city could de-realise itself, become that disintegrating world without substance that Kracauer speaks of. This is not so unrealistic as might at first appear. Consider for a moment that Paris (like other major cities of the West) has shifted from being a city of production to one of consumption (a process begun incidentally with the Haussmannisation of Paris). The next logical step is the cyber-city.

Paradoxically, cinema is one of the last *real* production industries to remain in Paris. Film, in the case of Paris, is a product of the metropolis – implanted in the city as an industry imaging the city as a product. Paris is the French film industry's number one product, in fact, and is immensely present. The camera and the spectator become two different spatial and temporal *flâneurs*/voyeurs. Both are visual consumers: the camera is the detached observer that strolls (for the most part unnoticed) around the city streets by day or by night. The spectator sits in the public sphere of the film theatre, ensconsed in the dark, viewing the imaginary private, often erotic, sphere of the filmed narrative on screen– our unconscious mirrored, reflected before us. As Giuliana Bruno puts it so eloquently 'cinema plays into the erotic journeys of the gaze' (1995, p. 151). The cinema-theatre of the 'now' substitutes for the iron and glass of the 19th-century arcade. In its first manifestations, such as the Gaumont or Omnia Pathé Palaces of the 1910s and the famous Rex of the 1930s, it is the new allegorical emblem of modernity. And in its later form, such as the cinema multiplex housed in the plastic mall of Les Halles, it is emblematic of multivalent postmodernity.

This filmed city is, however, the deformed city, the form divorced from the matter; a transubstantial virtual city of celluloid imaginings (a spectre, a ghost on screen), a disappearing world without substance. It can therefore be speeded up or sent to sleep (*Paris qui dort*, Clair 1923). The body of the city falls under the regime of photography: it becomes transposed into a series of signs, becoming, as it were, a 'corpus delecti' (to quote Tom Gunning out of context, 1995, p. 37). It was René Clair, then Jean Cocteau, and then Jean-Luc Godard, who said that to film life was to film death. What was the filmed body is no longer true of the present body as it is gone forever – the past, the process of death captured on film. Similarly, architecture has a relationship with death. First, it relies on decomposition to modernise: architecture kills to live, as many 1970s films make clear (for example *Le Chat*, Granier-Deferre, 1971). Second, architecture seeks to tame death by modernising or building monuments (to the dead often enough!), but what it puts in its place is already old. As we know, what is new in technology is already of the past. In a peculiar way, the city is its own graveyard – the body as city becomes ruins. In industrial and technological progress there is decay – the already dead.

Film reflects this paradox of modernity and the modernist city: the transient, the fleeting, the contingent *and* the eternal and immutable. The allegorical metropolis and the monumental metropolis. Film captures the now/now-gone of the 'then' city. The filmed city, because it films the passing of life (Barthes, 1981, p. 9), is like the architectural city – it is never of the 'now'. The city for architects is like a puzzle, an enigma that must be solved. But, just as the cinematic city (as I have already explained) is an enigma constantly probed and investigated by the camera but never resolved, so this is true for the architectural city. The city is an unresolvable riddle which makes architects (and the chattering classes, including Prince Charles) see the past and the future as better. As Donald says (1997, p. 184), architectural discourses perceive the city as a future-perfect (Lacan's *futur-antérieur*) which allows for a deresponsibilisation of the citizen: we accuse the city of the present of being polluted, dirty, noisy, chaotic as if we have nothing to do with it (others such as cars, dogs, vagrants etc do it). Architectural discourses then implicitly erase the present, and in their future-perfect perceptions they are nostalgic (they neo-classically long for the ordered Euclidean city), and/or futuristic (they post-modernly imagine the *ville radieuse* of Le Corbusier: the city as clean-machine). Dream cities come from these discourses, but they destroy the what-is-there to put in place the imaginings of the future-perfect, and by the time these are built they are already of the past and often the utopian ideal from which they emanated has turned into a dystopian reality. Godard's film of the mid-1960s, *Deux ou trois choses que je sais d'elle* (1966), points already to the effect of collective monumental housing. From the very opening titled sequence, the monumental crushes any sense of the communal; the space is an empty city space – no trees, no community in the streets (no streets to be seen, only through-ways). Compare that with a more recent film *LaHaine* (1995). We witness the same type of monumental housing, albeit with different residents (who are even less well-off than those of the 1960s). And we can see once again quite clearly the dehumanising effects of such a living environment. Change with no change. Ultimately the crisis of the monumental is the loss of meaning and therefore of memory, which in turn creates boredom. The space becomes a space of non-being, a breeding ground for phobias (often expressed in forms of violence) and no redemption. And the question becomes: 'where are the ethics of city planning in all of this?' The functional city has forgotten, it seems, the mental city as it has occluded the fact that the outer physical cityscape and the inner mental psychological state of the subject-citizen are self-perpetuating: that the city projects itself onto the subject and vice-versa.

We could take three cinematic examples from the late 1950s through to the early 1980s that usefully illustrate this crisis of the monumental, each one offering what might seem to be an image of a futuristic Paris but which is actually a recognisable Paris, imagined in the present. The first is the comic, but serious, *Mon Oncle* (Tati, 1958), in which the functionally and phobically clean, proto-Le Corbusian home represses both the body and emotion: little boys must be clean and not heard, food must be hygienically prepared and dispensed as if in a dentist's surgery, and so on. A clean home means a clean nation. The second example, *Alphaville* (Godard, 1965), shows a post-Fordian computer-controlled city, the dream city of Artificial Intelligence scientists that is so organised mankind is ultimately dispensable: the human body can be serially the same (the body of the female at least) and erased (for being curious, for having emotions) and replaced by the supreme rationality of Alpha 60. Finally, Besson's *Le Dernier combat* (1983) provides the logical last image of a futuristic barren city, a post-holocaust Paris, the nightmare city of the future where nothing will survive and where reproduction is a futile and meaningless gesture.

Film like architecture is very much a relationship of time and space. Film allows us to see space and time performing in the city, primarily (it has to be said) through the sexualisation of place: by that I mean through the presence of bodies – sexual bodies of all sorts – occupying and being in city spaces. We cannot actually imagine city space as it is beyond our imaginings (if only from the point of view of size), but as James Donald (1997, p. 183) says we can almost always imagine the city as a narrative, as a space and place where events take place. And ineluctably, in this context, we are led to think about how people act and perform in these spaces. In other words, the circulation of bodies, their interaction, is a major referent for our understanding of the city. We imagine this circulation of bodies based on what we know and see; whether these bodies be in cars charging around Paris, on boats going down the Seine, on foot, in the métro or on the bus, be they milling around monuments, skate-boarding at La Défense or in front of the Palais de Chaillot, sitting in cafés talking, or making love in bed, chatting in some apartment or another – whatever. These are examples of the primary narratives by which we imagine a city – in this case, Paris. These are also the primary narratives of cinema's representation of Paris. The body's movement and performance through the city makes the city readable.

But as the above makes clear, just as our own knowledge of the city is very limited – to monuments (the big), specific areas and the circulation of people within it (the small) – so too is cinema's representation of it. What is so intriguing is what is included as desirably visible and what is excluded. A survey of films from the beginning of sound cinema demonstrates that almost half the terrain of Paris is excluded! Even such a simple exercise as that shows how the city is the embodiment of power relations: there are places that are 'in' and those that are not. This means too that there are bodies that are 'in' and bodies that are not. Paris, like all major metropolises, is based in the principle of inclusion and exclusion – that is, it is a divided city, the complete opposite of its meaning, which is mother/city/democracy/nation (in short, metropolis).

The city, the polis, has always been hierarchically designed around the principle of segregation. Segregation based on gender dates back to pre-Christian times in the Western world – and one wonders how much this has really changed since the principle of segregation is still with us whether based on class, race, or ethnicity. Plato, in his *Republic,* talks of the negative effects of gender segregation, of this othering (exclusion of the female other) on the metropolis and in his later work, *Laws,* he goes on to refine his thinking on this matter. I will pause to summarise his thinking since it reveals how far we have yet to go. I am endebted here to Monique Canto and her illuminating essay *The Politics of Women's Bodies: Reflections on Plato* (1986) for the following synopsis of Plato's thoughts on the metropolis. In *The Republic* Plato spoke of an ideal polis (ideapolis) where men and women were equal, the only difference lying in the complementarity of their roles in procreation; and because the polis/city of men and women is in the first place political, then the idea of procreation must also necessarily be a political one. Procreation is then the first political act and also legitimises the identity and civic functions of men and women. Women, as much as men, are political bodies which means that within the city woman is in no way the representative of otherness. But the problem within this concept of the city is that it means that men and women work together to drive otherness to the periphery (or underground) of politics (as in polis/city) – men and women fight together as equals, and make war against those who would intrude into their city. This in turn means always being the same body politic; therefore a city that in remaining the same exists outside history and outside desire since all is the same and not subject to the unpredictability of history. In *Laws,* Plato greatly refines this already quite positive repositioning of woman as not other and comes up with a far more broad and diversified concept of the city. As we recall in *The Republic* the city constitutes itself by dissolving sexual difference but depends on its meaning by playing itself out in relation to otherness. In *Laws,* Plato recognises the need for difference if there is to be historical change: thus women must be there to reproduce and represent the political condition, but so too must otherness be present as a constitutive condition of political reality. In other words, life of the city (political reality, order, and value) is beyond gender – it is movement, circulation, encounter, a mixture of these differences and othernesses where history and desire are articulations of that circulation: a 'well-compounded bowl' as Plato puts it.

Plato's ideapolis is one of circulating otherness. Yet what do we in fact have? A sophisticated surveilled city, a polis that is policed. A capital for which only the circulation of capital really matters – where bodies circulating are perceived as the chaotic body that must be controlled. The city is a flow of capital and labour within a sharply and distinctively divided city. Paris is no exception. It is divided, first, in economic terms along an East/West axis – a division that is marked by the artery that goes north from the boulevard Saint-Michel up through the boulevard de Sébastopol. Secondly, the city is divided intellectually and politically according to its denomination into Left and Right Banks (rive gauche, rive droite). The city is not a body politic constituted for change. It relies on otherness to remain the same. Yet we know already that the city is in permanent flux (as exemplified, in the case of Paris, by the river Seine that runs right through the middle of the city – cleansing it, taking its excrescence away). And of course the city is deeply anxious about bodies that reflect the chaotic flux of urban life. In the 19th century it was the body of the prostitute and the working-class male that mostly worried– now it is the aged, sexualised, raced and ailing 'body-other' that causes concern and that must be policed, repressed and invisibilised. That city-life, by its very existence, resists the desired ordered Euclideancity-flow, the unified logical city of capital, the utopian city of modernity. But that city-life is the one pushed undergound or to the periphery. Today's urban imagineerings (more explicitly put: 'white male middle-class governmentality', Hesse, 1997, p. 100) are not far advanced from those of the past in that they still seek to erase history (as meant by Plato) through a desire to erase this otherness.

This is where a film like Mathieu Kassovitz's *La Haine* reveals just how important it is. Because it shows how 'otherness', in this case raced otherness, becomes problematised (by the polis, the body politic/police) within *and* beyond the city limits. Having placed the raced other outside the city limits (in low-cost high-rise housing) it becomes easier to objectify and then reify the other as 'the problem' that must always be kept outside. Thus the raced other is subject to surveillance (and beatings) not just outside the city limits (where 'they' belong/are pushed), but also within the city where 'they' ostensibly/visibly do not belong.

This is also why a film as difficultly narcissistic as *Les Nuits fauves* (Cyril Collard, 1993) is important because of the spectacle, the mise-en-scène it provides us with of homosexual sexuality. It shows us the night economy of capiton exchange and the performative rejection of reproduction, it shows us the labyrinthine space so associated with the underbelly of Paris, the dirty spaces where sex is both alluring and redolent with danger (to the danger of 19th century syphillis now corresponds 20th century AIDS).

Gay and lesbian sexualities are virtually absent from French cinema, even more so than from the city streets apparently. And in the only two contemporary examples of its filmic representation within Paris that come to my mind (one of which is *Les Nuits fauves*, the other being *Gazon maudit*, 1994, of which more in a minute), it has been within the night-time economy of the city that it has been imaged. Similarly, the sado-masochistic body is another sexual body of the night (unless we except *Belle de jour*, 1967). Claire Devers' film *Noir et blanc* (1986) challengingly puts on screen a set of sexualities (homo-erotic, sado-masochistic, single-sexed and cross-raced) that expresses itself at night, hushed away in private and invisible spaces until it spills out (literally through blood spilling) into the public domain. Deviant bodies, then, are associated with the underside of the city, the dark side of the capital economy – exchanges that we would rather not see. Yet at the turn of the century, lesbians were known as *les lionnes* in the avant-garde circles of those who admired them (including Baudelaire) – the lesbian body was seen as the heroine of the modern (Rita Felski, 1995, p. 20), as the exotic chic transgressor who made possible the imagining (for men) and the practice (for women) of new sexual pleasures. Interestingly, lesbian sexuality as represented in *Gazon maudit* once it is being practiced *not* in the city of Paris but in the South of France is very much seen in the daylight and as an articulation of desire. These few and far between films – which show us sexual practices that we fear – provoke and ask us questions. They take 'otherness' out of the space of our imaginings and perform it squarely before us as a projection on screen of our repressed unconscious (the corporeal city we dread, fear and deny).

Finally, this is why, amongst these contemporary films that matter, a film as excessive as *Les Amants du Pont-Neuf* must also be taken seriously since it shows us yet again that the 'othered' refuses to go away, always manages to penetrate through the rhetoric of the body politic that seeks to contain the threat of otherness. In this film we see street paupers back in the city in big numbers (as in the mid- to late-19th century), we see that they are young as well as old, abled and disabled, men and women. The film shows us also that, just as the Haussmannisation of Paris of the 19th century only veneered over the problem of city dirt and poverty in its attempts to cleanse the city of its dissidents, its poor and its rabble-rousers, so too Jacques Chirac's 20-year programme of cleaning up Paris (1970s-1990s) has failed to rid Paris of the unsuitable and in Euclidean terms the disordered body-non-politic.

In other words what we must value in this cinema is that it refuses the erasure of history, of desire, of sexuality, of ethnicity, of race; it goes on going on; it shows how it is that if you are not of the body politic then you can resist by becoming the body, and that you do this by seeking the last refuge and assertion of identity that is your own body. If, according to the body politic, you are invisible and cannot therefore perform the city so (paradoxically) any performance is possible. This cinema, then, disallows and disavows the safe legibility of the city as contained as clean, as clear and structured; furthermore, it exposes our nostalgia for collective relations (which we imagine to have existed) for what they are, namely, a way of coping with (even to the point of denying) the condition of existence of the city (as pleasure and pain/fear and desire) as we look to the past and the future (future-perfect) for an imagined utopian city. Finally, this cinema exposes the fact that we live in a circulation of commodities driven by capital which divides – that there are in the end no 'rights to the city' of Paris, contrary to what successive Presidents have promised since Giscard D'Estaing first pledged it to his electorate way back in 1974. This, then, is the other cinematic tale of the city of Paris. It is one of resistance, producing a corporeal body without end and therefore uncontainable – a corporeal Paris always going on – a corporeal Paris which, because it resists what is denied, lies between the future perfect and is therefore ireedemably of the always (already) present.

References

Barthes, R. *Camera Lucida: Reflections on Photography*, transl. Howard, R., New York, Hill & Wang, 1981.

Benjamin, W. *Charles Baudelaire, A Lyric Poet in the Era of High Capitalism*, transl. Zohn, H., London, New York, Verso, 1997.

Bruno, G. 'Streetwalking around Plato's Cave' in Pietropaolo, L. & Testaferri, A. (eds.) *Feminisms in the Cinema* (Bloomington & Indianapolis, Indiana University Press, 1995), pp. 146-167.

Canto, M. 'The Politics of Women's Bodies: Reflections on Plato' in Suleiman, S. R. *The Female Body in Western Culture* (Cambridge, Massachusetts, London, England, Harvard University Press, 1986), pp. 339-353.

Donald, J. 'THIS, HERE, NOW, Imagining the modern city' in Westwood, S. & Williams, J. (eds.) *Imagining Cities, scripts, signs, memories* (London, Routledge, 1997), pp. 181-201.

Felski, R. *The Gender of Modernity*, Cambridge, Massuchesetts & London, England, Harvard University Press, 1995.

Gunning, T. 'Tracing the Individual Body: Photography, Detectivesand Early Cinema' in Charney, L. & Schwartz, V. (eds.) *Cinema and the Invention of Modern Life* (Berkeley, Los Angeles, London, University of California Press, 1995), pp.15-45

Hansen, M. 'America, Paris, the Alps: Kracauer (and Benjamin)'in Charney, L. & Schwartz, V. (eds.) *Cinema and the Invention of Modern Life* (Berkeley, Los Angeles, London, University of California Press, 1995), pp. 362-402.

Hesse, B. 'White Governmentality: Urbanism, Nationalism,Racism' in Westwood, S. & Williams, J. (eds.) *Imagining Cities, scripts, signs, memories* (London, Routledge, 1997), pp.86-103.

Weiss, A. *Paris Was a Woman: Portraits from the Left Bank*, Hammersmith, London, San Francisco, California, Pandora, 1995.

Wilson, E. *The Sphinx in the City: Urban Life and the Control of Disorder and Women*, Berkeley, University of California Press, 1992.

Wilson, E. 'Looking Backward, Nostalgia andthe City' in Westwood, S. & Williams, J. (eds.) *Imagining Cities, scripts, signs, memories* (London, Routledge, 1997), pp. 127-39.

Virilio, P. 'Improbable Architecture', *Lost Dimension* (transl. Moshenberg, D., Brooklyn, New York, New York, Semiotext(e), 1991), pp. 69-100.

Subtext: Paris of Alexandre Trauner

Keith A. Reader

The role of the set designer must be among the most underrated in all of cinema. Stars, directors, scriptwriters, and composers all have their places in the various (real or imaginary) filmic halls of fame, yet asked to name even one major set designer it is likely that only a few sadly committed anorak-wearers could oblige, and the endangerment of the species as a result of computer-image generation will do little to change this situation. Since visiting the major exhibition of Alexandre Trauner's set designs held in Paris in 1986, I have been fascinated by one of the longest and most important careers (upwards of 50 years) in French and Hollywood cinema. For many readers of this book Trauner will not even be a name, yet that does not mean that they will not have encountered his work, above all the sets he designed for Marcel Carné. He left his native Budapest late in 1929, fleeing the proto-Fascist and violently anti-Semitic régime of Admiral Horthy, and like many another young artist, made for Paris. There, through a friend, he found work in the Épinay studios as assistant to Lazare Meerson, known above all for the sets he designed for René Clair. He worked with Meerson on *Le Million* (1931), where his watchword – as good an epigraph for his career as any – was 'suggérer la réalité et non la photographier.' ('to suggest reality, not to photograph it.') (Trauner, 1988, p. 18). This he put into practice in his work for Carné, whom he met through what appears to have been a classic bohemian, Rive-Gauche-bistro-based friendship with Carné's main scriptwriter, Jacques Prévert. Meerson died of a heart attack in 1938, while only in his late thirties, and Trauner was later to blame his death on the intense pressures of filming in an age when resources were restricted and scenes could normally be shot once only, and more particularly on the need to save time by bolting one's food at mealtimes, which in his account seems to have given virtually the entire industry permanent dyspepsia.

Trauner more or less immediately became Meerson's succesor, making his name above all through his work for Carné. Ironically, considering that he was to become known as the great designer of Parisian sets, his first two films for Carné, both scripted by Jacques Prévert, had non-Parisian settings. *Drôle de drame* (1937) takes place in a pastiche Victorian London influenced by the work of Dickens and the later nefarious reputation of Limehouse's Chinatown (which had been the setting for D. W. Griffith's *Broken Blossoms* of 1919). *Le Quai des brumes* (1938) transposed the action of Pierre MacOrlan's Montmartre-set novel to Le Havre, whose rôle in this film and in Sartre's *La Nausée* should make of it the unchallenged capital of French pre-War *malheur de vivre*. The relocation was Trauner's idea, so he claimed, and one which caused MacOrlan an unwelcome surprise when he attended the film's premiere. *Le Quai des brumes* is among the films most closely associated with what André Bazin was to call 'poetic realism' (more so than *Drôle de drame*, which is nearer to surrealism). The 'poetic' quality of Trauner's décor is perhaps more apparent today than its realism, if only because the destruction of Le Havre in the Second World War means that the city we know today bears scarcely any resemblance to that reconstructed in *Le Quai des brumes*.

'Trauner's Paris' makes its first major appearance in the Billancourt-shot *Hôtel du Nord* (1938), praised among others by Graham Greene for its reconstruction of the Canal Saint-Martin. Vigo's *L'Atalante* (to which *Hôtel du Nord* contains musical allusions) had shown four years before that in those days the Canal was quintessentially part of workaday proletarian Paris; it is now a favourite destination for tourist boat-trips in which Raymonde (Arletty)'s famous, and all but untranslatable, riposte to Edmond (Louis Jouvet): 'Atmosphère! Atmosphère! Est-ce que j'ai une gueule d'atmosphère?' ('Atmosphere! Atmosphere! Do I look like an atmosphere?)' is regularly invoked. Of the later films on which he was to work with Carné, only two were to be specifically set in Paris. The city in which *Le Jour se lève* of 1939 takes place is never identified (it could be Paris as it was supposedly modelled on one in the *zone* just outside the city limits, but might equally well be an industrial town somewhere in Northern France). *Les Visiteurs du soir* (1942) and *Juliette ou la clef des songes* (1951) construct fairy-tale worlds without realistic topography, while *La Marie du port* (1950) is set in the Normandy port-town of Cherbourg, close to which Prévert and Carné had adjacent houses. The Paris of Carné and Trauner, remarkably for such a cinematic legend, is thus confined to three films – *Hôtel du Nord*, *Les Enfants du paradis* and Carné's first post-War film, *Les Portes de la nuit* of 1947. The latter is the first of three appearances of the Paris Métro in Trauner's work (the others were to be Claude Berri's *Tchao Pantin*, starring Coluche, of 1983 and Luc Besson's 1985 *Subway*); widely criticised on its release, it marked the end of the Carné/Prévert collaboration. It is above all on the magnificent sets Trauner designed for *Les Enfants du paradis*, shot at the Victorine Studios in Nice in 1943 and 1944, that his reputation rests. These remain probably the best-known of all visual images of popular nineteenth-century Paris. Among more recent Parisian iconographies, the work of those who have come to be known as the 'Forum des Halles' directors – Jean-Jacques Beineix, Luc Besson and Léos Carax – has radically reshaped the image of the city, giving it a youthful post-modern turn which for a decade or so, until Mathieu Kassowitz's *La Haine* of 1995, dominated its cinematic representations. Particularly influential in this respect was *Subway*, whose sets were designed by the 78-year-old Trauner. Trauner also worked in Hollywood after the War, designing the sets for, among others, Hawks's *Land of the Pharaohs* (1955), Orson Welles's *Othello* (1959) and many of Billy Wilder's films, including the preternaturally vast, and Oscar-winning, office set for *The Apartment* (1960) and one of the defining Hollywood representations of Paris, *Irma la douce* of 1963.

This is clearly an extraordinary career, and the fulsome tributes that followed Trauner's death in 1993 in the Normandy village where he is buried next to Jacques Prévert make clear how respected and loved in the industry he was. Yet it has to be said, alas, that they do very little more than that. Dudley Andrew describes Trauner's work as 'much discussed' (Andrew, 1995, p. 187), but the major text he cites is an unpublished, and unreferenced, French doctoral thesis. I have looked in vain – even in the beautifully-presented and fascinatingly-documented, as well as forbiddingly pricey, *Alexandre Trauner*

– *décors de cinéma*, including interviews between Trauner and Jean-Pierre Berthomé – for any serious consideration of how the rôle of the set designer as part-auteur of a film might be articulated or conceptualised, of the part the hyper-real décors of *Subway* or *The Apartment* might play in the fixing of the viewing subject's position, or indeed of almost any aspect of Trauner's work beyond the biographical, not to say hagiographical, level. I hope that my necessarily tentative and provisional remarks here may mark the beginning of work along these lines, without unduly solemnising a man whose skill at cooking goulash with spätzle, Alsatian egg noodles, is affectionately evoked by another European Jewish expatriate, Billy Wilder, in his introduction to the Berthomé book. Two possible approaches to a theorisation of set design are suggested by, on the one hand, critiques of the notion of realism and, on the other, work on the importance of space in cinema. Jacques Leenhardt pays tribute to 'la justesse du rapport entre un espace et une action' ('the exactness of the relationship between space and action') in Trauner's work (Trauner, 1986 – this book does not have numbered pages). This suggests how work on cinematic space – I think in particular of Noël Burch's *Une praxis du cinéma* and André Gardies' *L'Espace au cinéma* – might contribute to a conceptualisation of the designer's role. Trauner's distaste (following Meerson) for 'primary realism' (Forbes, 1997, p. 20) evidently stood him in good stead when he had to design the sets of *Les Enfants du paradis* without being able to visit Paris. That city must be, after New York, the most frequently reproduced and celebrated in the history of cinema, Hollywood as well as European (several of Lubitsch's comedies, Minnelli's *An American in Paris*, Donen's *Funny Face* rank alongside *Irma la douce* as well-known examples). The French *Caisse nationale des monuments historiques et des sites* publishes a fascinating collection of photographs taken by the Séeberger brothers in the Paris of the late 1920s and early 1930s which were then dispatched to Hollywood production companies to help in the designing of their sets. The impact of these photographs seems to have outstripped the period during which they were taken, for images from Chaplin's *Monsieur Verdoux* (1947) and *An American in Paris* bear a strong resemblance to some of the Séeberger pictures. This is because such films 'donnent généralement de Paris une vision plus globale et mythique que documentaire' ('usually give us a vision of Paris that is global and mythical rather than documentary') (Salachas, 1994, p. 28). This is equally true of *Les Enfants du paradis*, and suggests a kind of second-degree realism, even hyper-realism, as the implicit aesthetic of much classic set design.

The hyper-reality of Trauner's design is its most important aspect – on that there is general agreement (Bazin describes the square and apartment block in *Le Jour se lève* 'not as a reproduction of reality, but as a work of art dependent upon the artistic economy of the film as a whole' – Carné/Prévert, 1970, p. 10). Andrew's assertion that 'he would characteristically seek a maximum reduction of objects on the screen, though making certain that everything that does remain is absolutely authentic to the period, class, and location the film is trying to represent (Andrew, 1995, p. 187) is nowhere better illustrated than in *Le Jour se lève* – the tellingly minimalist décor of François (Jean Gabin)'s room, the isolation of the apartment block from which François shouts his grief and eventually suicidal defiance. Trauner claims that he looked for a real block of flats to use – he was an assiduous scouter for locations when circumstances permitted – but without success.

Les Enfants du paradis   © Pathé Films

It would certainly be difficult to find a 'real-life' block like this, towering in solitary immensity over an otherwise largely denuded urban square, almost like the sole survivor of a bombing-raid. Could this be one reason why the film may now appear even more redolent of France's coming defeat than it did to audiences and critics at the time?

By the time *Les Enfants du paradis* came to be shot, of course, France had fallen and Jews were banned from working in the entertainment industry. Trauner's name, already upstaged in public prominence by those of Carné and Prévert, now had to disappear altogether, whence, among other reasons, the title 'Subtext' for this paper. He survived the years of Vichy and Occupation largely thanks to Prévert, who offered him shelter in his house on the Riviera (that same Riviera, we may recall, evoked as object of desire in *Le Jour se lève* by the inveterate seducer Valentin [Jules Berry]). This was hardly a disadvantage when it came to designing sets for the film, since its action is situated a hundred years before the time of its making. Jill Forbes astutely observes: 'Paradoxically, the success of the sets derives from their lack of inventiveness and from their conformity to an ideal "original" which we already carry in our mind's eye' (Forbes, 1997, p. 21). The characteristics of that 'ideal "original"' are rooted in, but emphatically not confined to, the Parisian topography of the July Monarchy in which the action of the film is set (see Forbes, 1997, pp. 18-26 for more on this). Integral to that are the Boulevard du Temple as focus of popular theatrical entertainment, the customs barriers set up around the city in 1784 and the *zone*, the 'low-life' area immediately beyond those barriers. The latter term is still used, often by those with no knowledge of its ancestry, to denote the socially marginal, in a clear indication of how far the cultural topography even of present-day Paris is saturated with the myths – the *sans-culottes*, the populist resonances of Belleville and Ménilmontant, the vastly different ethoses of Montmartre on the one hand, the Quartier Latin and Montparnasse on the other – that have gone into its making. It is this 'poetic-realist' Paris, hyperreal precisely through being real to the second degree, that *Les Enfants du paradis* at once calls upon and contributes to (though of course not all the instances I have cited occur in the course of the film).

The photographed prints and engravings from which Trauner worked were assiduously brought to the South from Paris by Carné, who had written an article for *Cinémagazine* in which: -

'(...) the capacity to film the city and its people is posited as the touchstone of cinema as a popular art, and set design is seen as the means by which cinema retained that capacity in the era of sound. In this way, the set serves not merely as a substitute for authentic locations but as a form of superior reality and a means of discovery.' (Forbes, 1997, p. 31).

The sets of *Les Enfants du paradis*, like those of *Le Quai des brumes*, do indeed serve for audiences as 'a means of discovery' of a city to which first-hand access is now impossible. Andrew's assertion that the cinema of poetic realism had replaced 'the theatrical model' with 'a novelistic, romantic aesthetic' (Andrew, 1995, p. 188) requires evident qualification in dealing with this film, which has theatricality at the heart of its diegesis – a theatricality romantically, even novelistically constructed in large part by Trauner's décor. (The overlapping of a theatrical and a novelistic aesthetic is less of a paradox than it may seem, as the work of Victor Hugo most graphically illustrates). Trauner's enforced invisibility during the shooting of *Les Enfants du paradis* metaphorically prefigures the neglect into which he was to fall, at least in France, during the heyday of the New Wave. Among the aspects of the *cinéma de qualité* – a term used, above all, by Truffaut in a very far from positive sense – most scorned by the *Cahiers* critics who were to become New Wave directors was its reliance on studio shooting. The low budgets with which Chabrol, Godard, Truffaut *et al*. were constrained to work combined with the wider availability of lightweight sound and camera equipment to make location filming an artistic statement at the same time as an economic necessity. Trauner was to pursue much of his subsequent career, with as we have seen great success, in Hollywood. It was not until the pendulum swung back towards studio filming, with the advent of the 'Forum des Halles' generation, that he was once more to come into his own in France. The hyperrealism I have mentioned as the major hallmark of his style links the Trauner of *Le Jour se lève* with that of *Subway*, which is emphatically not to imply any parity of quality or esteem between those two films.

Yet there is one film by a New Wave director – for all that the New Wave had long since ceased to exist as such by the time it was made – which seems to me unmistakably to bear Trauner's intertextual imprint. This is François Truffaut's *Le Dernier Métro* of 1980, the closest of his works to the *cinéma de qualité* he had so reviled as a critic – in the size of its budget, its use of established megastars (Catherine Deneuve and Gérard Depardieu) and its reliance on scripted studio shooting. It was also, and doubtless not coincidentally, his most financially successful work. The sets for *Le Dernier Métro* were designed by Jean-Pierre Cohut-Svelko (Truffaut's regular designer), yet the pressbook on Trauner held by the Bibliothèque André Malraux in Paris refers to it as being among Trauner's work. This is doubtless a genuine error, but not an insignificant one. My suspicion is that it came about because of the reference to the Métro in the film's title, which presumably suggested a parallel with *Subway* and Trauner's other Métro films.

The action of Truffaut's cinema backstage melodrama, *La Nuit américaine* (1973), actually takes place in the Victorine Studios in Nice where *Les Enfants du paradis* was shot. Truffaut also famously wrote in a letter to Carné, towards the end of his life, that he would give up all the films he had made to have done *Les Enfants du paradis* – this, from the great adversary of *cinéma de qualité*, and one for whom Renoir and emphatically not Carné had been the master of pre-War French cinema, a somewhat startling statement if not quite a recantation.

Les Enfants du paradis   © Pathé Films

Yet the echoes of *Les Enfants du paradis* in *Le Dernier Métro*, a film roughly contemporary with the letter to Carné, are not difficult to find. The film's setting in a popular boulevard theatre, the fact that much of its action takes place on stage, the calling into question or transgressing of the boundary between theatre and life – a theme dear to the Renoir of *Le Carrosse d'or*, but also to *Les Enfants du paradis* – all recall the earlier film. Individual episodes in the narration often have counterparts in *Les Enfants du paradis*. Bernard Granger (Depardieu) attacks the anti-semitic critic Daxiat (Jean-Louis Richard) (based on Pierre Gaxotte, also known as Lucien Rebatet, of Bardèche and Brasillach's collaborationist journal *Je suis partout*) in a literally more deadly serious version of Frédérick Lemaître (Pierre Brasseur)'s assault upon the theatre critics of *Les Enfants du paradis*. We see and hear the 'trois coups' before the action of *Le Dernier Métro*'s play-within-a-film much as we hear them at the beginning of each of the two halves/acts of *Les Enfants du paradis*. The theatre director Jean-Loup Cottins (Jean Poiret) is clearly homosexual like Carné and Prévert's Lacenaire (Marcel Herrand), while Bernard's inveterate womanising resembles a less successful version of Lemaître's. Marion Steiner (Catherine Deneuve), finally, is the object of the multiple desires that drive the plot of Truffaut's film much as Garance (Arletty) is in *Les Enfants du paradis*. These are to a large extent genre stereotypes of the backstage melodrama, but precisely thereby reveal how far Truffaut in this more than any of his other films except perhaps *L'Histoire d'Adèle H.* (1975) had moved away from the resolute non-theatricality of the New Wave.

Where is the Traunerian subtext in all this? The answer, I would contend, is precisely where Trauner himself was during the making of *Les Enfants du paradis* – underground, or more specifically under the stage where Marion Steiner's Jewish husband Lucas (Heinz Bennent) is forced to spend the Occupation years hiding (the topos of subterranean space as metaphor for the unconscious of history goes back at least as far as Victor Hugo's *Les Misérables*; a striking recent cinematic example is Emir Kusturica's *Underground* of 1995). Lucas continues to direct his plays at one remove, listening to the performances through a providentially-disposed heating vent and thus able to proffer advice through Marion who alone knows his whereabouts. At the same time, he hears in the emotional and erotic tension that builds between Bernard and Marion what is potentially an emotional death sentence for him to go with the literal one that he would undoubtedly incur if his hiding-place were discovered. 'Thus it is that the romantic and the historical plot of the film converge when the two men finally meet face to face' (Higgins, 1996, p. 160) – a scene whose obvious counterpart in *Les Enfants du paradis* is the 'face-off' between Garance and Nathalie (Maria Casarès), when both women proclaim their love for Baptiste (Jean-Louis Barrault). Whether or not Truffaut consciously intended *Le Dernier Métro* as a homage to *Les Enfants du paradis*, and whether or not the overtones of Trauner's situation in that of

Lucas Steiner were deliberate, I obviously have no means of knowing. Echoes of one text in another, however, are not reliant upon conscious or acknowledged authorial intention, as the work of Harold Bloom and Michael Riffaterre makes clear; there can be few of us who have not said or written something that we only later realise bears the imprint of another, preexistent text (done by students, that is plagiarism; done by authors and academics, intertextuality). The irony that one of the cinema's most remarkable evocations of Paris as imaginary space was produced in conditions of such spatial constraint and precariousness, for its designer at least, is, at all events, a suggestive one. The influence of Trauner could, on my hypothesis, be said not to have disappeared during the New Wave years so much as to have gone underground – a further reason for my choice of the title 'subtext.' I hope that his work will soon be lifted from the penumbra of subtext into the prominence and recognition he so mainfestly deserves.

References

Andrew, D., *Mists of Regret: Culture and Sensibility in Classic French Cinema*, Princeton, Princeton University Press, 1995.

Carné, M. & Prévert, J., *Le Jour se lève*, London, Lorrimer, 1990.

Forbes, J., *Les Enfants du paradis*, London, British Film Institute, 1997.

Higgins, L. A., *New Novel, New Wave, New Politics*, Lincoln/London, University of Nebraska Press, 1996.

Salachas, G., *Le Paris d'Hollywood: sur un air de réalité*, Paris, Caisse Nationale des Monuments Historiques et des Sites, 1994.

Trauner, A., *Alexandre Trauner: cinquante ans de cinéma*, Paris, La Cinémathèque Française, 1986.

Trauner, A., *Décors de cinéma: Entretiens avec Jean-Pierre Berthomé*, Paris, Jade-Flammarion, 1988.

Countryscape/Cityscape and Homelessness in Agnès Varda's *Sans toit ni loi* and Leos Carax's *Les Amants du Pont-Neuf*

Raynalle Udris

The importance given to the representation of space is a recurrent and essential feature in Agnès Varda's filmography. In many of Varda's short films the importance of space is prominent: one thinks of *Les Dites Cariatides* (1984), described by Sandy Flitterman-Lewis as 'an architectural documentary about buildings in Paris'; and in her 20-minute fiction film *7 Pièces*, we find 'a working of fantasy and imagination as they intersect with the reality of place'.[1] In *L'Opéra-Mouffe* (1958), the background is the impoverished quarter of the Rue Mouffetard in Paris explored through the eyes of a pregnant woman. 'In her characteristic dialectical spirit' writes Flitterman-Lewis, 'Varda interweaves the personal and the social, the subjective and the objective, into a detailed exploration of one specific milieu, and of one very particular point of view, and in so doing, delineates the constitutive elements of each' (p. 226). One of her feature films, *Cléo de 5 à 7* (1961), presents a 'ninety-minute portrait of a woman and a city in which important feminist themes intersect with an almost sociological regard for Parisian life' (p. 230). It is therefore no surprise that in *Sans toit ni loi*, Varda's 1985 film, space is also one of the essential elements in the construction of the film's subject-matter.

Straight from the credit sequence of *Sans toit ni loi*, with the representation of a winter rural landscape, the importance of space is evident. What characterises this shot is the presence of a very slow zoom, which 'allows time in between to perceive the shifting of planes, from foreground to background. Through this counter-cinematic practice,' rightly stresses Susan Hayward, 'the zoom becomes denaturalised and does not conform to the dominant ideology'.[2] This is indeed one aspect of Varda's film practice which links her work to the French New Wave.

For our concern with space here, the slow zoom functions, with its foregrounding of countryscape as metaphor, as a kind of *mise en abyme* of what the film is about. The slow diagonal movement of the camera, showing the bare landscape from the tree in the foreground to those in the background and ending up at the greenhouse, close to the ditch where the female character's dead body is lying, stresses the painterly quality of the image, while creating an impression of void, and draws attention to the broader countryscape. In doing so, the camera movement also alludes to one of the primary functions of space in *Sans toit ni loi* which is, as we shall see later, to expose bluntly the material conditions of existence of the homeless central female character, Mona. The interaction between character and environment also corresponds to one of Varda's principles of composition, in what she has called her *cinécriture*.[3]

The second shot, which logically follows the credit sequence and properly starts the film with the momentum of its contrasted silence, quickly brings the viewer, via the presence of a secondary character, to the ditch where Mona's body is lying. This reduction of the female figure to the gaze of the onlooker constitutes a first reification of Mona's body (though also the only one, in the context of the film's flashback). Such objectification announces the way Mona will be viewed throughout the film by the different people she has encountered in the few weeks before her death. The frozen body, reduced to an object in the frozen countryscape, blends with the earth in the ditch where she is found. Its female entity has disappeared, there remains only the frozen landscape; a meaning which may be seen as reinforcing the essential and potent presence of the countryscape, already shown in the credit sequence.

If, at one level, the fixity to which Mona is reduced in death, in the opening shots, reflects, as if it were its result, the process of objectification by the look she is submitted to by other characters later in the film, this fixity is nevertheless, on another level, the opposite of what the main character is about.

The film, as summarised by Varda, is a story about the 'adventures and solitude of a young vagabond (neither withdrawn nor talkative) told by those who had crossed her path, that winter in the South of France'.[4] This young vagabond, Mona, is not constructed in a psychological way. While in *Cléo de 5 à 7* the Paris cityscape plays an essential part in the self-discovery of the female character, in *Sans toit ni loi*, Mona's wandering in the southern French countryscape has nothing to do with a search for identity: 'son monde mental est en partie celui du fugitif qui ne connaît de la société que ce qu'il fuit', mentions Françoise Audé; 'elle ne sait d'elle-même qu'une certitude: il faut s'échapper.'[5] Mona's function, as the title *Sans toit ni loi* clearly indicates, is to wander.[6] What the film constructs, through a dialectical interaction between character and setting,[7] is a mythic figure of errancy. This mythic dimension is clearly stated by Varda's voice-over in an early sequence. The sequence acquires, with its voice-over and the association of the character with the sea, a strong Durassian tone and creates in the viewer a distancing effect, while presenting Mona as an enigmatic figure, almost an alien 'qui ne laisse pas de traces' ('who leaves no trace') (repeated later in the film) – her dead body is never claimed. In the rest of the narrative, Mona's constant uncompromising indifference to other peoples' reactions, her haphazard unsheltered errancy in the country, inscribes her character as a mythic figure, in the eyes particularly of other female characters in the film. In that sense, the film can certainly be read in relation to issues of femininity. 'The "Mona effect" is nothing other than the riddle of femininity politicised', claims Flitterman-Lewis (p. 245). The female character of *Sans toit ni loi* whose name, as Françoise Audé recalls in *Positif* (p. 65), comes from the Greek *monos*, meaning seul/unique, is, I quote, 'impenetrable, unforgettable like (the Mona of) Leonardo de Vinci, and as mysterious ... obstinate rather than in revolt' (my translation). Her rebellious stand, which leads her to look, for instance, at the built-up surroundings from the lorry-driver's cab and conclude simply 'c'est moche' ('it's ugly'), constantly propels her from space to space. Space then functions as the necessary material outlet for the articulation of her rebellious freedom, and as a primary agent of her eventual destruction, since the inhospitable countryscape in the grip of winter will finally claim her life.

Sans toit ni loi has a lot in common with a road movie, though as Susan Hayward signals, its composition goes against the canonical rules of the genre, since, for instance, 'the narration is a series of flashbacks all interwoven rather than an ordered sequence of events which lead inexorably to a bad end (*Easy Rider*) or a reasonable resolution (*Paris, Texas*)' (p. 290), and also, contrary to the laws of the genre, the roadster's point of view is not given but everyone else's instead. The construction of the narrative is based on a series of (eighteen) testimonies presented as interwoven flashbacks, interspersed with basic shots of Mona's wanderings in the landscape. The flashbacks partly contribute to identifying the characters' testimonies, while the shots of Mona in transit mostly serve to assert the female character's figure of rebellious freedom. While keeping in mind that Mona's existence only acquires its coherence in terms of its dialectical interaction with the setting in which it is pictured, we will now examine these two kinds of sequences in relation to the types of representation of space in *Sans toit ni loi*.

The contrast between enclosed and open space

The contrast between enclosed and open space in the film is particularly revealing of Mona's type of homelessness. Enclosed spaces, mostly houses, greenhouses, cafés, lorry cabins and cars, are portrayed in the context of peoples' memories and testimonies about Mona. Mona is rarely portrayed in these spaces, with the chief exception of Mme Lantier's car. It is interesting to note that she is never represented inside her tent – a place which could be seen as her private space – at most this is only shot from the outside by a fixed camera.

Enclosed areas are on the whole alien to her and when she enters such areas it is most often for survival purposes – to eat, to sleep, to earn money or to shelter from the cold. For instance, Mona enters cafés – typically 'male' domains – to ask for a sandwich or to be offered a beer. In the semi-open male space of the garage, where she temporarily earns a little money, she has to pay in sexual terms for compromising with social space. Man-made enclosed space functions for the representation of Mona's kind of homelessness as a necessary evil to be escaped from as soon as possible. There is one exception, however; that of the abandoned château in the sequence where she squats with a temporary travelling companion. The château, which could be seen as equivalent to the bridge of *Les Amants*, provides not only basic shelter but a space where the character can, albeit temporarily, recreate a private marginalised way of living.

The escape from solitude, a freedom lived in the warming company of sexual love, drugs and rock music, the comfort of the chateau's past glory, all constitute the necessary ingredients for what becomes a mythic marginal space in the eyes of a beholder, like those of the secondary character Yolande. The temptation of fixity, of settlement in a space, does not last long since external events soon send Mona back on the road. Another temptation of marginalised settlement will later occur with her encounter with the shepherds' marginal lifestyle. The shepherd farm, and the offer she receives of a little land and a caravan, represents the most realistic alternative to Mona's life of wandering, a way of living which initially seems to attract her. Such a way of living could have provided, if only temporarily, a settlement for Mona, but even the 'radical' shepherd cannot cope with her uncompromising marginality. It is his reaction of rejection, and cogent summary of the limitations of her world-view, which puts her back on the road. The shepherd, like many others in the film, cannot accept her filth, laziness, indifference and determination to live the way she wants to.

Nîmes station at the end of the film, another enclosed space where Mona takes refuge, is, together with the squat she then briefly inhabits, the only urban space represented in the film. It is worth noting that Mona, increasingly weak and tired, forced into enclosed spaces by the rigours of winter, has gravitated towards the town. It is also significant that it is from this point that her decline accelerates.

> The representation of enclosed space, which encompasses the testimonies about Mona, functions therefore (with the exception of her tent) as a symbol of life in society, and more often the sign of society's rejection of her marginality. Enclosed space provides a framework for the representation of reactions to Mona's homelessness and it is in this sense that the film acquires its sociological dimension. We know indeed that for *Sans toit ni loi*, Varda was inspired by the real story of a homeless woman: 'I have made several films' she has said, 'around this kind of research into what we feel, what we see, what emotions we experience in relation to other views, other feelings, other choices, and this chain reaction has finally resulted in *Sans toit ni loi*'.[8] The examination of space within this social exploration is undeniable, as Flitterman-Lewis writes: 'In her almost sociological cinematic explorations of cultural situations, Varda has consistently emphasised the effects of place on the social relations she analyses; this has been a recurrent thread in her work from *La Pointe courte* onwards' (p. 237).

The representation of enclosed social areas in villages or towns, which generally become for Mona the symbol of rejection, is interspersed and contrasted with shots of open countryscape which mostly picture Mona on the move and which give her situation of homelessness a more positive, though mythic, dimension of freedom. 'Seule c'est bien' ('It's good, being alone') and 'je m'en fous, je bouge' ('I don't care, I'm on the move'), confirms Mona in her conversation with the shepherd. However, as winter deepens, the representation of Mona in the open countryscape increasingly takes on a more dramatic tone.

The representation of open space in *Sans toit ni loi* corresponds to two types of shots: the static shots in which the character is caught in a temporary lack of movement and, more significantly, the moving shots in which Mona is captured in the continuous movement of roaming around the landscape. The first type of shot, where a static camera records a temporary interruption to her wandering movement, generally stresses some specific action: Mona repairing her boot, rolling a cigarette, fixing her tent-pegs or eating soup, actions which aid her survival in an inhospitable landscape. These static shots are a kind of punctuation in Mona's long solitary journey and provide a counterpoint to the other kind of shot. The moving shots in *Sans toit ni loi* are signalled by the presence of some 14 tracking shots. Varda has described the film 'as a long tracking shot ... we cut it up into pieces, we separate the pieces and in between them are the "adventures"'.[9] Hayward recalls that 'the tracking shot is a natural icon for a road movie' (p. 290). However, as she stresses, a significant number of these shots go against the rules of the genre since Mona's movement is filmed from right to left. Hayward sees in this movement 'a metaphor for the flashback, and even more significantly, death' (p. 288), while Alain Bergala in *Cahiers du Cinéma* viewed the tracking shot as a filmic technique which resolves the contradiction between controlling the character and keeping her at a distance.[10] As far as our study of space is concerned here, it is noticeable that in most of the tracking shots the camera does not focus on the character but foregrounds the countryscape instead. The camera movement either catches up with Mona's walking or starts panning the landscape when Mona enters the frame. When she does not leave the frame, it is the camera which abandons her to finish its movement on a static object, like a gate, a closed door, some deserted agricultural machinery, a ruined wall or abandoned boxes; objects which can clearly be seen as symbols of Mona's situation of dereliction and solitude which characterise her homelessness.

Though, as Hayward emphasises, the tracking shots, often accompanied by bleak, non-harmonious music, are the 'sign' of Mona (p. 288), nonetheless this filmic technique tends to relativise the character's importance by giving greater status to the material landscape in which she is portrayed. What matters is the representation of the space covered by Mona's wandering, and the very action of solitary walking rather than where she is going.

This foregrounding of countryscape throughout the film echoes the opening shots of the film and clearly signals space as one main element of the film's subject-matter. Space which gives a character its justification, and which also acquires importance in its own right, is indeed an intrinsic part of the film's diegesis. The space of homelessness, the open countryscape of *Sans toit ni loi* is varied, non-habitable, increasingly harsh and inhospitable. There is little sign of private life or settled marginality in any one space as there is in *Les Amants du Pont-Neuf*. Homelessness in *Sans toit ni loi* is represented as incessant free movement, congruent with the character's deliberate, rebellious and uncompromising choice. Her movement in space is a pure wandering which leads nowhere since Mona follows a kind of circular trajectory which brings her back to the same areas. Her walking has no linearity except that which brings her to her death.

As a contrast and as the name of the famous bridge of the title clearly indicates, the Cityscape is the referential space of *Les Amants du Pont-Neuf*.[11] As Keith Reader states in 'Cinematic Representations of Paris', 'the modern city has had an obvious and enduring appeal to film-makers ... and Paris has probably embodied more of that appeal than any of its rivals'.[12] Reader also recalls that the film-makers who have used Paris are many, from Vigo with *Zéro de conduite* and *L'Atalante* to Truffaut and *Les Quatre-cent coups*, to which one could of course add Varda's *Cléo de 5 à 7*, Carné's *Hôtel du nord* or Godard's *A Bout de souffle*, among many others. As a result, Reader deduces that 'any consideration of how Paris is depicted in the cinema will necessarily be an intertextual one' (p. 409). *Les Amants* does contain many references to other cinematic works, though one could argue, with Thomas Bourguignon in *Positif*, that the cinematic and literary references are far from being the best in Carax's film, because they often have no emotional or diegetic value.[12] The intertextual link for the study of space in *Les Amants*, though no doubt important, may in fact be less revealing than the close examination of the referential space undertaken in the film.

The representation of the city of Paris in *Les Amants*, no doubt influenced by the conditions of the film's production and by modern cinematic developments in the representation of city space, contributes to the 'blurred image of the cities' described by Pierre Sorlin in his book *European Cinema, European Societies*.[13] The cinematic destruction of city space was noticeably begun in 1967 with Antonioni's *Blow-up* and Godard's *Deux ou trois choses que je sais d'elle* – films that offered only vague representations of cities, without any added narrative meaning: 'such notions as urban atmosphere, city life, which were central to the cinema of the 1950s are abolished' writes Sorlin (p. 134). He continues, 'after 1965 or so (other) cinematographers were no longer able to tell, or see what towns were and created a blurred image of cities' (p. 135). In *Les Amants*, in spite of a crudely realistic early sequence shot in the Nanterre shelter for the homeless, the cityscape of Paris is elsewhere flattened, reduced to prosaic clichés like that of the neon sign of 'La Samaritaine',[14] megastore symbol of capitalist Paris.

However, if the representation of the cityscape in *Les Amants* contributes to the modern transference of collective visual characteristics, to the general 'cinematic destruction of cities' as Sorlin would put it, we do observe a displacement of referential meaning. If, in line with the contemporary tendency, the cityscape in *Les Amants* is not given any specific diegetic role, a leading historical symbol, Le Pont-neuf is, as the title clearly indicates, central to the narrative. Its pivotal presence in the film functions as a metonymic displacement of the diegetic importance of the city, 'since beyond this very closed and yet open space, it is Paris as a whole which is here mobilised. Paris as a locus for cinema and as a locus for fiction.'[15] (my translation).

The image of the bridge could to some degree be viewed as an equivalent to the filmic depiction of the shanty-towns from the 1950s, mentioned by Sorlin, which were portrayed as existing for themselves, in their own right, but the intensive collective life, symbolic of hardship and of freedom, is replaced in *Les Amants* by a more contemporary individualised form of marginal living. The bridge, closed to the public for renovation works and colonised by Alex and his homeless companions, is represented here as a no-man's land. Its presence frames the plot; a symbol of marginal space, it enters into a dialectical interaction with the cityscape as a whole, itself represented, as already mentioned, as a vague entity. It is in this sense that we can assert that space, more exactly marginal space, acquires a diegetic value in *Les Amants*. Like the town in Godard's and Antonioni's early-1960s films, the bridge is 'alive and glamorous enough', as Sorlin would again put it, 'to add supplementary meaning to the story' (p. 131), and one could go further and say that the film's story depends on this space.

The plot of *Les Amants* constantly underlines the opposition between city and marginal place, an opposition constitutive of its subject-matter. While the closed bridge is the symbol of an 'inside' private marginal space, of disorder with recourse to drugs and alcohol, of madness, fantasy and movement, the city is portrayed as a contrast, as the outside public space, the domain of law, order and control, and of respectability. One place belonging to the city does escape these symbolic characteristics: the Paris Underground is pictured several times, and could possibly be viewed as an alternative to the marginal space of the bridge.

In *Les Amants* the two main characters are representative of the two irreconcilable types of space. Michelle belongs to the city, her presence on the bridge is due to a kind of accident, an act of despair: after an unfortunate love story, losing her sight and deprived of hope, she has taken to the street. She originally came from the city when she met Alex, who had collapsed in the middle of the road, after trying desperately to follow the straight line in the middle of the road, itself an impossible symbolic attempt in the context of the character's marginality. Temporarily homeless, Michelle remains normalising when she tries to get Alex away from drugs, and is herself normalised when, for instance, she decides to get rid of her dangerous gun. Contrary to the anonymity of other city homeless, Michelle is individualised, unlike Mona in *Sans toit ni loi*, whose dead body is never claimed. The city later attempts to regain Michelle through the many posters which cover the city and underground walls and through the radio appeal which she inadvertently ends up hearing. Her marriage to the doctor who saves her sight towards the end of the film signals the triumph of the city and of normalised life. To this extent, rather than being a social depiction of homelessness, the film's narrative could be seen as a struggle to keep Michelle on the bridge.

Alex belongs to the marginal space of the bridge. Whenever he finds himself away from the bridge, one is reminded of the Nanterre shelter or the prison; his recurrent motto is 'let's go back to the bridge', even if, as Keith Reader signals, 'it is an attachment which is clearly destroying him' (p. 314). Alex tries to keep or regain Michelle on the bridge, the most obvious instances being when he burns the van containing the posters of Michelle's face or when, on his release from prison, rather than planning to meet Michelle in the city, as the possible symbol of the start of a new life, he insists on meeting her on the bridge – even if the bridge as he knew it has completely disappeared, since it is now open to the traffic, and he has become, so to speak, twice homeless.

Hence the logic of the last sequence. As Michelle and Alex fall into the water, the opposition between city and marginal space, the lovers' dilemma, is resolved. This 'unrealistic' ending contributes to giving the film its mythic seal. Leaving the city behind is prefigured earlier in the film by temporary escapes to the sea or to snowy landscapes. These short, isolated sequences picture spaces of fantasy, a mythic return to nature and innocence. The ambiguity of the last sequence (seen as a direct reminder of Vigo's *L'Atalante* by many film critics) can symbolically be read as death or as rebirth (which in Bakhtin's carnivalesque amounts to more or less the same thing...).[16] The couple's fall into the water and their implausible rescue by a barge sailing towards Le Havre, a seaport whose name signifies 'haven', can be read as the final escape from the city and a mythical rebirth into love, innocence and freedom.

As already suggested earlier, the portrayal of marginal space in *Les Amants* is not really convincing in terms of social representation. Despite the crude realism of the early sequences, such as that at the Nanterre shelter, the film pictures, as Bourguignon stresses, 'an artificial Paris'; hence 'this heterogeneous aspect of the work, which does not always succeed in marrying two alien worlds, that of the documentary and that of pure illusion' (p. 37, my translation). As for the tracking shots of Mona's walking in *Sans toit ni loi*, the function of the representation of space in *Les Amants* appears mostly to foreground the characters' need for endless movement. One thinks of the chase sequence in the Underground, the lovers running on the beach or the water-skiing on the Seine. The marginal space of the bridge, though functioning to some degree as a realist shelter, is also an excuse for the characters' physical exultation of life, with their running, pacing up and down, and jumping around the parapets. A most noticeable sequence, that of the Paris Bicentenary firework display, transforms the bridge into a space for bodily excess, movement and fantasy. It is interesting to note that in *Les Amants*, the hardship of the homeless condition is not so much registered in the depiction of the spatial environment, but on the character's body. This displacement, also to some extent present with Mona in *Sans toit ni loi* and Michelle in *Les Amants*, is most striking in Alex, whose body's gradual destruction, gruesomely represented in the film, is stopped in the first instance by his stay in prison and, later, artificially prevented from recurring.

Referential space in *Les Amants* is therefore mostly represented as a space of excess and fantasy, emphasised by the many visual effects of the image, mostly colours and lights, and by the dazzling recurrent presence of fire. The fireworks sequence on the bridge is the most striking example. 'It may not have a lot to do with real life under the bridge,' concludes Nick Jones in *City Limits*, 'but it is a fresh-eyed incandescent wonder of cinema' (in Reader, p. 413).

The difference between the two films in the representation of space and homelessness is also to a significant degree inscribed in the historical conditions of their production. Mona's story of spatial wandering is answerable to the ethos of rebellion, among other features, which aligns the film to the New Wave tradition. While the emphasis on visual effects in Carax's film – effects which in several sequences seem to take the subject over – is inscribed in what could be called 'the cinema of the look', Carax's *Les Amants du Pont-Neuf* is, with the cinema of Beneix and Besson, very much a cinema of the 1990s.

But whether the countryscape of *Sans toit ni loi* serves to construct a figure of radical otherness or whether the city-space of *Les Amants* functions as a celebration of marginality, we find in both films a pregnant celebration of freedom. It is in this sense that Bergala, in *Cahiers du Cinéma*, sees *Vagabond* as a film from which one comes out comforted and stimulated: 'it is a film which accrues self-confidence ... a joyful challenge to any self-pity ... even if its tone is far from being blissfully optimistic' (p. 5).

The valorisation of marginal space, at both the referential and diegetic level, be it the bridge in the Paris cityscape or the winter South of France countryscape, gives these films their ideological dimension. Homelessness is not so much treated at the economic or material level, but is rather treated as a symbol of exclusion and of potential revolutionary power, in a society which values fixed settlement and material security. The viewer, together with other characters in *Sans toit ni loi*, is prompted to react and to reassess her/his own assumptions in front of the blatant representation of the character's uncompromising marginality. We could argue that the principle of reality is safe and that the victory of societal order is obvious in both films, with the explicit or imagined deaths of the main characters and their respective symbolic return to water or to earth. Nevertheless with Mona in *Sans toit ni loi* the mythic power of her marginal existence makes of her spatial wandering a potent ingredient which haunts the spectators (viewers and other characters) and ultimately questions the foundations of the societal order.

Notes

1 Flitterman-Lewis, S., *To Desire Differently*, New York, Columbia University Press, 1996, p. 228.

2 Hayward, S., 'Beyond the Gaze and into Femme-Film Ecriture', in Hayward, S. and Vincendeau, G. (eds.) *French Film Texts and Contexts* (London & New York, Routledge, 1990) p. 292.

3 *Cinécriture* means cinematic writing; Agnès Varda explains specifically that it is '...not illustrating a screenplay, not adapting a novel, not getting the gags of a good play, not any of this. I have fought so much since I started, since *La Pointe courte*, for something that comes from emotion, sound emotion, feeling, and finding a shape for that, and a shape which has to do with cinema and nothing else.' ('Agnès Varda: A Conversation with Barbara Quart', in *Film Quarterly* Vol.40 no.2 (Winter 1986/87) p. 4, quoted in Flitterman-Lewis, p. 219).

4 Agnès Varda, publicity release for *Ciné Tamaris*, 1985.

5 *Positif*, no.299 (January 1986) p. 65.

6 Errancy was already present in Varda's earlier film, for instance in *Murs murs* (1980) and *Documentar* (1982), two films which picture Hollywood and which were also fictions of solitary wanderers.

7 The dialectical interaction between Mona and the countryscape in *Sans toit ni loi* is the counterpart of another interaction, this time between the cityscape and its inhabitants, in *Murs murs*, in which Varda starts from the townscape: 'l'habitat explique l'habitant, le décor ici explique le ou les décorateurs (car ces fresques sont le produit collectif ou individuel des californiens du centre ou des quartiers, l'expression de tribus et de gangs qui signent par là leur existence et leur identité.' ('The habitat explains the inhabitant, here the decor explains the creator(s) – since these frescoes are the collective or individual products of californians from the entre or the suburbs, the expression of tribes and gangs who thus testify to their existence and identity.' (my translation) (Dubroux, D., in *Cahiers du Cinéma*, no 331 (January 1982) p. 48).

8 Varda, A., 'Entretien', *Cinébulles* p. 7 (quoted by Flitterman-Lewis, op.cit. p. 228).

9 *Cinématographe*, no.114 (1985) p. 19 (quoted by Hayward, p. 290).

10 Bergala, A., 'La Repousse', *Cahiers du Cinéma* no.378 (December 1985) p. 6.

11 Made in 1991, *Les Amants du Pont-neuf* is the hallucinatory love-story of a 28-year old fire-eater and of a young woman who is going blind, set on the oldest bridge in Paris. After *Boy Meets Girl* and *Mauvais sang*, *Les Amants*, the third feature film by Leos Carax, was described by Carax himself as 'the last film of

a trilogy: over eight years I have made three films with the character of Alex, I had to put an end to it.' (my translation; in *Cahiers du Cinéma*, Hors-série M1089 (1991) p. 75) The shooting of the film, twice interrupted in the course of three years, was epic in itself. Because of an accident involving the co-star Denis Lavant, the renowned bridge could not be used during the three weeks previously booked. An artificial replica of the bridge had to be built (in Montpellier): as Thierry Jousse concludes: 'the object of every desire and every kind of envy, the famous bridge was first of all the stake in an aesthetic as well as an economic battle' (my translation; in *Cahiers du Cinéma*, no.448 [October 1991] p. 25).

12   Reader, K., 'Cinematic Representations of Paris', in *Modern Contemporary France*, no.4 (1993) p. 409.

13 'Carax nous embarque dans sa planète 'cinéma', qui, vue à travers l'œil de sa caméra, se peuple de références cinéphiliques et livresques qui sont loin d'être le meilleur de son film, car elles n'ont bien souvent aucune valeur émotionnelle ou diégétique.' ('Carax takes us to his planet Cinema which, seen through the camera-eye, is peopled with filmic and literary references which are far from being the best part of his film since they often have no emotional or diegetic value.' (my translation; Bourguignon, T., *Positif* , no 369 (November 1991) p. 37)

14 Sorlin, P., 'The Blurred Image of Cities', in *European Cinemas, European Societies 1939-1990* (London, Routledge, 1991).

15 'The unmissable Samaritaine, honoured to be suddenly raised to the rank of metaphor: that of the film, a gigantic cinema megastore where Carax wanders with his camera...' (my translation; Strauss, F., in *Cahiers du Cinéma* no.448, p. 24)

16 Jousse, p. 25. 'Car au-delà de ce lieu clos en plein air, c'est Paris tout entier qui est ici mobilisé. Paris comme lieu de cinéma et comme lieu de fiction.'

17 Bakhtin, M., *Rabelais and his World*, Cambridge Mass., MIT, 1968: '...the earth's motherhood and burial as a return to her womb' (p. 327). Bakhtin also refers to 'pregnant death' (p. 359).

Anxious Spaces in German Expressionist Films

Carol Diethe

For the purposes of this chapter, I shall use the word 'space' in the sense of external space or 'outdoors', a space little used in Expressionist film for a variety of reasons, most prominent of which was the Expressionist preoccupation with the city which left little room for the contemplation of its environment. I shall seek to show that the rare shots of 'outdoors' (sometimes shot *indoors*) reflect a heightened anxiety on the part of the character in the film; and this heightened anxiety can communicate itself to the spectator. Of course, there is nothing new in the association of anxiety with Expressionism. Without descending to cliché, one can legitimately say that the neurotic gloom permeating German Expressionism can scarcely be overstressed. Just why the urgent need to express the angst of the period overcame first the poets and dramatists (especially from 1910–20) and then, after the Great War, the film-makers in Germany is more difficult to explain. Of course, there was first an apprehension of war throughout the cultural life of the country, and then the experience of the real thing. And other nations besides Germany produced artists who expressed their fears in jagged distortions – in fact, Edvard Munch's *The Scream* (1894) became iconographic for the whole mood which would envelop Expressionism. But there were factors in German society itself which brought about a mood of hysterical despair amongst the German avant-garde, and these must be addressed for us to understand the way in which these fears were transferred to the silver screen. Though the anxieties often stem from a fear of technology and urbanisation, by far the most frequent expression of anxiety in Expressionist films occurs as a result of the male protagonists' fears of sexually attractive women.[1] Though the iconoclastic Expressionists, who were nearly all male, appeared to be hurtling into the future at great speed, their collective fear of female sexuality is as old that found in Genesis in the story of Eve and the apple. These fears are encrypted in the loci: as a rule, the male is king in an outdoor space and the reverse is true of an interior space, especially a domestic domain. This order is often subverted in the films discussed below.

As in Britain, women's freedom to express themselves had flourished briefly in Germany too during the Romantic period only to be quashed by the pressures of a newly-industrialised society when Bismarck founded the Reich in 1871. As the century turned, legally and constitutionally Germany went backwards. Germany's dash for colonies alongside Kaiser Wilhelm's undisguised belligerence, especially towards Britain, set the tone for the pre-war generation. The bureaucratic status of teachers and university lecturers ensured that organised alternative policies could seldom enter mainstream intellectual debate, and remained largely the preserve of the socialists. On the whole, men and women, whatever their social position, accepted that the bourgeois family, where the man went out to work to keep his family, was the desirable norm. Paradoxically, the constitution of 1898 actually stated (Paragraph 1,356) that a wife had a legal duty to help in her husband's business, should such help be necessary, as well as doing her housework. This ominous 'as well as' provides the key to the otherwise inscrutable significance of the role of the *Hausfrau* in Germany: such work was enshrined in the law of the land and, even if only subliminally, slipshod housekeeping was held to be tantamount to a criminal act. Against this coercive attitude towards female domesticity, it is almost farcical to reflect that Germany was at the same time the fulcrum for advanced debate on sexuality, yet Richard von Krafft-Ebing, Magnus Hirschfeld and Ivan Bloch were by this time renowned pioneers of the new science of sexology.[2]

We should not be fooled by the fact that the new science of sexology was first conducted in the German language: nothing was more inimical to Wilhelmine society than the notion that a respectable woman might harbour sexual passion. More prudish than their Victorian cousins, the Wilhelmines clung tightly to the ideal of woman as the moral guardian of the hearth as though their very nation depended on it. Perhaps, in a way, it did. The Austrian Sigmund Freud would soon shock genteel sensibilities by arguing that the repression of sexuality led to inhibitions and neuroses. Were women to be excluded from this discussion as well? Yes, argued Freud. Women were not rational, like men. Biologically incomplete, they were unable to progress through the Oedipal stage of development and were condemned to be defined by penis envy. German-speaking writers and artists, mindful that revenge often results from envy, depicted the battle of the sexes with undisguised alarm. If Freud's arguments were sound, women who repressed their libido would be dangerous and potentially destructive. Though a bourgeois home is hardly ever depicted in an Expressionist film, the reassuring *rightness* of the bourgeois family is always present in the background.

If Germany had a political spectrum which moved increasingly to the right, it had a women's movement which refused to be politicised, whereas in Britain, 'The Cause' was nothing if not political. Add to this the promulgation of the new constitution in 1896 (which, though much modified, is still in force), and the stage was set for the institutionalised marginalisation of German women, whose official 'space' was the kitchen. The women's movement itself, dominated as it was by bourgeois feminists who endorsed woman's domestic role, made only one clearly radical appeal – for women's education – and that was only dictated by the perceived need for women to be better companions to their spouses. By eschewing radicalism for the most part, German feminists ensured that a political solution to women's patent inequality would not even be looked for, let alone found. These remarks on the women's movement, though necessarily brief, are by no means of casual importance. The movement's acceptance of the *völkisch* rhetoric which reached its apotheosis not in the Great War, but in the Third Reich, was a decisive factor in Germany's collective cold shoulder to liberal principles which began in 1871 and steadily accelerated, scarcely diminishing in the Weimar Republic which purported to represent liberal politics within the coalition. I shall argue that although the new Weimar Republic had come into force in 1919 at the cessation of hostilities, the first such state in Germany's history, the underlying conflicts in German society remained unaddressed.

It is not clear why creative artists remained staunchly Wilhelmine in their attitude towards the opposite sex, when Wilhelmine manners were otherwise a complete anathema to them. Possibly the misogyny of Nietzsche, their mentor in so many matters, had a decisive and prolonged effect. There is insufficient space here to dwell upon Nietzsche's own anxieties and inconsistencies towards women. Suffice to say that from the mid-1890s for at least three decades, Nietzsche's influence in all the arts, including the nascent film industry, was massive, so much so that the popularity of a given work by Nietzsche remains as reliable an indicator as any of what writers and artists were thinking at the time. For example, at the turn of the century, *The Birth of Tragedy* (1872) competed for top rank neck and neck with *Thus Spoke Zarathustra* (1883-85); the creative artist modelled himself on either the sexually ambiguous mythological god Dionysus or the chauvinist warlord Zarathustra, and sometimes, as with the crazy *Kosmiker* in Munich, on both at the same time. The Dionysians loved to depict woman as a natural hetaera, but other artists mistrusted the sexually attractive woman. In the avant-garde German art world of Ludwig Kirchner, for example, the pictures of rapacious vamps are so common that it seems churlish to point out that the narrow-minded respectable German *Bürger* also thought that sexually attractive women were rapacious vamps – so what was new? What was new was the simultaneous arrival of the new woman and the silver screen after the Great War.

I would like to apply the above observations to a number of scenes in German Expressionist films which the camera captures in order to convey anxiety. Put briefly, the film-makers sensed that there was something inherently wrong with German society – and in the light of hindsight, they were right. They ought to have had full freedom in a post-Wilhelmine state run by the social democrats. Instead, they were hidebound by censorship rules which restricted decency to that which the 'average citizen' would recognise as such.[3] Meanwhile, the shaky democratic government was pounded with hostility from luminaries such as Thomas Mann, who thought Germany would go to the dogs under the weak leadership of a republic.[4] In fact, a worse bogey man than any of them could think up was waiting out there in the crowd. I shall now examine a number of outdoor scenes in order to assess to what extent an action in such scenes can reflect the anxiety of the actor, or the film-maker, or both, and to judge what effect this might have on the capacity of the film to convey anxiety. We shall find that space – outdoor space – is used consistently to unsettle. Never at ease when portraying the natural world, Expressionist film-makers depict an external world in which men are not necessarily in control and there are comparable indoor scenes in which women are not reassuringly domesticated. These subtle indicators show a world out of kilter – a society ill-at-ease with itself and with the roles assigned to each sex.

Let us take the example of the first truly great expressionist film, Wiene's *The Cabinet of Dr. Caligari* (1920), which was shot completely in the studio, so that 'outdoor' scenes maintained the principles of Expressionist drama through diagonal lines, minimal props and a stunning use of chiaroscuro. In this film, we have Cesare's attempted murder of Jane, Cesare having been first hypnotised by Caligari. Unable to kill the sleeping Jane because he finds her too attractive, Cesare – hotly pursued by a number of men – runs off with her along a road that consists of broad jagged lines painted onto the studio floor. Weakened by his coffin-like entombment in Caligari's tent, Cesare twists and turns, staggers and finally drops Jane and (as we learn later through Jane's fiancé Francis) dies. Why is this scene so compelling? We suspend the knowledge that the painted lines are not a road (indeed are nothing like a road: with one diagonal bound, Cesare could be caught by his pursuers), and we are captivated by Cesare's struggle to carry the swooning Jane, his manifest weakness, and by his subsequent collapse. In the external space signalled by the fake road and imaginary landscape, Cesare briefly inhabits the male world of activity and bravado: he tries to be Tarzan, carrying off his Jane. Dehumanised by his master, emasculated by being shut inside for most of the time and mocked by his very name, Cesare has nevertheless not entirely lost his manhood. And we, the spectators, are forced to confront our own conflicting responses to Cesare, whom Kracauer describes as 'not so much a guilty murderer as Caligari's innocent victim'.[5]

The original film script by Hans Janowitz and Carl Mayer demonised Caligari as a madman impersonating a doctor; Robert Wiene, ignoring the protests of Janowitz and Mayer, subsequently placed the central story within a frame which transformed Francis and Jane into reminiscing lunatics in the care of a benevolent Caligari. Significantly, Cesare's function in the film is not affected by the framework which does such violence to the rest of the film. Our disquiet at finding that we sympathise with Cesare lingers long after the shenanigans of 'who is Caligari?' are resolved. Whatever interpretation we put on the character of the haunted Cesare, his desperate flight along the zigzag road and his subsequent death arguably convey and arouse more angst than all the evil theatricality of Caligari. The same phony road later provides a fittingly dislocated scenario for Francis' pursuit of the fraught Caligari when the latter anxiously searches for Cesare. In contrast, the sleeping Jane in the privacy of her bedroom radiates a serenity which literally disarms the programmed killer, Cesare. It goes without saying that the intrusion of a potential murderer into such serenity is calculated to convey anxiety.

Let us now take the example of *Nosferatu* (1922), and let us remind ourselves that the legend behind Richard Wagner's *Der Fleigende Holländer* (1843), which depicts a lost soul who cannot die until the love of a woman releases him from his nomadic torment, was 'sometimes referred to as "the English legend"'.[6] Bram Stoker in his novel *Dracula* (1895) drew on 'the English legend' as well as Wagner's opera,[7] and Murnau drew on Bram Stoker. Stoker had embellished the plot of his novel with a melodramatic portrayal of a sexually attractive woman, Lucy Westenra, and a morally virtuous matron, Mina Harker. Lucy, once bitten, goes to the bad – unlike the virtuous Mina who, though bitten, retains her integrity. Murnau's undead Nosferatu can only be released from his desperate predatory nocturnal activity through the love of a pure woman, encapsulated in one innocent female figure (as in Wagner's opera), and in Murnau's case, Mina. The outdoor scenes in *Nosferatu* provide ample space for male bravado, in contrast to the reassuring internal scenes where bourgeois domesticity dominates, but this is an illusion. In the famous scene in which Harker, not yet bitten but in perilous danger, travels to Nosferatu's castle, the film is speeded up and in one place filmed in the negative in order to highlight the perilous severity of the situation. The anxiety awakened in the spectator is heightened by the knowledge that the vampire's bite brings permanent pollution into the victim's body; it is similar to Aids in that both contaminate the blood and are often deadly. Harker's spooky ride is parodied later in the film when Nosferatu's familiar escapes from jail and leaps though the fields, bounding, singing and dancing ecstatically, all because the Master is near. His joy contrasts starkly with the ominous tone which has been built up during the film to accompany shots of Nosferatu. The outdoor space is claimed as the rightful domain of male activity, but anxiety is aroused by the strange and, in Dracula's case, predatory activity of these perverse males.

The final paradox of this film comes in the closing scenes. The cosy bourgeois security of the Harkers' home, which has been labouriously built up in layers throughout the film, is destroyed when the pregnant Mina attracts the vampire into her room and detains him beyond dawn. Murnau departs from Stoker's ending, where Mina Harker survives the rigours of trapping and destroying Count Dracula. Murnau also invented the notion that sunlight destroys a vampire.[8] Though Mina effectively commits suicide when she 'saves the world', one of the most unsettling things about this film, as with *The Cabinet of Dr. Caligari*, is that we are more likely to feel sorry for the criminal than the victim and disapprove of the trap laid for the revolting vampire by the virtuous self-sacrificing Mina. Although the role of the virtuous woman is ostensibly praised in the film, the underlying dynamics of the plot force attention to be shifted away from the idealised woman whose function in the plot is that of a cipher, and focuses on the sufferings of the (male) victim, even so monstrous a victim as Nosferatu, as being more interesting. There is also a complicated web of sexual attraction, with Mina sighing for Nosferatu,[9] which Murnau sketches too lightly but which the viewer uneasily senses.[10]

In *Metropolis* (1927), the external world 'outdoors' is viewed as so extraneous, so 'foreign', that the ruler's palatial home has a mock roof garden, complete with incongruous ornamental birds, where Freder plays hide and seek with ladies dressed in bizarre outfits. When the 'good' Maria first bursts upon this scene, she brings with her a crowd of small children who look as out of place in this male-dominated scenario as the storks (see Figure 1). In stark contrast, the cityscape is crammed full of technological wizardry: high-level motorways and so many little aeroplanes that a crash is surely imminent. If this external world is alienating for the dwellers of Metropolis, the city underground is worse. When the underground dwellers go 'outside', they swop one internal space for another by hurrying to the catacombs underneath the cathedral. Only in Maria's tale of the building of the Tower of Babel do we glimpse a natural world beyond the reach of the tyrannical city and its machinery, but it is a natural world where – as in Metropolis – the workers are driven beyond their capacity by the unreasonable demands of the rulers. The caption title reads: 'the hymns of praise of the few became the curses of the many'. This 'outdoor' scene thus underlines two conflicting themes: the demonisation of mass industrial life and its simultaneous projection as a stylised utopia.[11]

All the main actions of the film take place underground: the breaking of the machinery, 'good' Maria's rescue of the workers' children and the ritual burning of the witch, the 'bad' Maria, in an indoor scene which clearly ought to be outdoors (see Figure 2). Finally, as Freder and his father Fredersen stand outside the cathedral, Rotwang appears on the roof, precariously balancing the 'good' Maria in his arms in a virtual re-enactment of the scene already discussed with regard to Cesare and Jane in *The Cabinet of Dr. Caligari*, since it was also Lang's original intention to portray Rotwang as a victim. Predictably, the 'good' Maria is saved for Freder just as Jane is saved for Francis in *The Cabinet of Dr. Caligari*, and as in *The Cabinet of Caligari*, late changes to the plot make the end of the film confusing. In the case of *Metropolis*, Lang's proto-Fascist wife, Thea von Harbou, tacked on a message of brotherhood between masters and men which the burden of the film has not generated, though Kracauer notes sourly that 'Maria happily consecrates this symbolic alliance between labor and

Figure 1. A Scene from Metropolis *– '(Maria) brings with her a crowd of small children who look as out of place in this male-dominated scenario as the storks'*   (© *Films Sans Frontières*)

Figure 2. A scene from Metropolis – '. . . *the ritual burning of the witch, the 'bad' Maria, in an indoor scene which clearly ought to be outdoors'*   (© *Films Sans Frontières*)

capital'.[12] My point is that Maria herself, and not just her message of mediation, is out of place in this external scene.

Thea von Harbou also demonised the character of the Jew Rotwang, rendering the plot dense to the point of being inscrutable. In the original version of the film, Rotwang suffered a personality breakdown when Fredersen inveigled away Rotwang's wife, Hel, who subsequently gave birth to Freder. A still of Rotwang in front of the shrine erected to Hel on her death was in the original film, but later cut in deference to the wishes of the makers of the American version of the film,[13] so that the present film makes no reference to her. Only if the shadowy Hel is added to the equation is the underlying guilt felt by Fredersen towards Rotwang explicable to the spectator. Without the information, Rotwang is too important to ignore and too convoluted a character to understand. Hence the bathos at the end of this film. The muted excitement of the rooftop chase, which with a proper delineation of the figure of Rotwang could have been truly thrilling, collapses into the Fascist version of agit-prop as engineer and master shake hands. It is no accident that this male bonding takes place in the open air outside the cathedral. The activities of both versions of Maria took place underground. Most notably, the 'good' Maria is associated with motherly attributes for which indoor scenarios are appropriate, and Kracauer's reservations about her role as mediator are perhaps more justified than he realised.

Technically a masterpiece, *Metropolis* suffers from chronic internal fractures which all but destroy the film's narrative in its closing moments. Exactly the same confusion occurs at the end of Pabst's *Pandora's Box* (1929). Pabst invents the opening scene in which Lulu opens the door to the meter man. She stands poised between external and internal worlds, as Thomas Elsaesser has pointed out:

> The two doors, front door and apartment door, suggest a rather theatrical proscenium space, but it is the effect of the editing and the dynamic of the point-of-view shots which establish the illusion of a real space, while at the same time undercutting it, making it imaginary. Juxtaposed to this imaginary space, and counteracting the spectator's disorientation (and one shared with the meter man), is the image of Lulu, framed by the door and offering the spectator, too, a radiant smile and the promise of pleasure and plenitude.[14]

In fact, Lulu belongs neither to the internal nor the external domain, for she is not, and can never be, a *Hausfrau*. Pabst also ignores the ending of Frank Wedekind's play,[15] where Alwa is murdered, and sends Alwa and Schigolch in search of plum pudding whilst Lulu is left to prowl the streets for custom. The internal world is Lulu's domain; to roam the streets is to court disaster in the person of Jack the Ripper. These are real Berlin streets (pretending to be foggy London streets) down which the salvation army marches after the murder of Lulu, with an abject Jack sloping in the rear, the whole scene a complete and sentimental invention which Wedekind would have loathed. Nor does the spurious religiosity throw light on the character of Jack the Ripper. Is the spectator to infer that even a sinner like Jack can be saved? Throughout *Pandora's Box* and *Metropolis* the action takes place indoors, with the result that the outdoor ending, especially in *Pandora's Box*, leaves the spectator ill at ease. In both cases, the film-maker has diverged from his source material to reclaim the outside world as the sphere of activity for the male protagonist, ignoring any inner discrepancy with the plot. Wedekind's play ends with Jack murdering Countess Geschwitz for good measure. He then carefully washes his hands, drying them on Geschwitz's petticoat for lack of a towel, a sublimely psychopathic action whereby Jack profanes Lulu's space, humble lodging though this might be.[16]

Outdoor scenes restore male protagonists to their rightful positions and domestic indoor scenes threaten them. The opposite can be true with female characters: to venture outdoors can be lethal. In *M* (1931), Fritz Lang's first 'talkie', Elsie is quite safe at home with her mother, but in terrible danger when seduced into the world outdoors by 'M', the killer. The security of domestic space is reinforced by the camera lingering on reassuring images before panning to show the uncertainty of the world outdoors, where Elsie is abroad with the killer, 'M'. As Lottie Eisner points out, spatial dimensions can be reinforced by a shrewd use of sound:

> Lang's counterpointing of sound and image is done with supreme mastery: the sound actually enhances the image. When Elsie's mother leans over the desperately empty staircase to call her name, the little girl's absence is impressed upon us by the images – the table with a place set before an empty chair – and the inexorable ticking of the clock.

The mother's calls ring out in the deserted attic. Then the murder is suggested elliptically by the ball rolling away and the balloon getting caught on the telegraph wire, while the mother's cry against these images rings on, and dies.[17]

In *The Cabinet of Dr. Caligari*, 'outdoors' is corrupted by the presence of a fair, and the fun of the fair jars with the actions taking place on screen, reinforcing the menace of the unbounded space outdoors in comparison with the safety indoors. Precisely *because* indoors is viewed as safe, the seduction of Jane from the safe haven of her bedroom in *The Cabinet of Dr. Caligari* is perceived as shocking. And precisely *because* the German *Hausfrau* is awarded the position of cook, and cook only, the failure of the child to appear for lunch in *M* is so shocking. Apart from the Harker couple in *Nosferatu*, there has been a consistent lack of any happy bourgeois family in the films so far discussed, a typical feature of Expressionist film which indicates that the film-makers were reluctant to portray something they considered sacrosanct. It should be noted that even in *M*, the family consists of mother and daughter only, implying, perhaps, that the absence of a father opens up a weak flank in the family which makes the tragic murder possible.

The antidote to such considerations can be found in the film *Kuhle Wampe* (1932) upon which Bert Brecht collaborated with Slatan Dudov, though it should be noted that Brecht is very much a marginal figure in German Expressionism. In *Kuhle Wampe* we see in painful close-up a lower-middle-class family who have happened upon bad times. Brecht paints the bourgeois mother as a monstrous creation who is more interested in her shopping list than in the suicide of her son. Even more alarming is the ease with which Frau Bönike takes her ideology with her when she moves out of her flat, with her husband and daughter, to stay with the daughter's boyfriend in the shantytown of holiday homes just outside the city. Meanwhile, her daughter goes off into the fields with her boyfriend. The field grass waves back and forth in mock fallacy: Brecht seems to hoot with laughter at the very idea of a country retreat or the balm of relaxation in nature. The sporting scenes at the end of the film, which Marc Silberman finds '[b]y far the most didactically structured section',[18] show Brecht's idea that even when off duty, the worker should be marshalled into activity. Never one to appreciate nature for its own sake, Brecht uses the alien rural setting (as it is to him) to debunk the bourgeois family. And this he does to great effect. Unfortunately, his treatment of the question of abortion (which Anni rules out) was censored out of the film (Silberman, 1995, p. 256, n. 21). Though Expressionist film-makers intuitively used external scenes to produce alienation and anxiety in the knowledge that sudden unfamiliarity would introduce a distortion into the plot, it was a mistake for them to assume that this in itself would make up for inconsistencies of plot or character. The lack of anything resembling normal family life creates a curious vacuum at the heart of Expressionism film which is also relevant to the movement in general. Only with Brecht's *Kuhle Wampe* do we have an authorial raspberry blown at the cosy domesticity so coveted by Germans in the Weimar Republic. The gold standard of 'the family' officially purported to place the wife and mother on a pedestal; simultaneously, of course, she became aesthetically boring unless, as with Brecht's Frau Bönike in *Kuhle Wampe*, the role was subjected to persiflage.

Much more interesting to the German Expressionist film-maker was the sexually attractive woman, such as the 'bad' Maria in *Metropolis* or Lulu in *Pandora's Box*. Unfortunately, such women could not be allowed to survive at the end of the film, just as in the field of literature, a fallen woman was never allowed to survive at the end of a novel or play. Theodor Fontane's *Effi Briest* (1895) (the subject of Fassbinder's *Effi Briest*, 1974) and Wedekind's 'Lulu' plays are indicative of this tendency, and however iconoclastic Wedekind *felt* he was his plots are actually conventional in this regard. A really iconoclastic denouement would present us with a Lulu who survived the rigours of her (sex) life and was actually alive at the end of the play. Pabst tries to do this in *Diary of a Lost Girl* (1929).[19] He is successful to the extent that Thymian is allowed to survive the experience of a reformatory for fallen women, and at the end of the film, now a dowager countess, she is actually the personification of virtue in her charitable endeavours for seduced girls and their babies, though her own baby dies. There is a world of difference, however, between a seduced girl, the victim of a man, and a loose woman, a predator on man and by extension a disruptive element to the safe, indoor world of hearth and home. Thus the spectator is expected to share the various anxieties experienced by characters in early German films at the depiction of a 'loose woman'. It goes without saying that such films will invariably convey a covert thrill of illicit pleasure as well as, simultaneously, overt disapproval of the vamp's disruption of the safety of the home.

Especially in outdoor scenes, in an unfamiliar space, women in German Expressionist films are shown to be vulnerable, and by the same token a male character who tries to usurp the sanctity of a virtuous woman's hallowed indoor space can be thereby unmanned, as discussed in relation to Count Dracula's doomed invasion of Nina's bedroom in *Nosferatu*. Though in the first decades of the 20th Century, German family life no doubt seethed with the stresses identified by Freud, especially in the field of father-son conflicts which were often dramatised,[20] liberally-minded Wilhelmines still yearned for the security of family values even when they were in the process of attacking the limitations of bourgeois domesticity. As we have seen in relation to *M*, the mere lack of a domestic patriarch is sufficient to render a family dysfunctional in the view of a film-maker as avant-garde as Lang. Paradoxically, though, the most successful scenes in German Expressionist films occur in the rare outdoor scenes where male icons, however monstrous, steal the limelight, as in *The Golem* (1920),[21] where the Golem's powers are neutralised by the unknowing touch of a child (a symbol of home and domestic security). The outside arena is where interesting, non-domestic, *dangerous* events occur, as in *King Kong* (1933), a film which borrows elements of gothic horror straight from German Expressionist film. Although Jane dangles perilously from the Empire State Building, the audience sympathises with the rampantly priapic King Kong, perceiving him as less brutish than the men who shoot him down. The fact that men, or icons of male dominance, do not find it easy to dominate the world outdoors in German Expressionist film is part and parcel of the anxiety which brought Expressionism into being. Expressionist films thus use indoor and outdoor space to build an iconography whereby the underlying structures and beliefs of society, where a woman presides in the home (that haven of peace) while a man is active and dominant in the world at large, are affirmed; even when they appear to be most at threat from sexy vamps or monstrous men who do not know their place.

Notes

1   See Penley, C. (ed.), *Feminism and Film Theory*, New York – London, Routledge, 1988, for a full discussion of the topic and (p. 196ff) a useful bibliography.

2   See Diethe, C., *Some Aspects of Distorted Sexual Attitudes in German Expressionist Drama*, New York, Bern, Frankfurt am Main and Paris, Peter Lang, 1988, pp. 35-43.

3   Barbian, J.-P., 'Filme mit Lücken. Die Lichtspielzensur in der Weimarer Republik: von der sozialethischen Schutzmaßnahme zum politischen Instrument', in Jung, U. (ed.), *Der deutsche Film. Aspekte seiner Geschichte von den Anfängen bis zur Gegenwart* (Trier, Wissenschaftlicher Verlag, 1993), 2 vols, I, pp. 59-78, p. 59.

4   Thomas Mann's reactionary politics dominate his *Betrachtungen eines Unpolitischen* (*Observations of a Non-Political Man*), written during the war and published in 1918. Gay, P., *Weimar Culture: The Outsider as Insider*, Harmondsworth, Penguin, 1992, 4th edn., p. 77, writes: 'When in the 1920s Thomas Mann underwent his conversion to the Republic and democracy … there were many who interpreted Mann's change of front as treason or sheer irresponsibility …'.

5   Kracauer, S., *From Caligari to Hitler: A Psychological History of the German Film*, Princeton, Princeton University Press, 1966 (1947), p. 65.

6   Osborne, C., *The Complete Operas of Wagner: A Critical Guide*, London, Victor Gollancz, 1992, p. 68.

7   Bram Stoker was a fervent amanuensis to Henry Irving, actor and impresario at the Lyceum theatre in London. In 1878 Irving had put on the stage play *Vanderdecken* by H.G.Wills and Percy Fitzgerald, a version of Captain Marryat's novel, *The Phantom Ship* (1839), based on the legend of the flying Dutchman. In 1876, the Lyceum had put on Wagner's *The Flying Dutchman* (1843).

8   'Traditionally, film-makers have loved the Murnau final twist of Dracula surprised by sunlight and turning first to gorgonzola and then to bones and sawdust. It makes wonderful cinema.' Sutherland, J., *Is Heathcliff a Murderer? Puzzles in Nineteenth-Century Fiction*, Oxford, Oxford University Press, 1996, p. 234.

9   'The yearning body language with which Nina draws the count towards her invites us to speculate upon the eroticism she anticipates, albeit subconsciously, in his embrace'. Diethe, C., 'Beauty and the Beast: An investigation into the role and function of women in German expressionist film', in Meskimmon, M. & West, S. (eds.), *Visions of the 'Neue Frau': Women and the Visual Arts in Weimar Germany* (Aldershot, Scolar Press, 1995), pp. 108-123, p. 113.

10 According to Frayling, C., *Vampyres: Lord Byron to Count Dracula*, London, Faber and Faber, 1991, p. 388: ' … the whole question of vampire manifestations is also a question of sexual repression'.

11 Möbius, H. & Vogt, G., *Drehort Stadt. Das Thema 'Großstadt' im deutschen Film*, Marburg, Hitzeroth, 1990, p. 14.

12 Kracauer, 1966, p. 163. Kracauer goes on to say that 'Maria's demand that the heart mediate between hand and brain could well have been formulated by Goebbels' (pp.163-64).

13 Patalas, E., '*Metropolis*, Bild 103', in Ledig, E. (ed.), *Der Stummfilm. Konstruktion und Rekonstruktion* (Munich, Schauder, Bauer and Ledig, 1988), pp. 153-162, p. 161.

14 Elsaesser, T., 'Pabst's *Pandora's Box*', in *German Film and Literature: Adaptations and Transformations*, Rentschler, E. (ed.), (New York – London, Methuen, 1986), pp. 40-59, p. 44.

15 Frank Wedekind published *Erdgeist* (*Earth Spirit*) in 1894 and *Die Büchse der Pandora* (*Pandora's Box*) in 1902.

16 Jack: 'They haven't even got a towel! A miserable hole!' (Wedekind, F., *Pandora's Box* in *The Lulu Plays and Other Sex Tragedies*, trs. by Stephen Spender (London, John Calder, 1972), 2nd edn., p. 175). The volume also contains *Earth Spirit*, the first of the two 'Lulu Plays'.

17 Eisner, L., *The Haunted Screen*, trs. by Robert Greaves (London, Secker and Warburg, 1973), 3rd edition (1952: in French), pp. 320-21.

18 Silberman, M., 'The Rhetoric of the Image: Slatan Dudov and Bert Brecht's *Kuhle Wampe* or *Who Owns the World*?' in *German Cinema: Texts in Context*, Detroit, Wayne State University Press, 1995, pp. 34-48, p. 45.

19 *Das Tagebuch einer Verlorenen* (1929), Pabst's last silent movie, starred Louise Brooks, who had played Lulu in *Pandora's Box*. Pabst's protegée later fell on hard times, recounted in Brooks, L., *Lulu in Hollywood*, London, Hamish Hamilton, 1982.

20 For example, Walter Hasenclever's *Der Sohn* (*The Son*) (1914) and Arnolt Bronnen's *Vatermord* (*Parricide*) (1920).

21 The full title is *Der Golem, wie er in die Welt kam* (*The Golem: How He Came Into the World*).

Turkish Women on German Streets: Closure and Exposure in Transnational Cinema

Deniz Göktürk

Trapped at Home – Out on the Town

1986 – A woman pleads with her husband to take her for a walk in the city. The place is Hamburg, she has been living there for some months since her arrival from Turkey, but she has never left the flat where he keeps her enclosed. Turna (meaning 'the crane'), is reduced to '40m² of Germany', the world outside is beyond imagination and her dreams keep drifting back to her home village. The camera captures the actress Özay Fecht in long takes and often underexposed frames – in front of the mirror, cutting off her braids, or through the window, overlooking a grey courtyard. The view of the street beyond is restricted, but we can see a woman pacing up and down there – a prostitute, the archetypal urban streetwalker, diametrically opposite to the housewife who remains confined to the domestic sphere. Turna will dress up in bright rural attire on Sunday and wait forever, but her husband will forget his promise to take her out and go off to spend the day with friends. At the end of the film, the death of the husband will finally drive her out into an alien world, where she will fail to communicate. Once again, she will appear framed in a doorway, and the credits will start running before she has a chance to step out on the street. Tevfik Başer's 'Kammerspielfilm' *40m² Deutschland* is characteristic of the 1980's mode of depicting migrants, especially women, in the German context, and perhaps more broadly speaking in Western Europe. In cinema, and more generally in the popular imagination, they tended to appear trapped in claustrophobic spaces and scenarios of imprisonment.

1996 – Two girls walk along a street, facing the camera, smiling at each other. Instead of their conversation we hear the opening of a hiphop song by Juks (Savaş Yiğit) and DJ Hype which was already playing at the beginning of the film. The credits start running while the vocals come in: '… and I can't say what my place was … because I'm just passing …' Music is instrumental in configuring space and in establishing a feel of urban circulation. No big happy end, but still, in its low-key manner the film manages to finish on a somewhat hopeful note. The place is Berlin-Kreuzberg, and the two girls in motion seem very much in place on this street. We have grown familiar with Leyla and Sevim over the past 84 minutes. The amateur performance of Serpil Turhan and Mariam El Awad (who is a Kreuzberg resident of Arabic origin, but volunteered to play a Turkish character), is fresh and natural, except for some stiltedness in dialogues. We have seen the girls at work together in a sewing factory, we have listened in on their conversations (mostly in German with the occasional phrase in Turkish), we know that they like going out together and that they dream of moving in with each other once they are eighteen. Leyla is of mixed descent, the youngest daughter of a German mother and a Turkish father. Her two brothers could not be more different. Erol (Tamer Yiğit), the eldest, is a drop-out from school, a fan of Bruce Lee, a petty-thief and dealer who owes money to everybody and who sees a chance of ecape when he receives his draft papers to do military service in Turkey. Ahmet, the younger, wears the same fashionable baggy trousers, but goes to high school and likes to read. He doesn't think much of the Turkish army or any other kind of fighting. Thomas Arslan's film *Geschwister* (Siblings) signals a new mode of depicting immigrants and their hybrid offspring by following their diverging pathways through their neighbourhood, letting them drift along and casually observing their encounters in various 'contact zones' such as the family dinner table, the working place, the boxing studio, the nightclub, and primarily the street.

This shift in the representation of migrants corresponds with recent trends in theory. We have come to appreciate the migrant as the 'modern metropolitan figure' – not dwelling worlds apart from modernity, but moving right at its centre. Cities today, more than ever, suggest an 'implosive disorder, sometimes liberating, often bewildering', a 'multiform, heterotopic, diasporic' reality.[1] Urban circulation cannot be contained in a stable sense of space, as it disperses into a multitude of encounters and 'contact zones'.[2] This seems particularly true of Berlin, a city which has been remodelled on a major scale over the past ten years. Paradoxically, the removal of the visible border running through the city has in many ways reinforced differences which emerge in daily life encounters.

The urban space which offers a multitude of casual, often strange encounters can be seen as a microcosm of a world increasingly determined by mobility and rootlessness, by the clash or amalgamation of cultures – where 'the pure products are going crazy', as cultural anthropologist James Clifford has put it, echoing a 1923 dada poem by William Carlos Williams, in which the young doctor and poet falls into nostalgic pondering about the desolate state of culture at the sight of Elsie, a young house-maid with 'a dash of Indian blood … ungainly hips and flopping breast' (obviously an offspring of miscegenation), stranded in a middle-class home in a New Jersey suburb. It is the uneasiness of the white male at the sight of this vagrant and somewhat impure female presence which Clifford takes as a point of departure for his analysis of rootlessness and mobility, of loss of purity and authenticity as crucial experiences of modernity.[3] No matter whether we regard it as loss or gain, in an increasingly urban, multinational world of travelling cultures and conflicting voices, identity and difference can no longer be defined as fixed, stable and confined within one coherent culture or language. Routes/roots are subject to constant negotiation, home and belonging become difficult to determine, and we understand that there is 'no place like *Heimat*'.[4]

Discourses about migrants and diasporas, however, are often still informed by a social worker's perspective and haunted by residual notions of cultural purity, community and authenticity. Between national entrenchment and transnational globalisation, ethnic minorities are often 'imagined' as outsiders on a subnational level. Postcolonial studies have critiqued the reductive objectification of third world women to the status of the 'subaltern'.[5] Turkish women in Germany, in particular, have often been subject to 'double othering'.[6] They are assumed to find a voice and space which is supposedly denied to them in their oppressive partiarchal culture of origin. The critical interest devoted to them often serves to confirm hypocritical narratives of rescue, liberation and Westernisation. The Elsies and Leylas of our time are only just beginning to establish a more self-confident and appealing presence on streets and screens.

Over the past years, there has been a growing worldwide interest in films which visualise experiences of migration and displacement. These films have been described as a new genre of 'postcolonial hybrid films'[7] or as an 'independent transnational cinema'[8] and can be found in video stores on a shelf labelled as 'world cinema' – a label on the lines of 'world music', which signals the universality of diversity and mobility, compared to older, separatist categories such as 'third cinema' or 'sub-state cinema'.[9] If the space assigned to migrants in the cultural imaginary has been shifting from 'subnational' to 'transnational' over the past decade, we can begin to take on board films by and about migrants as a challenge to rethink established notions of a 'national cinema'.

Is it possible to incorporate into this broadening picture the Turkish 'guestworker', who has usually been imagined as the 'seventh man' – an incommensurable, alienated, speechless victim without any voice, lusting for blonde women and hardly respecting the independence of his wife or daughter?[10] Is there a transnational cinema emerging in Germany, where over two million people of Turkish origin are living today, who are increasingly applying for full citizenship and claiming their place as 'Inländer' (as opposed to 'Ausländer')?[11] What spaces do women occupy in Turkish-German film culture? Are they trapped at home or out on the town? In order to answer these questions, let us briefly recapitulate the 1970s and 1980s, before we move on to contemplate some new developments in the 1990s.

Ghettos of Subsidy

The New German Cinema of 'rebellious' auteurs, declaring the death of 'daddy's cinema' and confronting the nation with revisions of its past, emerged at a time when popular European cinemas were dying while Hollywood was gaining a stronghold on European markets and television had reached a mass audience. The New German Cinema relied heavily on public funding, on televison co-productions and on the acclaim for European 'art cinema' on the international festival circuit.[12] This framework of social mission and public funding opened up spaces for 'minority views', for exploring differences and articulating 'otherness', first in terms of gender and gradually also ethnicity. However, schemes of film funding ('Filmförderung') on a federal or regional level as well as co-productions with television, mainly with the public broadcasting channel ZDF (*Das kleine Fernsehspiel*) have sometimes proved to be counterproductive and limiting, in the sense of reinforcing a patronising and marginalising attitude towards 'Ausländerkultur', the culture of foreigners. Film-makers from an immigrant or minority background often saw themselves reduced to producers of 'a cinema of duty'.[13] In order to receive funding, film-makers were expected to make films about the problems of their people and represent the 'other' culture in terms of common assumptions and popular misconceptions. In consequence, a kind of ghetto culture emerged which was at great pains to promote politics of integration, but rarely achieved much popularity.

Back in the late 1960s and early 1970s, directors of New German Cinema had shown some interest in immigrants. Fassbinder who staged himself in *Katzelmacher* (1969) as 'ein Griech aus Griechenland' ('a Greek from Greece'), shot *Angst Essen Seele Auf (Fear Eats the Soul)* (1973) under the working title of 'Alle Türken heißen Ali' ('All Turks are called Ali') – all North Africans as well, one might add, because the film did not feature any Turks, but a black man (Ben Hedi El-Saalem) as an object of desire and erotic projection. While the first imaginary 'Turks' were appearing on the screen, the cinema audience was also undergoing major changes and many cinemas became venues for soft-core pornographic films. Thus the legendary mute and lecherous *Gastarbeiter* makes an unexpected reappearance as a spectator in the standard history of New German Cinema – 'a volatile and furtive but none the less numerically quite sizeable clientèle began to oust, indeed eradicate, the last remnants of the family audience.' (Elsaesser, 1989, p. 67)

While the male *Gastarbeiter* were imagined to satisfy their needs as porn spectators, women tended to be victimised on screen. Many films centred around the problems of Turkish women who were oppressed by their patriarchal fathers, brothers or husbands, excluded from the public sphere and confined in enclosed spaces. Helma Sanders' *Shirins Hochzeit (Shirin's Wedding)* (1975), for example, less well-known than her *Deutschland, Bleiche Mutter (Germany, Pale Mother)* (1979), is a black and white film with neorealist aspirations about Shirin (Ayten Erten) who leaves her Anatolian village and travels to Cologne in search for her fiance Mahmut. The fiancé was played by Aras Ören, who was around the same time becoming known as a writer of Berlin-poems such as *Was will Niyazi in der Naunynstraße (What is Niyazi doing in Naunynstrasse)* (1973). Shirin ends up on the street as a prostitute and is killed by her pimp in the end, her fate commented upon elegically by Helma Sander's voice-over, universalising the suffering of womanhood.[14]

In the 1980s, pictures of victimisation and closure continued to circulate, and were replicated in the work of Turkish directors living in Germany. Tevfik Başer received the Bundesfilmpreis in 1987 for his *40m² Deutschland* (1986), an award given by the Federal Ministry of Internal Affairs – dutiful national acknowledgement, which paradoxically seemed to cement the subnational status of 'Ausländerkultur'. In his second film *Abschied vom falschen Paradies (Farewell to a false paradise)* (1988) the Hamburg-based director Tevfik Başer followed a similar pattern of staging women's confinement in enclosed spaces, photographed in dark, often underexposed long takes. Elif, a young

Turkish woman in a German prison, tries to commit suicide in her cell just before her release. Her story is presented in flashback. Being sentenced to six years in prison for killing her husband, paradoxically, her experience of imprisonment becomes an experience of liberation. Her integration into German society is achieved in prison where she learns fluent German from a dictionary and finds a safe haven in the supportive community of women, reminiscent of the women's community in her village in Turkey. In this film, the Turkish woman interacts with German society, but only within the confined space of the prison. The liberation and Westernisation, or Germanification, of the Turkish village woman (performed by Zuhal Olcay, an actress familiar in Turkey from sophisticated theatre and film productions, usually in roles of modern urban women characters) is reached all too smoothly in the 'fake paradise' of the prison.

The prison which film-makers in exile have tended to use as a key symbolic space is thus re-evaluated in a dubiously positive sense by Başer.[15] His heroines can only escape enclosure and confinement by retreating into their subjectivity, into flashback memories and dreams. When Elif is feverish in her cell and longingly looks out through the iron bars of the window, rain brings back memories of the clean and clear waters back home. Home is associated with women bathing and doing the washing, with water, purity, and nature. The scene offers a somewhat purified version of the Turkish village film genre, made consumable for Western audiences in ways beyond the use of Western-style flute and violin music. The community of women back in the village is idealised in bright colours and contrasted with the harsh reality of German prison life, although in the course of the film the community of women in prison gradually grows stronger and develops into a second home. In the end, it remains unclear whether the 'false paradise' is the pure and authentic homeland back in Turkey or the claustrophobic space of the German prison which Elif is reluctant to leave behind. But beyond the indeterminacy of the title the film offers little critical reflection about the fake warmth of closed communities. *Goodbye to a False Paradise* illustrates the cinematic imprisonment of immigrants within the parameters of well-meaning multiculturalism feeding on binary oppositions and integrationist desires.

Among the German productions of the 1980s dealing with experiences of immigrants, *Yasemin* (1988) has proved the most popular. It features on almost every German-Turkish film programme and is circulated by the Goethe-Institutes even in Thailand and India. *Yasemin* was released in 1988 and directed by Hark Bohm, a German director also living in Hamburg. His films emerged from a political engagement common to a much of New German Cinema, in fact he is slightly mocked as social consciousness personified. In *Yasemin* he took up current debates about the problems of Turks in Germany. Yasemin (Ayşe Romey) embodies the total split between German and Turkish culture which was summed up in an exhibition title of those years: 'Morgens Deutschland – Abends Türkei' ('Germany in the morning – Turkey at night'). The double identity is also rendered in the linguistic mix of family conversations, featuring Emine Sevgi Özdamar as the mother, an actress who has meanwhile made a career as a writer of hybrid German with *Mutterzunge (Mother Tounge)* (1990) and *Das Leben ist eine Karawanserei hat zwei Türen aus einer kam ich rein aus der anderen ging ich raus (Life is a Caravanserail …)* (1992). Yasemin is active in a Judo club where she fights with great ability. In fact, she is just like her German classmates at high school, where her teacher encourages her to proceed with her studies and prepare for university. But when she returns from school to the family's greengrocery shop, she is the dutiful Turkish daughter who helps with the business and always has to be chaperoned by her cousin when she goes out. Initially, her transitions from one sphere to the other are staged with some pleasure and sense for costume. She lowers her skirt and covers herself up on the way home from school to mark the shift from one sphere to the other, and switches gracefully from Western to 'Oriental' style when she dances with her father at her sister's wedding – a scene from which her German admirer Jan (Uwe Bohm) is excluded and which he watches through a window from outside, thus providing a point of view for the voyeuristic ethnographic gaze of the camera on the Turkish wedding. Eventually, the culture clash explodes. The kindly father, being concerned about his honour, switches into a brutal patriarch who rejects his elder daughter and proposes to ship Yasemin back to Turkey. Whereas the promoters of this film claimed to foster cross-cultural understanding, it really reproduced and generated common stereotypes and confirmed the view that German society in general is more civilised and enlightened than the archaic Turkish community. Integration in this binary model could only be achieved by a split between first and second generation immigrants. The popularity of the film draws on the common phantasy of victimised Turkish women who, especially when young and beautiful, need to be rescued from their patriarchal community. Within the parameters of this discourse, Yasemin does the right thing, when in the end she leaves the Turkish men behind and is carried off by Jan on the backseat of his motorbike.

In general, narratives about Turks in German society have tended to centre around gender relations. The liberation of poor Turkish women from enclosure, oppression, subordination or even prostitution has been a popular fantasy. Although ethnic cinema, third cinema, and minority discourse in general, are usually presented and perceived as some kind of authentic expression of the real-life experiences of a group to which the director belongs, there does not seem to be a fundamental difference between a German director's and a Turkish director's depiction of German-Turkish encounters. Tevfik Başer, Hark Bohm and Helma Sanders all participate of the common discourse about the victimisation of Turkish women and confirm the subnational positioning of the immigrant.

Reinventing Berlin in Berlin – through Turkish eyes

Have there been any new departures in the 1990s? Are the exiles still in prison, or have they managed to break out? Is the cultural production of migrants still confined to niches, or has it meanwhile become centre stage? Can we find celebrations of mobility and mutual exposure, rather than victimisation and closure in recent Turkish-German productions? *Berlin in Berlin* (1993) might be considered a step in this direction. This rather trashy movie offers a bizarre and entertaining view of intercultural encounters, and ironically subverts some of the established stereotypes and models. It was produced in Turkey, although with a Turkish-German team and partly shot on location in Berlin. Its fast pace and cinematic style appear to be influenced by director Sinan Çetin's work in advertising. The film is a genre mix, incorporating elements of thriller, melodrama, and comedy. The camera playfully engages in an investigation of voyeurism and dissects the power of the ethnographic gaze. In Turkey, the film was a box office hit in 1993, predominantly because it features Hülya Avşar, an actress and singer popular on Turkish television, as Dilber in a masturbation scene.

The 'multicultural melodrama'[16] is set in Berlin. The establishing shots, initially aerial, then followed by scenes from the Alexanderplatz in the Eastern part of the city, point to a setting in the new reunified Berlin. The city at this time is a huge building site, and thus the story begins on a building site which is rendered as a potentially dangerous space. Thomas (Armin Block), an engineer and amateur photographer, follows the wife of a Turkish colleague with his camera and takes pictures without her noticing. The camera adopts the voyeuristic gaze of the photographer on the Turkish woman. Despite her headscarf, she becomes an object of erotic attraction and is objectified by the camera. When finally she looks back into the telephoto lens her gaze, too, appears to be somewhat threatening. The loud clicking of the camera underlines the thriller atmosphere. Later, the photographer hangs up the enlarged photographs in the office. When the husband sees them he is infuriated by this liberty taken with his wife. He assumes that she has deliberately posed for the camera and exposed herself to the gaze of a stranger – an offence against his honour. He rushes out to confront his wife. The photographer comes in on the row and tries to pacify the couple. In the resulting fight the husband is pushed against an iron bar and thus killed by accident. Fake blood dribbles from the corner of his mouth.

Three months later, we see the photographer doing push-ups facing the photographs of the woman while memorising Turkish sentences from a dictionary: 'Bu bir kaza. Ben katil değilim.' ('It was an accident. I am no murderer.'). He travels by the underground in search of the woman and sits opposite her house in Berlin-Kreuzberg in a café which is run by her brothers-in-law. When he finally gets hold of her and attempts to explain that he did not intend to kill her husband, he finds himself chased by the dead man's brothers. Ironically, his flight leads him into the flat of the very same family where he hides on top of the wardrobe in Dilber's bedroom.

Along with the intruder the spectator is introduced into the diegetic space of 'Berlin in Berlin' – a city within the city, namely the home of an extended Turkish family in Kreuzberg. The matriarch of the family wakes up to the muezzin's call for prayers. A tapestry image of Mecca is hanging on the wall behind her bed. German voices mingle into the prayer call. The camera then moves to a portable mosque-shaped clock, the source of the muezzin's voice which is competing with a German commercial for a nail cure. This originates from the television set in front of which the father is just waking up. The use of diegetic sound and the delayed revelation of its sources gradually introduces the spectator into the hybrid space of 'Berlin in Berlin' – a place where the day begins with competing voices and languages.

Meanwhile, the intruder is discovered on top of the wardrobe. Mürtüz, the angry young man (played by popular talk show star Cem Özer), claims that the stranger has murdered his brother and threatens to kill him with his pistol. The chase is stopped, just in time, by the father and the grandmother (Aliye Rona) who pronounce that this German is a guest, 'sent to them by God' as a 'trial', and therefore cannot be harmed while inside their home. The young avenger has to bow to the authority of the elders. The displaced German is thus granted asylum in the Turkish family, settling on the floor for a life in 'Berlin in Berlin' or '40m^2 of Germany'.[17]

It is this reversal of the situation of foreign 'guests' seeking asylum on German territory which makes this film potentially interesting, and which transgresses performances of duty which have determined most German attempts to produce 'Ausländerkultur'. In one scene, Thomas lingers on the doorstep, staring at Dilber, not daring to come in or to go out. His performance points to the borders running right through Berlin, while at the same time his lack of resolve subverts these boundaries and makes them appear ridiculous. What follows is a bizarre symbiosis between the German 'foreigner' and the extended Turkish family. Four generations are living together in this flat (grandmother, father and mother, three sons and the daughter-in-law – the dead man's wife – with her son) and they all display different modes of interaction with their surroundings and with the intruder. The eldest brother Mürtüz (Cem Özer) is a caricature of the Turkish macho, playing around with his gun and screaming for revenge. Mostly, he insists on speaking Turkish and on keeping up Turkish customs, but he likes whisky and blondes as much as he adores his beautiful sister-in-law. The younger brothers who tend to speak German are more ready to fraternise with their guest.

Thomas is gradually incorporated into family life. He is given a plate of food, handed a guitar, appreciated for fixing the television set during an important football match of Germany vs Turkey, he befriends the grandmother and learns Turkish songs from her, familiarises himself with the customs such as the passing around of *eau de cologne* and Turkish delight, and even kisses everybody's hand on Kurban Bayramı, a religious festival. In this enforced symbiosis, the voyeurist ethnographic gaze is gradually reversed. It is now the Turks who are watching the German, almost like a circus animal and who stare at him in claustrophobic close-ups. When all the relatives come to visit, Thomas is the chief attraction. The uncle who does a great belly dance to a German popsong, keeps bending down towards this odd stranger, asking why on earth he is sitting on the floor. While Thomas mingles with the brothers, Dilber finds herself interrogated about the circumstances of her husband's death. The discovery of the photographs makes her position within the family increasingly problematic. The film ends by pairing Thomas with Dilber. They leave the flat and walk hand in hand along a street into an unknown future. Once again a Turkish woman liberated by a German man? The ending seems slightly forced. On the whole, however, the reversal of the asylum situation and the resulting symbiosis in *Berlin in Berlin* opened up possibilities of exploring German-Turkish encounters through mutual exposure. This is probably due to the 'outsider' perspective which this film can afford to adopt, as *Berlin in Berlin* was produced in Turkey, largely outside the German framework of subsidy.

New German Cinema Made By Young Turks

In the fall of 1998, there was a considerable breakthrough in Turkish-German film production. A new generation of film-makers and actors emerged, mostly based in Hamburg or Berlin. *Kurz und Schmerzlos (Short Sharp Shock)*, the acclaimed debut of Hamburg-based director Fatih Akın, which has been nominated for the German Film Prize, was even shown in London in December 1998 at the German Film Festival in the West End as well as the Turkish Film Festival at the Rio Cinema in Dalston, both within the same week. This interesting overlap points to the transnational nature of films like this. *Kurz und Schmerzlos* is a fast-paced thriller about three friends: Gabriel the Turk (Mehmet Kurtuluş), Costa the Greek (Adam Bousdoukos) and Bobby the Serb (Aleksandar Jovanovic) who shared the best actor's prize at the Locarno Film Festival. This film about angry young men, somewhat similar to the French film *La Haine* (1995), attempts to mix ethnicities and focus on social position at the margins of the urban underworld. Unlike *La Haine* or *Berlin in Berlin*, however, this is a straightforward thriller in Scorsese-style, which does not foreground reflections about conventions and possibilities of media representations. This film, like a number of other new productions, focuses on young men. Nevertheless, it leaves some space for new women on the streets. The actress İdil Üner, who only has a minor role, comes across as independent and strong-minded. Furthermore, *Kurz und Schmerzlos* reinvents Hamburg as a generic gangster movie location.

   Regional film funding is seen as a way of promoting the city. Films produced with Hamburg money have to be shot and produced in Hamburg. *Aprilkinder (April Children)* (1998), directed by Yüksel Yavuz, is another example. This trilingual melodrama depicts a Kurdish immigrant family with somewhat wayward offspring. The oldest son Cem (well acted by Erdal Yıldız, encountering the world with a slightly bewildered and puzzled look) works in a slaughterhouse as a pork butcher and falls in love with a German prostitute of somewhat androgynous appearance, while the younger brother Mehmet is dealing drugs and their streetwise little sister Dilan has an eye for his partner in crime. This film is also primarily an exploration of young male subjectivity, culminating in a swirl of the camera at the wedding when Cem is finally married off to a girl from the war torn village back home. There are some autobiographical elements in this film by Yüksel Yavuz whose first experience of 'Germanistan' was a 12m² shed which he had to share with his father, leaving 6m² for him.[18]

   Kanak Attack, a gangster movie which is based on Feridun Zaimoğlu's novel *Abschaum (Trash)* (1997) and which director Lars Becker was shooting at the time this chapter was written, is likely to maintain the focus on angry young men. For a more female focus we might have to wait for an adaptation of Zaimoğlu's latest book *Koppstoff (Headstuff)* (1998) which is a collection of female voices 'from the margins of society'. Furthermore, there are new women directors emerging. Ayşe Polat, also based in Hamburg, who has had international success with short films such as *Fremdennacht (Stranger's Night)* (1991), *Ein Fest für Beyhan (A Celebration for Beyhan)* (1994), *Gräfin Sophia Hatun (Countess Sophia Hatun)* (1997), fantastic, dream-like miniatures on the situation of exile, has just completed her first feature *Die Auslandstournee*. In Berlin, Aysun Bademsoy has made several documentaries depicting self-confident young girls on German streets such as *Mädchen im Ring* (about a female boxer who is beautiful, intelligent and articulate) or *Mädchen am Ball* and *Nach dem Spiel* (both about the only Turkish girls' football team in Berlin-Kreuzberg).

Meanwhile, the discourse of victimisation of Turkish girls 'between two cultures' still persists. *Yara* (1998), a German-Turkish-Swiss co-production with Eurimages funding by director Yılmaz Arslan, is like a sequel to *Yasemin*. Hülya (Yelda Reynaud), a fragile young girl who suffers from disorientation is taken back to Turkey against her will to stay with some relatives, runs away and ends up in a psychiatric clinic. Her mother (played by Özay Fecht, familiar from her role as an imprisoned housewife in *40m² Deutschland*), who has left the family and remarried in Turkey, disowns her. Finally, she finds herself back on a German street, feeling alienated, not knowing where she belongs. The attempts to render the subjective visions and dreams of this disturbed girl, however, are staged like fashion photography and appear rather implausible.

Ich Chef, Du Turnschuh (Me Boss, You Running Shoe) (1998), directed by Hussi Kutlucan who also plays the main part, is one of the few comedies in this realm. The adventures of the asylum-seeker Dudie take us from a refugee-camp in Hamburg to the building site at the centre of Berlin. Özay Fecht figures once again in a minor role as Dudie's beloved who decides to secure the right to a better life for herself by leaving him and marrying an unknown German, a choice which is determined by pragmatic and economic rather than 'cultural' reasons. This film is notable for some scenes which clearly show masquerade and performance of ethnicity (an asylum seeker from Turkey masquerades as an Indian, a German child has his hair coloured brown and accordingly starts talking in broken German). The building site at Potsdamer Platz is populated by illegal workers who decide to claim a patch of land to protest for their pay and have a wild celebration against the back-drop of the unfinished Reichstag building, thus proposing a rather messy and subversive view on the state of the Republic.

At the Berlin Film Festival in February 1999, while debates about double citizenship were at their peak, many of these films were shown as 'New German Films' and two brand-new Turkish-German productions were presented with great critical acclaim.[19] Thomas Arslan's new film *Dealer*, co-produced with ZDF – *Das kleine Fernsehspiel*, like his previous film *Geschwister*, and once again staring Tamer Yiğit, offers rather unglamourous, minimalist visions of Berlin, staging the main character against the background of housing estates, green parks or pointilistic traffic lights. Encounters in private and public spaces are acted in a subdued, chilled manner, somewhat characteristic of the stagnant atmosphere in quarters which appear to be light years away from the big-scale remodelling of the reunified capital.

Kutluğ Ataman's *Lola und Bilidikid*, which was the opening film of the Panorama section of the festival, is a flamboyant family melodrama and thriller set in the gay and transvestite scene of Berlin, using a great deal of location shooting. The Istanbul-based director with a degree from UCLA has his characters take over the urban space. He stages them on streets, in nightclubs, public toilets, parks, derelict industrial buildings, in front of a poster announcing some event of 'diaspora' culture or around nationally significant momuments such as the Olympia Stadion or the Victory Column in the Tiergarten. Lola is a perfect belly-dancer and the leading lady of a transvestite group ironically called 'Die Gastarbeiterinnen'. She has been disowned by her family, but her gay little brother Murat discovers her and her lover Billidikid. When Lola is later found dead, floating in a canal, it is he who figures out that she was murdered not by Neo-Nazis, but by their elder macho brother Osman who was trying to cover up his own homosexual inclinations. While the exploration of family relations and machismo seems exaggerated and does fall back into ethnic stereotyping at some points, the transgender performance nonetheless succeeds in dissolving essentialist identities, quite in line with recent theoretical dismantlings of sexual identity in favor of performative qualities of gender.[20] The Turkish women on German streets in *Lola und Bilidikid* are really men, reminding us, perhaps, that binary oppositions such male/female or German/Turkish are constructions on shift-sand. The film was shown in cinemas throughout Berlin for several weeks after the festival, and its world distribution is handled by Good Machine International, the same company that distributed Ang Lee's *The Wedding Banquet* (1993) – another signal that Turkish-German film might be breaking out of its subnational status and venturing into the realm of transnational cinema which has recently discovered global diasporas as subject and market.

We seem to have reached a stage where film-makers are less concerned with closure than with exposure – in terms of lighting and *mise en scène* as well as performance and representation. Turna, Elif and their sisters remained trapped in subaltern positions, in claustrophobic spaces, in '40m² of Germany', and were framed in underexposed shots which reflected their lack of exposure to adventures and encounters in the urban space. There is hope, however, that the films to come will employ more mobile scenarios and travelling shots to depict vagrant women. 'Die Gastarbeiterinnen' in *Lola und Bilidikid* are out on the town, subverting bourgeois morality, performing gender as well as ethnicity, and dismantling 'woman as artifact' by their use of wigs, make-up, clothes and their irreverent speech and gestures. Although one of them ends up as a murder victim, they generally resist closure, engage in provocative encounters, venture out of dimly lit in-door locations and unsettle any simplistic resolution of identity and belonging.

Notes

1   ~~Chambers, I., *Migrancy, Culture, Identity*~~, London-New York, Routledge, 1994, p. 93.

2   Pratt, M. L., *Imperial Eyes: Travel Writing and Transculturation*, London-New York, Routledge, 1992. Pratt uses the term 'contact zone' to describe 'spaces of colonial encounters' where 'subordinate or marginal groups select and invent from materials transmitted to them by a dominant or metropolitan culture', but also with reference to 'transculturation from the colonies to the metropolis'. (p. 6)

3   Clifford, J., *The Predicament of Culture: Twentieth-Century Ethnography, Literature, and Art*, Cambridge, Mass.-London, Harvard University Press, 1988: 'Introduction: The Pure Products Go Crazy', pp. 1-17.

4   Morley D. & Robins, K., 'No Place like Heimat: Images of Home(land)', in *Spaces of Identity: Global Media, Electronic Landscapes and Cultural Boundaries* (London-New York, Routledge, 1995), pp. 85-104.

5   Spivak, G. C., *In Other Worlds: Essays in Cultural Politics*, London-New York, Methuen Press, 1987.

6   Adelson, L., 'The Price of Feminism: Of Women and Turks', in Herminghouse, P. & Mueller, M. (eds.), *Gender and Germanness: Cultural Productions of the Nation* (Oxford-New York, Berghahn, 1997), pp. 305-19.

Also Göktürk, D., 'Kennzeichen: weiblich / türkisch / deutsch, Beruf: Sozialarbeiterin / Schriftstellerin / Schauspielerin', in Gnüg, H. & Möhrmann, R. (eds.), *Frauen Literatur Geschichte: Schreibende Frauen vom Mittelalter bis zur Gegenwart* (Stuttgart-Weimar, Metzler, 1999), pp. 516-32.

7   Shohat, E. & Stam, R., *Unthinking Eurocentrism: Multiculturalism and the Media*, London-New York, Routledge, 1994, p. 42.

8   Naficy, H., 'Phobic Spaces and Liminal Panics: Independent Transnational Film Genre', in Wilson, R. & Dissanayake, W. (eds.), *Global/Local: Cultural Productions and the Transnational Imaginary* (Durham-London: Duke University Press, 1996), pp. 119-44.

9   These categories still continue to be used, for example by Crofts, S., 'Concepts of national cinema', in *The Oxford Guide to Film Studies*, Hill, J. & Church Gibson, P. (eds.) (Oxford-New York: Oxford University Press, 1998), pp. 385-94.

10 The prototypical Turkish 'guestworker' in Germany makes a passing appearance in H. Bhabha, 'DissemiNation: time, narrative, and the margins of the modern nation', in Bhabha, H. (ed.), *Nation and Narration*, London-New York, Routledge, 1990, pp. 315-17. The figure of the 'seventh man' stems from Berger, J., *A Seventh Man*, Harmondsworth, Penguin, 1975, a book documenting the experiences of migrant workers in Europe with texts and photos. The 'seventh man' does not only appear in Germany and other Western European countries, but can also be found back in Turkey where there is a high rate of migration from rural areas to the cities. Oóuz Makal considers the continuity between these migration processes and their respresentation in cinema: Oóuz Makal, *Sinemada Yedinci Adam. Türk sinemasında iç ve dış göç olayı* (The Seventh Man in Cinema. Migration within and abroad in Turkish cinema), Izmir, Ege Yayıncılık, 1994).

11 Cem Özdemir, who represents the Green Party in Parlament, sums up the new spirit of claiming one's place in the title of his book: *Ich bin Inländer. Ein anatolischer Schwabe im Bundestag*, München, dtv, 1997.

12 For a detailed description of these structures cf. Elsaesser, T., *New German Cinema: A History*, New Brunswick-New Jersey, Rutgers University Press, 1989.

13 The 'cinema of duty' has also been criticised in Britain by Malik, S.,'Beyond "The Cinema of Duty"? The Pleasures of Hybridity: Black British Film of the 1980s and 1990s', in Higson, A., (ed.), *Dissolving Views: Key Writings on British Cinema*, London, Cassel, 1996, pp. 202-15. Malik argues that there has been a shift from the 'cinema of duty' to the 'pleasures of hybridity' in some 1990s productions such as *Bhaji on the Beach* (1993) or *Wild West* (1992).

14 Cf. Brauerhoch, A., 'Die Heimat des Geschlechts – oder mit der fremden Geschichte die eigene erzählen: Zu *Shirins Hochzeit* von Helma Sanders-Brahms', in Karpf, E., Kiesel, D. & Visarius, K. (eds.), *'Getürkte Bilder': Zur Inszenierung von Fremden im Film* (Marburg, Schüren, 1995), pp. 109-15.

15 Hamid Naficy (1996) has decribed the configuration of claustrophobic spaces as an iconography which is characteristic to exilic cinema.

16 Cf. Martenstein, H., 'Das multikulturelle Melodram', *Der Tagesspiegel*, 13.5.1994.

17 Cf. Reinecke, S., 'Vier Quadratmeter Türkei: *Berlin in Berlin* – ein Kinomelodram von Sinan Çetin', *Frankfurter Rundschau*, 20.5.1994.

18 Kiontke, J., 'Sechs m^2 in Germanistan. Der Regisseur Yüksel Yavuz und sein Film *Aprilkinder*', *Filmforum*, February/March 1999, pp. 12-4.

19 Martenstein, H., 'Ich Chef, du Turnschuh. Filme mit doppelter Staatsbürgerschaft: türkisches Kino auf dem Weg in die deutsche Gegenwart', *Der Tagesspiegel*, 11.2.1999, p. 31. Martenstein concluded that perhaps the Turks were the only ones in Germany these days to make political movies on present day issues. Others joined into the praise of Turks making the most interesting German films and breaking out

of the ghetto, but nevertheless could not resist falling back into the rhetoric of 'between two cultures'. Hallensleben, S. & Noack, F., 'Auferstanden aus dem Ghetto. Die spannendsten deutschen Filme werden derzeit von Türken gedreht: *Dealer* und *Lola und Bilidikid* erzählen vom Leben zwischen zwei Welten', *Der Tagesspiegel*, 11.2.1999, p. 23. See also Tuncay Kulaoólu, 'Der neue 'deutsche' Film ist 'Türkisch'? Eine neue Generation bringt Leben in die Filmlandschaft', *Filmforum*, February/March 1999, pp. 8-11.

20 Butler, J., *Gender Trouble: Feminism and the Subversion of Identity*, London-New York, Routledge, 1990, and Butler, J., *Bodies that matter: On the discursive limits of 'sex'*, London-New York, Routledge, 1993.

The Sky over Berlin as Transcendental Space: Wenders, Döblin and the 'Angel of History'

Martin Jesinghausen

The New York sky has no stars.
They are all on the ground.

Lou Reed

1. From Benjamin to Wenders: Aura and Filmic Space

In his seminal essay 'The Work of Art in the Age of Mechanical Reproduction', Walter Benjamin establishes some theoretical parameters for a debate on film. One of the central aspects of this text is the problematic concept of *aura* in art and literature. What is aura? Can film have one? Can it feature in an investigation of film and space, such as the one intended in the present volume?

According to Benjamin, auratic experience of art provides a sense of 'distancing'. Defined by him as 'the unique phenomenon of a distance, however close it may be',[1] aura involves a spatial idea of three-dimensionality. Space features in auratic experience in an almost Brechtian sense of metaphysical *Verfremdung*, a 'strange' rendering of that which is familiar – what is so close is faraway. The auratic work of art puts a reflexive distance between the subjectivity of the recipient and the world of objects in space. Aura as Benjamin sees it has much in common with the transcendental aesthetic project of 'romanticising reality' advocated by the early German romantics. For Novalis, this project entails 'investing the commonplace with a lofty significance, the ordinary with a mysterious aspect, the familiar with the prestige of the unfamiliar, the finite with the semblance of infinity'.[2] Thus the auratic experience is a translation process – a carrying across – from the physical realm of reality to the metaphysical and back again. What has this process got to do with film?

Benjamin does not make that clear. The initial stumbling block in linking aura and film is that it runs contrary to Benjamin's own intentions. In his essay, he invests considerable effort in denying the auratic nature of film. Based on revolutionised cultural production processes, film for Benjamin as a new medium has overcome the dependence on auratic experience characteristic of art and literature of the bygone bourgeois and earlier periods. Film is in the vanguard of modernist art: it can break the spell of ritualistic production and reception; it demystifies; through its specific aesthetics, it contributes towards lifting the fog of capitalist and fascist ideology. The loss of aura in film is thus the precondition for its gain as a politically emancipatory medium.

Benjamin's text initiated a lively, and still on-going, discussion about film and aura. His friend and co-critic of the Frankfurt Institute of Sociology, Theodor W. Adorno, contradicts Benjamin's view of aura and film on three counts. First and foremost, he holds that film, as a product of the capitalist culture industry, cannot be instrumental in bringing about the downfall of capitalism; secondly, Adorno challenges Benjamin's assumption that film precludes aura; finally, Adorno thus fundamentally disagrees with Benjamin's contention that the loss of aura is the precondition for the freeing-up of the liberating potential of film. Adorno holds that not only can aura and film co-exist, but, what is more, film is an essentially auratic art form. For him, this has totally negative implications. In support of his point of view, he cites Kracauer who views Chaplin's films as an example of aura in film. Kracauer adulates Chaplin as an auratic hero. In principal, Adorno agrees with Kracauer on the auratic nature of film, but he deplores the industrially produced meretriciousness of aura, especially of the Chaplinesque one. He therefore writes to Benjamin that film, 'if anything, does have an auratic character, it is surely the (sic) film which possesses it to an extreme and highly suspect degree'.[3] Because of the nature of film's industrially produced aura, he argues that film is unworthy to be considered as a serious art form, let alone a weapon in the struggle against 'wrong consciousness'.

Thus the issue of aura and film has been a highly contentious one since the publication of Benjamin's text. It leads Adorno to question Benjamin's colours as a true critical theorist and provokes him to accuse Benjamin of being insufficiently dialectic in his approach to both bourgeois and mechanically reproduced art, a shattering verdict for any Marxist historian of culture, and especially hard-hitting given Benjamin's fragile academic persona. As Pierre Missac (one of Benjamin's more perceptive French friends) has shown, there is however another way of assessing Benjamin's stance on the issue – by reading his text more sympathetically than Adorno. Missac argues that Benjamin's attitude towards aura is at least ambivalent since he 'both dreads and wishes for' its disappearance.[4] Missac apparently believes himself to be unearthing and amplifying Benjamin's secret nostalgia for aura and fulfilling his hidden agenda in claiming that not only can aura be present in film but it can also have positive potential:

> what about an involuntary reappearance of the aura, so to speak, added to the cinematographic work as an excess, as an example of the 'plus' that, as in the 'Theses on the Philosophy of History', crowns the cultural and helps dialectical materialism to avoid falling into *plumpes Denken*. A half century after the essay on the work of art, the question has not been settled, whether film can have a high quality aura, or whether in film the aura necessarily has an archaic and regressive character.
>
> (Missac, 1995, pp.100-1)

In an attempt to clarify Benjamin's ambivalent position, Missac's argument is that film and aura can indeed go together and may well achieve a positive synergy.

The present essay tries to go one step further in suggesting that a positive auratic experience of *metaphysical* space in film can be created by specific filmic uses of *physical* space. One of the fundamental aesthetic features of film as a 'new' artistic medium is its specific use of space, its intrinsic spatial realism. Film, it is argued here, achieves the auratic experience of metaphysical space through a manipulation of filmic space – 'real', physical space, spatial relationships between 'real' objects, people and (often geographically identifiable) places. This can be illustrated by considering treatments of space, and in particular urban space, in European cinema. In the portrayal of urban space in city films, the link between film and aura is particularly evident because a productive tension comes to the fore between filmic realism of space and the need for symbolic stylisation of space. Exploration of urban space dates from the very beginnings of cinema, (for example, in the Lumière brothers' *aperçus* of city life), and continues right up to the present through films such as Patrick Keillor's *London* via Rosselini's *Roma città aperta* or Fellini's *La dolce vita*, Reed's *The Third Man*, or Jean-Luc Godard's *Une ou deux choses que je sais d'elle*. Within this genre and in a German context, films about Berlin feature prominently, and are regarded by later German film directors as potentially supplying the foundations of a national German cinema. Ruttmann's *Berlin. Symphonie einer Großstadt* (1927) is an early attempt of shape filmic space as metaphysical space. Berlin is here the modernist metropolis at the centre of the modern experience. The first filmic rendition of Döblin's *Berlin Alexanderplatz* (Piel Jutzi, 1931) also belongs to this tradition, as does Fassbinder's 1979-80 adaptation. More recently von Trotta's *Das Versprechen* (1994) can be added to the list of important films exploring this city.

Wim Wenders has made it clear in his writings and city films, and most strikingly in his two Berlin films, that he perceives his work as standing in the Benjamin-inspired tradition. In *Wings of Desire* and *Faraway, So Close*, Wenders has succeeded in creating auratic film in the best possible sense as advocated by Missac – he takes physical urban space and transforms it successfully through cinematic alchemy into metaphysical space, thus creating the filmic auratic experience. As for Ruttmann, Berlin for Wenders represents an archetypal site where the cinematic miracle of metaphysical distancing can be performed. Berlin, especially postwar Berlin, is fertile symbolic terrain, and Wenders recognises this quality and translates the highly-charged geography of Berlin into a new metaphysical language of film. In attempting to contribute to the debate on film and aura, this essay explores Berlin as transcendental space in Wenders's Berlin films, and in tracing some of his geographical and cultural references, opens up vistas of Berlin's crooked history itself.

2. Berlin: Negative City-Prose or Transcendental Poetry of Salvation?

In 1987, shortly before the fall of the Berlin Wall, Wim Wenders film *Wings of Desire* was premiered, and was followed, two years after re-unification, by the arguably less convincing sequel *Faraway, So Close*. This essay moves back from Wenders by roughly

60 years to Alfred Döblin's novel *Berlin Alexanderplatz*, published in 1931. Added to film and novel will be a theoretical text – Walter Benjamin's 'Theses on the Philosophy of History' written in 1940.

Wenders

On the surface, *Wings of Desire* is about pre-reunification Berlin, the divided city between East and West. The sequel *Faraway So Close* carries the story of Berlin forward beyond reunification, overturning the basic assumption of *Wings of Desire* that there is no prospect of overcoming the 40-year history of political division. Between the two instalments of the film, history had intervened. Whereas the original movie had to acknowledge the fact that divisions, literally set in concrete, were real and permanent and could at most be transcendentally overcome, *Faraway, So Close* has to restate the problem and deals with the totally unexpected reality of unification. This moving of the historical goal posts may be one of the reasons why *Faraway, So Close* is a less powerful film than *Wings of Desire*.

In *Wings of Desire* the reality of divisions is the main driving force. Here, Berlin is identical with division. Originally not having liked Berlin much, Wenders went on a series of visits to Berlin in the mid-1980s, which constituted his 'only true experiences of Germany in twenty years'.[5] By the time of the making of *Wings of Desire* he was living in a Kreuzberg flat overlooking the Wall.

The politico-cultural angle of symbolic significance of Berlin to Wenders is only one aspect of the relevance of Berlin for the film. *Wings of Desire* is about divisions in a higher sense as well. The reality of division is the platform for lift-off into the transcendental perspective of the film. The 'real' Berlin is only a pretext to unfold a large-scale phenomenology of division on a meta-level of reality behind the concrete one: past and present, individual and political, human and divine, childhood and adulthood, male and female, physicality and spirituality, art and reality, black and white and colour, etc.

The film covers many symptomatic localities – the Gedächtniskirche, National Library, Europa-Center, Potsdamer Platz, and the Wall. As an example of the film's play with different levels of reality, the Potsdamer Platz scene is particularly graphic.[6] In *Wings of Desire*, Potsdamer Platz is symbolically charged territory: the 'first-hand', the 'hard' reality of this space is so evocative that it releases the 'second', the transcendental or meta-level of perspective. From Potsdamer Platz, this filmic epic takes wing. Potdamer Platz is central to the aesthetics of this film – its methodological engine room. The dead square works as a multifunctional symbol. Exposure to the storms of history has destroyed this space; against the backdrop of this devastation, the contrasting vision of meaningful cultural continuity is set. The Homer character muses on the destructiveness of time, and puts forward his alternative concept of a positive 'epic narrative of peace', verbalising the programmatic intention of the film as a whole:

> No one has been able to strike up an epic of peace. What is it about peace, that in the long run it fails to impassion, and that it does not lend itself to narrative? Should I give up

now? If I give up, then mankind will lose its storyteller. And when mankind has lost its storyteller, it will also have lost its childhood.

Potsdamer Platz is like a black hole of history where negative matter is transformed into spirituality, a time warp triggering the flow of collective memory, a kind of *Wesensschau* in the German philosophical tradition of spiritual reality behind tangible reality. A process takes place here, embodying the epistemology of the film as a whole. It could be called *transcendental condensation* of reality induced by the particularly unreal or super-real atmosphere of urban space.

Wings of Desire is a filmic essay on divisions. Structurally, it is in itself based on a central division. There are two Berlins here: the physical cityscape, which is drab, dingy, desperate and forlorn, and the *Sky over Berlin* (the original German title) with Berlin as a transcendental space where angels roam, hope predominates, love triumphs and collective memory has its field day. Two worlds are juxtaposed, the first being a historico-political, visible, documentable reality with condensed negativity, and the second a vision of consolation with positive vibrations of meaningfulness and sensuous radiation visible only to children, angels and the viewer. The second world, emanating from the first, mirrors it as its ontological and historiological recognition. We follow the film like unspoilt children into the beyond and onto the higher plane of angelic view.

Marion, the trapeze artist, meets Damiel, the guardian angel: divine spirituality with an earth-wish unites with gravity-bound physicality aspiring to levitate. Because Marion wants to fly and Damiel is longing for the gravity of the body they are drawn to one another. Marion's love of Damiel overcomes the restrictions of gravity. Damiel's love of Marion overcomes the limitations of his bodiless spirituality. The material and spiritual worlds merge.

The film contrasts positive transcendental unification against negative political division. It has been argued that it reduces the historico-political dimensions of urban division of Berlin to mere props for the real drama of division and unification which is one of the soul. 'The whole movie is saying, "If only I could express myself like a child or an American moviemaker! Then I could unify the divided German soul, or, at least, my own soul"'.[7] Unification then is not envisaged in the political arena at all, but takes place in the realm of the heightened reality of the soul, instigated by love and divine supervision.

When the unification of the souls becomes the hard reality of the film, the real reality divide remains stubbornly resistant to reconciliation. After his downfall into material humanity, Damiel finds himself in the West. He is walking the streets of Charlottenburg and not those of, for instance, Berlin Mitte in the East. The final colour section of the film illuminates the West in its melancholy glory. The graffiti of the Wall come into central view as the first sensual touchstone of Damiels's new-found gravitas in life. Now the East of the city is almost forgotten. It is no more than a dark memory in the black and white of alien territory.

The happy ending narrows down the universal perspective of the film: it ends up as a glorification of one side of the divide – West Berlin – where two Charlottenburg

Schickimickies are about to have a good time. The division of the city is unintentionally sanctioned through the plot. The real Berlin is sacrificed to Wenders's reconciliatory 'epic of peace'. In the filmic vision of soulful equilibrium where spirituality turns physical and physicality turns spiritual, the urban political divide, which the vision of peace was originally meant to heal, is taken for granted. It is left behind as the unfathomable remainder, which the film proceeds to ignore. Ironically, the Wall was to come down two years later. Political unity emerged precisely at the moment when divisions appeared at their most insurmountable and it was taken to be common-sense to assume that they were here to stay.[8]

What is new about Wenders's films (new in the context of post-war German film, as well as regards the wider German cultural situation) is their special style of 'New Subjectivity', characterised by the courage to be positive and symbolic, by epic-narrative expansiveness and the curiosity to explore a new cultural situation which had changed greatly since the austerity of the 1950s and early 1960s, now marked by a new diversity and vibrancy in the wake of the student rebellion. Wenders's big theme, also powerfully put forward elsewhere (for example in *Alice in the Cities* and *Kings of the Road*) is that of overcoming the negative status quo through the power of positive humanity. For Wenders, identity and continuity is possible despite alienation and divisions.

Döblin and Wenders

In an essay on German film history, Volker Schlöndorff demands that film become an epic narrative of space and time, defined as a technique of 'free association which makes its way across the length and the breadth of the world, rather than clinging to some narrow ideologically circumscribed action'. In support, he cites Siegfried Kracauer who in 1931 had written an article on *Berlin Alexanderplatz*, regarding it as a literary role model for epic narrative in film. Kracauer's observation that Döblin and the social novels of Balzac and Zola are "examples of an epic narrative style missing in German film" is quoted by Schlöndorff and thus transplanted into the postmodern 1980s. Kracauer says:

> That is how every film that is a real film ambles along. It draws its suspense from the largeness of the camera, which only fulfils its task when it conspicuously kaleidoscopes its way through the environment, and draws in the world around us piece by piece.[9]

As experiments in film style, Wenders's films are identity strategies of the New German Cinema. *Wings of Desire* in particular could be regarded as seminal in that it comes close to fulfilling Schlöndorff's and Kracauer's demand for a new epic narrative as the new identifiable style of German national cinema. Its declared goal is to realise the assumption that an 'epic of peace' is possible. Truly kaleidoscopic, it proceeds gradually in the unfolding of its temporally and spatially broad vision. It has 'the largeness of camera' demanded by Kracauer.

Schlöndorff's demand regarding epic narrative style links *Wings of Desire* with Döblin's portrayal of Alexanderplatz. Like Fassbinder's massive adaptation of Döblin's novel, *Wings of Desire* can be located in the tradition of the modernist epic style; Döblin's novel plays a central role in the very creation of it. With references to Rilke, the photographer Otto Sander, Benjamin, modernist architecture etc., *Wings of Desire* is also a kaleidoscopic re-assessment of German modernist culture which renders it a postmodern retrospective of modernism, an attempt to carry modernism forward into the late twentieth century.

There are also direct references to Döblin's novel in the film which it would be difficult to dismiss as mere coincidence. In *Berlin Alexanderplatz*, a narrative of the intersection of biography and urban space, the square is the symbol of city life as the theatre of modernist mass individuals. The life of Franz Biberkopf, a representative common man, is set on Alexanderplatz. Like Potsdamer Platz in the film, this square is the locus of paradigmatic city space, extending beyond this city, the national situation and even the real, taking us into the metaphysics of twentieth century history.

The perception of the transcendental homelessness of modern life is central to both novel and film; and both hold out the promise of spiritual homecoming. In the film, Berliners' lives are watched over by two guardian angels Cassiel and Damiel; in the novel, Biberkopf is also monitored by two guardian angels, Terah and Sarug. There are remarkable similarities between these two pairs of angels, their characters being based on an allegorical mixture of traits – they are at the same time real as contemporary commentators and unreal as mythical Christian archetypes. In both film and novel, the angels intervene in the characters' lives and motivate the epic progression towards a positive outcome: 'Yes, this tale of Franz Biberkopf, of his hard, true, and revealing existence, has now progressed thus far. Everything is growing clearer and clearer, the more Franz Biberkopf rears and rages. We are nearing the point where everything will become clear. (…) "This man is on the brink of a vision." (…) "So you have hope for this man?" "Yes."'[10] The parallels are striking: the dualism of the two worlds, the impact of the transcendental on the real world, and the reference to children's perceptive powers all reveal Wenders's debt to Döblin.

Benjamin, Döblin, and Wenders

Walter Benjamin occupies a special place in Wenders' universe and could be regarded as a formative influence.[11] There are links on various levels. First, regarding subject matter, Wenders and Benjamin share an interest in charting the experience of the city. Some of Wenders's films are panoramic *Städtebilder* like Benjamin's. Second, the methodology of filmic narrative in Wenders has a distinctly Benjaminian ring to it. He embraces Benjamin's principles of storytelling, defined as 'epic remembrance'.[12] Handke's eulogy of the purity of the child's perception in *Wings of Desire* echoes Benjamin's involvement with children's literature. For Wenders, film is the medium of the postmodern storyteller: 'Only a story can give meaning and a moral to an image.'[13] Third, for Wenders, film has a similar function as essay writing for Benjamin.[14] *Wings of Desire* and its sequel amount to essays on Berlin. Wenders's films are self-referential, exploring film's possibilities of communication and liberation.

Fourth, the Benjaminian concept of aura is of central importance for Wenders's cinema, a cinema which implicitly provides a positive response to Missac's initial question as to whether film can have a high-quality aura. Wenders's conscious creation of a filmic aura and his aspirations for a new epic narrative style in German cinema go hand in hand. The title *Faraway, So Close* can be read as a programmatic reference to Benjamin's concept of aura, since it is a concise summary of his own definition quoted above. It is not an exaggeration to say that Wenders's cinema stands in the tradition of critical theory initiated by Benjamin and the Frankfurt School, mediated through the events of 1968. As cinema essays on issues such as the culture industry and its impact on subjectivity, his films provide a link between modernist theorising on the role of art in revolution and the postmodernist play with art and reality.

Fifth, Wenders borrows from Benjamin the main principles of aesthetics and cultural theory. In the true Benjaminian tradition, he gives allegorical expression to these principles. The most relevant example for the Berlin films is Benjamin's angel of history. In *Wings of Desire* and *Faraway, So Close*, Benjamin's image of Klee's angel of history is recognisable as a major ingredient in the portrayal of the guardian angels (for example, in the initial scene of *Wings of Desire*, an angel looks down from the Gedächtniskirche on the 'debris of history'). Wenders, however, misinterprets this aspect of Benjamin's cultural philosophy: the angelic principle in the Berlin films admittedly represents a recourse to Benjamin's angel of history, but this is based on a misreading by Wenders and Handke of an important aspect of the angel. What follows is a more detailed discussion of this misunderstanding, but we should note at the outset that, even though of some consequence for the structure of the two Berlin films, it in no way diminishes the creative interaction between Benjamin and the films' scriptwriter and director.

The 'Theses on the Philosophy of History', the last text Benjamin completed, were a desperate attempt to make sense of the inevitable breakdown of Western civilisation. Eerily prophetic, the ninth thesis anticipates the 'pile of debris' Berlin was to turn into five years later. The *Theses* were written in Paris, the interpretation of Klee's angel as the angel of history is associated with Berlin.

> A Klee painting named *Angelus novus* shows an angel looking as though he is about to move away from something he is fixedly contemplating. His eyes are staring, his mouth is open, his wings are spread. This is how one pictures the angel of history. His face is turned toward the past. Where we perceive a chain of' events, he sees one single catastrophe which keeps piling wreckage upon wreckage and hurls it in front of his feet. The angel would like to stay, awaken the dead, and make whole what has been smashed. But a storm is blowing from Paradise; it has got caught in his wings with such violence that the angel can no longer close them. This storm irresistibly propels him into the future to which his back is turned, while the pile of debris before him grows skyward. This storm is what we call progress.[15]

The similarities between Benjamin's *Angelus novus* and the guardian angels in *Wings of Desire* has been emphasised by critics.[16] Cook for instance compares them, stressing their similarity in that neither set is:

84

able to alter the course of history; they only observe and verify it as they accompany it into the future with a painful countenance. (…) As pessimistic as Benjamin's description of the *Angelus novus* seems, and as negative as the film's depiction of Berlin's reconstruction since 1945 may be, *Wings of Desire* is a film imbued with the spirit of hope for new beginnings. One finds similar hope in Benjamin' s essay. (Cook, 1997, p. 185)

This comparison makes only limited sense. Although Wenders was probably inspired by Benjamin's *Theses*, the angel trope is only meaningful in the context of his 'epic of peace' narrative. This was never Benjamin's intention, certainly not at this time of war and ensuing personal crisis. It is evident from the moment *Wings of Desire* moves from black and white into colour, that the course of history *is* altered in a positive sense through angelic intervention. The possibility of reconciling the public with the private through benevolent influence of the spiritual over the real would have been out of reach for Benjamin. The film's suggestion that salvation is possible links it more closely to Döblin's model than to Benjamin's. While Damiel's chief ambition is 'to be able to say "now" and "now" and not like always "forever" and "in eternity"', to leave eternity and enter time, Benjamin's *Angelus* cannot and does not wish to do so. What lands at Damiel's feet is not the wreckage of a catastrophic past but (with a humorous clanking of iron and an ironic nod in Benjamin's direction) the pathetic armour of his heavenly existence. Incorporation is an escape from eternal time and a return into limited time. In contrast, the *Angelus novus* is forced to move on forever. According to Benjamin's rules of negative dialectic, the angel has himself become a victim of the process he had watched over. Whereas Benjamin projects eternal homelessness, Wenders suggests a possible homecoming in the here and now. Because of the storm of history, the *Angelus* cannot even close his wings to fly at all, let alone home, and he cannot prevent himself being blown into the future.

The reason for the misunderstanding of the relationship of the angels apparently lies in the fact that Benjamin's *Angelus novus* thesis is mostly quoted without his friend Scholem's prefatory motto:

Ready to fly, my wings are spread
To return I'd be glad
For, if living time I'd stay instead
My luck would soon turn bad

Gershom Scholem – (Greetings from the Angelus)

Cook's comparison suffers from this omission. Ironically, it is Wenders's and Handke's misinterpretation of this poem in its context that establishes the link between Wenders's two Berlin films and Benjamin's 'Theses...'. The change of title from *Sky over Berlin* to *Wings of Desire* additionally emphasises the reference to the Scholem motto where Angel's wings facilitate the desired return. With the stylised closure of an angels wings in flight both films move on from one episode to the next. This must have been intended as a conscious reference back to the motto, suggesting that Benjamin's allegory of negative divine exposure can be reconciled, if not altogether interpreted in a positive light, through the utopian image of homecoming represented by the angel of the poem. That homecoming is deemed possible in the merger of Damiel's with Marion's world suggests the misunderstanding of Benjamin's *Thesis* where the desire to return is regarded as powerless and uncalled for.

It is at this point where the misunderstanding has crept in. Cook does not understand the link between Benjamin and Wenders because he neglects the fundamental difference of outlook between the thesis and the films, and because he omits the motto where the true link can be established. If the assumption were right that the reference is based on this thesis and particularly Scholem's motto, the conclusion would have to be drawn that Wenders and Handke have misunderstood Benjamin's message. A closer look at the significance of the motto might reveal Benjamin's method of dialectical composition of juxtaposing the logical alternatives of transcendental returning (desire, motto) and dislocation (disillusion, prose text).

The prose text both presents the allegory of history from the point of view of the failure of the 'now' *and* provides Scholem with a belated answer to his invitation that Benjamin leave Europe and join him in the safety of Palestine.[17] The *Angelus novus* allegory contains an element of personal justification: it is also the explanation of his reason to stay in Europe. Benjamin interprets the meaning of Klee's picture differently from Scholem. To him the *Angelus novus* has to 'stay living time'; this meaning links Klee's angel with Benjamin's biography. Benjamin, like the angel, cannot tear himself away. In the face of breakdown of European civilisation, returning is not an option for two reasons. First, the historian cannot go back in time like a historicist – even the 'tiger leap into history' is impossible. The historical perspective is now fixed in an empty gaze. Second, the persecuted European Jew cannot go to the homeland Palestine as did Scholem (Scholem, 1975, especially pp. 191-95). The only way forward for this angel is to look back, take a battering from the storm of history, and thus be driven towards the future.

This portrait of the Angel then is Benjamin's despairing acknowledgement of the Dialectic of Enlightenment, contrasted with a theological vision of homecoming. It recognises the destructive force of progress, governed by 'instrumental reason'. That the prophetic 'pile of debris, growing skyward' has a literal application to the destruction caused by the war (and particularly to Berlin) is one of the saddest of the ironies in Benjamin's writings. Their historical involvement and postmodern legacy literally culminates on the Mont Klamott.

3. Urban Experience as Transcendental Paradigm of History: Paris or Berlin?

Benjamin's major critical achievement is the methodology of urban iconology, first explored in *One Way Street*, and more fully formulated in the *Arcades Project*,[18] with its focus as Paris. The intention is to formulate a 'modern mythology' and lay the foundations of an archaeology of modernity. Going back into nineteenth century Paris was for him the 'tiger leap into history', since it was from this period that an understanding of the immediate contemporary situation could be gleaned.

If Paris is obviously the critical focus of Benjamin's last creative period, how is it possible to construct a kinship between Wenders and Benjamin on the basis of common Berlin experience? One of the most interesting aspects of Benjamin's work is the curious imbalance between Berlin and Paris when Benjamin deals with urban experience in writing.

For Benjamin, Paris is the rational projection of the Berlin experience, often too immediate to be rendered objectively.[19] Benjamin does not fully acknowledge the formative significance of his Berlin experience for his interpretation of Paris. Or perhaps Berlin features less significantly than Paris on the level of the critique of urban culture. As his two main essays on Berlin demonstrate, the Berlin experience is not taken into the contemporary. Both works break off on the level of memoir of a youthful past. The urban experience of Paris is transcendentally heightened: Paris becomes the 'Capital of the Nineteenth Century'. Berlin, in contrast, remains as a real-life urban situation, too close for comfort.

There is a circular shift of perspective at work in Benjamin's view of Paris and Berlin. The Berlin experience is projected onto Paris and thereby verbally rationalised. The Paris experience clarifies the significance of Berlin and puts his Berlin-life in slightly nostalgic perspective.[20] One side of this paradox is that Benjamin's interpretation of Paris is pre-structured by his experience of Berlin; the other that Paris features as the medium through which Benjamin's urban experience of Berlin takes rational shape. Whereas Berlin is the formative framework of experience in the background of Benjamin's criticism, Paris occupies its foreground as a representative critical medium.

Evidence for this paradox is that he illustrates the Berlin experience through Paris references even when he is writing about Berlin, as in *A Berlin Chronicle and A Berlin Childhood*. In the Parisian perspective, many of the central *Ur*-experiences of Berlin present themselves more sharply outlined than in Berlin. A good example of this perspective oscillation between Paris and Berlin is the following account of an 'illumination', taken from *A Berlin Chronicle*, written in 1932. Highlighted in the following excerpt is the decisive principle of a 'momentarily occurring condensation (*Zusammenschiessen*) of meaning', through an increased awareness of the essence of urban experience. It culminates in the realisation that the city is the 'symbolic form' of modern life. The revelatory event happened in Paris and is representative in that Benjamin regards it as symptomatic of similar occurrences that might have also taken place in Berlin.

> The more frequently I return to these memories, the less fortuitous it seems to me how slight a role is played in them by people: I think of an afternoon in Paris to which I owe insights into my life that came in a flash, with the force of an illumination. It was on this very afternoon that my biographical relationships to people (…) were revealed to me in their most vivid and hidden intertwinings. I tell myself it had to be in Paris, where the walls and quays, the places to pause, the collections and the rubbish, the railings and the squares, the arcades and the kiosks, teach a language so singular that our relations to people attain, in the solitude encompassing us in our immersion in that world of things, the depths of a sleep in which the dream image waits to show the people their true faces.

> I wish to write of this afternoon because it made so apparent what kind of regime cities keep over imagination, and why the city, where people make the most ruthless demands on one another (…) grant the individual not a single moment of contemplation, indemnifies itself in memory, and why the veil it has covertly woven out of our lives shows the images of people less than those of the sites of our encounters with others or ourselves. Now on the afternoon in question I was sitting inside the Café des Deux Magots at St.-Germain-des-Prés, where I was waiting – I forget for whom. Suddenly, and with compelling force, I was struck by the idea of drawing a diagram of my life, and knew at the same moment exactly how it was to be done. With a very simple question I interrogated my past life, and the answers were inscribed, as if of their own accord, on a sheet of paper that I had with me.

It is striking that in an account of his earlier life in Berlin, the existentially striking experiences were initiated in Paris. Berlin revealed its true nature through Paris.

The reason for this lesser role allocated to Berlin in Benjamin's later work is only partly to be found in this personal dimension and cannot be fully explained by the fact that he was not living in Berlin anymore. Instead, it is a feature of Berlin itself and points to the principle of its history: for Benjamin, Berlin was not 'text' in the same way as Paris, for the obvious reason that Berlin was not yet legible as text in the same way. Berlin had not yet finished becoming a capital of the twentieth century. The full understanding of its significance arguably emerged only after 1945 and the events of 1989/90. Wenders's two Berlin films make that clear.

4. History Viewed From The End: Material History of the City and Metaphysical Meaning

The City at Constant Breaking Point

As the Wall had been attractive as a piece of political architecture and a Berlin symbol, the fall of the Wall evoked a new interest in Berlin. The chequered city history of Berlin came back into full view.[21] It became clear how Berlin had turned into a belated capital of a belated nation and the most recent of great European metropolises; how the course of European and world history in the first half of this century had been shaped from within its palaces, parliaments and bunkers; how the city had been battered in the fallout from the explosions that had been originated in it.

The renewed interest after reunification was caused by Berlin's history becoming patently visible. It had come full circle from unification to re-unification. History was almost complete, in a Fukuyamaian sense. Berlin emerged as subject and object of twentieth century history, as a historical protagonist and suffering victim. Berlin had made history, history had been made in Berlin, and history had made something of Berlin. Some of the main features of Berlin's historical uniqueness need to be stated.

First, its belatedness. With hindsight, we can see that no other capital in the world has developed as Berlin has. One of the roots of its uniqueness is its belatedness. No other European city is so inextricably linked up with its recent history. Berlin became what it is today in the course of little more than a hundred years. Whereas Paris was fully developed as a metropolis by the end of the 19th century, Berlin's growth only took off after Paris had arrived.

Second, 'hemmed-in-ness' and speed of urban development. Paradoxically, Berlin's historical belatedness is also the reason for an acceleration of the speed of its historical development. Within decades rather than centuries, Berlin developed from being a provincial German town into a major centre of German nationalism and a cosmopolitan metropolis. It was hemmed in culturally between Moscow and Paris; and economically and politically between the colliding eastern and western hemispheres, protectionist agrarian feudalism and the laissez-faire culture of capitalist modernisation. Its modern cultural cityscape bears the signs of a wild fluctuation between authoritarianism and anarchy – Prussian, Wilheminian and Fascist domination on the one hand, the sprawl of mass culture and the typical characteristics of big city anarchy on the other. It was torn between the conflicting excesses of a politically prescriptive culture of representation and spontaneously growing metropolitan culture. Unlike any other European capital, Berlin has never enjoyed any extensive consecutive periods of gradual metropolitan growth (or decline). Any changes in status came about with unique suddenness, mostly as strategically planned governmental interventions and part of the wider German phenomenon of 'Revolution from Above'. Examples here are the foundation of Berlin's university in 1806, the Wilhelminian building programme of the suburbs, the East-West-Axis as an initial phase of the monumental fascist re-invention of the city, and – another Speer project – the building of the Olympic stadium.

Third, non-identity as discontinuity. Looking back at Berlin's history from the end of the twentieth century, it seems that the development of Berlin's cityscape has followed a programme of discontinuity and non-identity. The city moved from

- being a provincial Prussian capital (caesura: Franco/Prussian Wars and annexation of Southern Germany through Bismarck's Prussian armies 1870/71) to being a megalopolis and national seat of empire (caesura: First World War),
- being the centre of national republican life (caesura: Treaty of Versailles/ World Economic Crisis) to a fascist fortress; from being one of the world centres of diverse city culture (caesura: fascist takeover of 1933) to a testing ground for the fascist cultural experiment, based on megalomaniac persecution, censorship, book- and art-burning (caesura: Second World War); and
- suffering total urban destruction to becoming a divided city (caesura: monetary reform, Berlin Blockade and building of the Wall) and back, not quite full circle, to a national republican capital (caesura: Silent Revolution/Fall of the Wall and Communism).

Winged Beasts – half Divine, half Human: Berlin's Transcendental Cyberspace

To the cultural historian, Berlin reveals itself emblematically through the icon of the winged transcendental messenger. The city is teaming with them. There are the winged goddesses; for example, Victoria as the charioteer of the Quadriga (part of Schadow's Bronze on the Brandenburg Gate), and the same creature also on the Victory Column;[22]

all kinds of modernist angels, Prussian and fascist eagles. The equivalent of the series of ruthless interventions of history in the recent career of the city is a tradition of mythological imagery, creating what could be called Berlin's *transcendental cyberspace*. These hybrid winged beasts, half human, half divine, are the emblems of Berlin's *genius loci*. They signify the presence of divine forces accompanying the city's fateful career, inciting, listening, commenting, commiserating. Wenders has assembled these gods, demigods and angels together in a historical picture atlas of divine fragments: *Götterklein* Mournfully, providence looks down upon a landscape of ruins.

Wender's films complete Benjamin's necessarily incomplete assessment of Berlin, by applying to Berlin Benjamin's methodology of urban iconography essayed on Paris. From Wenders's *post-histoire* point of view, the history of Berlin's urban iconographical transcendentalism comes to make symbolic sense. The films have uncovered this tradition and provide a retrospective, a form of archaeology of the twentieth century. *Faraway, So Close*: the transcendental powers of twentieth century history are tangibly immediate in Berlin.

5. Filmic Space as Auratic Space in Wenders's Two Berlin Films

By focussing on Berlin as subject matter and transforming one of Berlin's cultural-historical icons- the angel trope, and in particular Benjamin's angel of history – into a major structuring device in the two films' creation of a metaphysical via a physical reality, Wenders has made a significant contribution to a new language of film. In doing so, he has also gone some way towards fulfilling aspirations for the creation of a national German cinema advocated by Schlöndorff and other New German film-makers, a process which in their view demands a return to the sources of German cinema and the German cultural tradition in general. What these films have also achieved paradigmatically – the overarching perspective of this article – is a demonstration of the auratic nature of film in its most positive form. Wenders's films are auratic because they body forth the interpenetration of spiritual reality as metaphysical space and physical urban space. The films may not have grasped the full meaning of Benjamin's angel of history as 'living time', but they have perhaps addressed a more central problem with regard to Benjamin's standing as a critic in contemporary debates on film and culture. The two works can be cited in support of the claim that film is a fundamentally auratic medium: the intrinsic force of filmic aura brings about a process of distancing where it is possible for viewers to put reflexive and emotional space between themselves and their living space. Perhaps we can re-establish Benjamin's notion of film as a politically emancipatory art form if it manages, contrary to Benjamin's own declarations of intent, as in the two Berlin works discussed, consciously to create what is inherently one of its central aesthetic principles – the filmic aura. Wenders has demonstrated that film, far from being a medium bereft of aura, in fact achieves its inherent aesthetic *raison d'être* when it capitalises on aura's potential – close, so faraway.

Notes

1 'The Work of Art in the Age of Mechanical Reproduction', in *Illuminations*, London, Fontana, 1973, p.216.

2 Novalis, 'Fragmente des Jahres 1798', *Gesammelte Werke*, No 879, vol. III, p.38, cited in Furst, L. A., *European Romanticism. Self Definition*, London, Methuen, 1980, p.3.

3 Adorno, letter to Benjamin, London, 18 March 1936, quoted in Brooker, P. *Modernism/Postmodernism*, London, Longman, 1992, p.54.

4 The controversy gets even more byzantine in its affiliations when Missac quotes Adorno as being in agreement with Benjamin's position that 'film was by its very nature allergic and hostile to aura' (Missac, P., *Walter Benjamin's Passages*, London, MIT, 1995, p.100)

5 Wenders, W., *TheLogic of Images. Essays and Conversations*, London – Boston, Faber and Faber, 1991, p. 94.

6 In *Faraway, So Close*, Potsdamer Platz is beginning to change appearance in the direction it is going at present: it is depicted here as a massive building site.

7 Kael, P., New Yorker, 30.5.1988.

8 William Garton Ash has suggested that an irony of history is at work in the fall of the Wall: that the common acceptance of the division in the seventies and eighties could have been one of the main factors in overcoming it in 1989/90. "Now, just as they (the architects of Ostpolitik, MJ) had thoroughly buried the hope (for unification, MJ), just as not only they but the Christian Democrats who took over their GDR-policy had become soberly convinced that it would not happen in their lifetime – it happened." *In Europe's Name. Germany and the Divided Continent*, London, Vintage, 1994, p. 203. The status quo of division was changed "by first fully recognising it" (p.367). Wenders's film is situated in this paradoxical cultural environment of the last Cold War days.

9 Schlöndorff, V., 'Discovering and Preserving German Film History', in Rentschler, E. (ed.), *West German Film-makers on Film. Visions and Voices* (London, Holmes and Meier, 1988), p.110.

10 Döblin, A., *Berlin Alexanderplatz. The Story of Franz Biberkopf*, New York, Continuum, 1996, pp. 549-51.

11 See Cook, R. F., 'Angels, Fiction and History in Berlin', in Cook, R. F. & Gemünden, G. (eds.), *The Cinema of Wim Wenders. Image, Narrative and the Postmodern Condition* (Detroit, Wayne State University Press), 1997, pp.163-90.

12 Put forward in the early essay on Leskow: 'The Storyteller', in *Illuminations*, London, Fontana Press. 1973, p. 97.

13 Quoted after Kaes, A., 'Wim Wenders', in *Oxford History of World Cinema*, Oxford, Oxford University Press, 1996, p. 623.

14 See Kaes above, who points out the symbiotic relationship of Essay-writing and film-making in Wenders's work. "Wenders has concerned himself overtly with the theoretical issues involved with cinematic representation" (p. 624).

15 Benjamin, W., 'Theses on the Philosophy of History', in *Illuminations*, p. 249.

16 See Cook, especially pp. 181-87. See also for example Kolditz, S., 'Kommentierte Filmografie', in *Wim Wenders*, Munich, Hanser, 1991, p. 281.

17 Scholem's Angelus Novus-verse forms part of a longer doodle-type poem, sent to Benjamin in Berlin in 1921 from Scholem in Munich who had borrowed the Klee picture from Benjamin, shortly after he had bought it. See *Briefe I*, Scholem, G. & Adorno, T. W. (eds.), Frankfurt/M., Suhrkamp, 1978, letters 101 to 104. Seven years later the invitation to go to Jerusalem was made. And it is around this time that their friendship floundered, because Benjamin, after an initial period of indecision, finally decided against leaving, having gratefully received a lump sum as a gift to finance his stay in Jerusalem. Scholem can

hardly conceal his anger in commenting on the loss of his friend, even with the distance of nearly five decades between the event and Scholem's chronicle. See Scholem, G., *Walter Benjamin, Die Geschichte einer Freundschaft,* Frankfurt/M., Suhrkamp, 1975, pp. 179-95.

18 See comparatively recently Buck-Morss, S., *The Dialectics of Seeing. Walter Benjamin and the Arcades Project,* London, MIT, 1989.

19 As Benjamin's correspondence with Scholem and Scholem's often patronising comments show very clearly during many periods and junctures of Benjamin's life, Berlin to Benjamin was linked with the make-or-break struggle of everyday existence, often too extreme or complicated to be expressed. More often than not the day-to-day goings-on cannot be sorted out verbally, or even in a letter to a close friend, let alone in publishable texts. Berlin for Benjamin is the place of crisis, happiness and dithering, also a hiding place where he can protect himself from too close a scrutiny of his personal affairs by his friends. See for example the crucial conflict between Scholem's Palestine plans, which he had devised for Benjamin, and the arrival of Asja Lacis in Berlin, spoiling Scholem's stratagems. For Scholem, it is Berlin that leads Benjamin astray. In the end, when all his plans for Benjamin's transformation into a career devoted to Jewish scholarship come to nothing, he has really lost Benjamin to Berlin.

20 In a letter of 1 May 1938, Benjamin writes from Paris: 'In 1932 I started to write a slender book with the title *Berlin Childhood around 1900.* Perhaps you have noticed parts of it, published before Hitler in the *Frankfurter Zeitung.* Over the last weeks I expanded and increasingly revised the book. Owing to its subject matter, it will be difficult to find a publisher for it. (…) It will be appealing to thousands of exiled Germans.' (*Briefe II,* see above, pp.756-7, my translation, MJ) Benjamin, W., 'Berlin Childhood', in *One Way Street and Other Writings,* London, NLB, 1979, p. 96.

21 See for example Read, A. & Fisher, D., *Berlin. The Biography of a City,* London, Pimlico, 1994, or more recently: Taylor, R., *Berlin and its Culture,* London, Yale University Press, 1997, and most recently and best of all: Richie, A., *Faust's Metropolis. A History of Berlin,* London, HarperCollins, 1998.

22 Between 1807 to 1814, this sculpture was abducted by Napoleon and taken to Paris. On its return in a triumphal procession, reportedly watched over by Hegel and other luminaries of the idealist community, the population danced in the streets. The Victory Column is symbolic of the material fabric of the city coming under the influence of chauvinistic pan-German nationalist identity strategies, erected to reassert Prussian/German supremacy over France. It was commissioned as early as 1865, actually six years before the actual event, to commemorate Prussian annexations of parts of Denmark and the victory over France in the Franco-Prussian War of 1870/71. The monument was put up in 1873 in the presence of the Kaiser, then on the Königsplatz, now Platz der Republik. During the First World War, the plinth was refurbished with ornamentally arranged metal from German gun barrels. In 1938 it shifted to the Platz Grosser Stern in the Tiergartenviertel as part of Albert Speer's monumental plan to restructure the geography of Berlin. Benjamin devotes a passage to it in *Berlin Chronicle.* For quick overview see Reclams Kunstführer Deutschland, Band VII *Berlin, Kunstdenkmäler und Museen,* Stuttgart, Reclam, 1980, pp. 119-21 (Brandenburg Gate) and p. 329 (Victory Column).

The Rome of Mussolini:

An Entrenched Stereotype in Film

Leonardo Ciacci

The fact that a Rome of Mussolini ever existed or, worse, actually exists, is without a shadow of doubt a commonplace devoid of any concrete reality. Nevertheless, the conviction that twenty years of Mussolini rule were sufficient to give concrete urban form to the politics of Fascism has long been part of common belief, as it is in the impressions of visitors and, at times, the opinion of experts.[1]

It is possible to back up this claim in more than one way. Firstly, it is possible to compare what is commonly regarded as being the specific, innovative initiative of a political government subject, with all that this has inherited from its predecessors. The monument to the unknown soldier in Piazza Venezia, better known as the Altare della Patria than as a monument dedicated to King Vittorio Emanuele II, and which constitutes one of the preferred backdrops to Mussolini's Rome, has actually been in place since 1911.[2] Cases of new urban initiatives, along with projects already underway or previously effected by others, are very important aspects in the history of the city of Rome, as they are in every city. In this case it was the isolation of the 'Vittoriano' from the buildings which blocked its view on the right side (in 1932) and its renewed positioning at the entrance to the new Via dei Fori Imperiali. Old projects successively become part of a new, at times alternative, political programme, which usually adopts the 'shell', transforming its meanings and confusing their attribution in the collective memory. This is nothing unusual, it is rather a recurring situation and one usually intimately linked to the amount of time the project involves. If the urban policies of the twenty-year Fascist period are compared first with the actions of the liberal-monarchical and then with those of the democratic-republican governments, it is not difficult to see the evident continuity. The same thing naturally occurs in other European countries, though the need to isolate a political period by cultural forms and by such negative and compromising outcomes is not so strong. Finally, a comparison between the events of different countries and disciplinary cultures may also allow the specific nature of an attribution as powerful as that which opened this essay to be placed in the right perspective.[3]

Nevertheless, concrete facts and actual events are one thing, while the meanings that finish up taking root on those same facts to the point of distorting historical truth, via the memory of images, are another. The Fascist regime in Italy undoubtedly paid particular attention to ensuring that the images of individual efforts to transform the city in Italy and the images of the *Duce* and the 'Fascist revolution' were overlaid.

93

However, interventions on the city in Italy cannot be said to have produced any significant form of innovation, neither in town planning practices (if not in the sense of the preservation of historic patrimony kept longer than elsewhere in the buildings and in entire parts of the city) nor in the choice of town planning themes to include in the urban transformation programme. In the years of Fascism, these were incisive if not significant in number. Even a necessarily superficial reading does not seem able to identify anything new and characteristic in the demolition of the blocks of Medieval cottages at the entrance to the big Piazza di San Pietro to open up the new Via della Conciliazione, between the Tiber and Bernini's colonnade. Similar operations had been carried out for decades throughout Europe after Baron Hausmann, prefect of the Seine, had so sensationally demonstrated procedure and result in Paris in the 1850s and 1860s. Italian cities had in any case already tried out the practice of 'alignment plans', as shown, for example, by the hoary affair of the opening up of Via Rizzoli in Bologna.[4] The same could be said of Piazza Venezia (isolation of already existing buildings) or of the 'garden city' of Garbatella in Rome and the new cities of Agro Pontino, constructed on planned redevelopment programmes to decades old schemes, and EUR, the modern new urban quarter built by Mussolini on the outskirts of Rome in 1942.[5]

Despite this, there is at least one document in which 'the Rome of Mussolini' is explicitly spoken of and, not without reason, this is kept in the archive of cinematographic images produced and left by the twenty years of Fascism as an incredible legacy of documents for history.[6] The text that follows is based on the analysis of a single, short 'film' lasting a few minutes; a newsreel explicitly dedicated to illustrating the new 'Rome of Mussolini'. Indeed, this is precisely how the off-screen narrator defines 'the capital in the sixteenth year of the Fascist era', in this 1937 newsreel.[7] The film was screened in January of that year in cinemas around the country,[8] and simply entitled 'Roma'. The first words of the commentary, which opens with *Risveglio di una metropoli* (*Awakening of a metropolis*) as a kind of poetic subtitle, are more significant. This is actually a very nice piece of cinema, of which, alas, the author remains anonymous (this is also true of the whole vast collection of Luce newsreels, due to a lack of documents). On just 77 metres of film (including titles) and in a little under three minutes, it describes the first hours of an ordinary day in the life of the capital, from the first light of dawn to when the workers go into their offices. Even now, this brief 'news item' seems so insistent and convincing that the viewer is not in any way inclined to resist accepting the fact that he is really watching the representation of a new, fascinating and definitive reality. It is exactly here, in the film's capacity for persuasion, that it is possible and correct to look for the meaning of the 'urban' construction Mussolini and his 'Fascist revolution' undoubtedly created, in spite of the film's obvious propaganda function and the several obvious lies it transmits.

'The sun has just appeared on the horizon of the eternal city, and already finds it pulsing with the dynamic, multiform rhythm that typifies the life of the capital in the sixteenth year of the Fascist era. From the first hours of dawn, the army of municipal street cleaners washes and sweeps the asphalt of the streets, which will shortly begin filling up with vehicles and pedestrians.'[9] The screen is at first dark and black, like the night about to end, then suddenly a real 'army' of street cleaners floods a street in the city centre with hoses. With the street cleaned of the previous day's dirt, the water runs effortlessly into the Tiber, murky as usual, but now controlled and enclosed within new embankments on which important new roads aimed at 'speeding up' the traffic of the capital have been opened. I don't think I have exaggerated in describing the first sequence of the film in such an allusive manner. The allusion is present in every single frame that crosses the screen. In the intention of the screenplay, the awakening of the metropolis is effectively the awakening of a country, of a nation, in the year the war is about to begin. A war that will 'return' Italy to those lands in Africa where there are still clear signs of the 'Romanism' that sustains a good part of Fascist rhetoric and in which other countries, stronger than fragile Italy, have already long established colonies.

The city was in general a great allegorical symbol in the years between the two wars, and particularly so in the images of the illustrated press and the cinema. This was the case in all the main European countries, not only in Italy, superimposing itself from time to time over one or other of the themes that all led to the construction of a new general contract to be drawn up between the social orders.

As Lewis Mumford was to write the following year (1938) in his *The Culture of Cities,* the capital cities had a special role to play in this.[10] Capital cities, according to Mumford, had by then become physical places completely separate from the geographic conditions of the regions from which they had sprung. Dangerously reduced to being 'paper' entities, they seemed increasingly less distinguishable from the 'collective utopia of the National State', of which he had written sixteen years earlier in his *The Story of Utopias*.[11] The Italian newsreels of the 1928–37 decade decisively confirm this interpretation.[12] Other cities naturally appear in them, such as Naples and the redevelopment works to its centre, the new, modern 'Via Roma' in Turin, the construction of the central railway station in Milan, and Venice, several times, with its new lagoon bridge. Forlì, a city dear to Mussolini due to its proximity to his birthplace, is given a privileged place in the newsreels. But no Italian city is comparable to Rome and to the frequency with which it is featured. It is not just the 'Urbe' of the 'eternal city'. Rome is the city symbol, the city that allows every Italian, every inhabitant of the country of 'a hundred cities' to identify with the great 'workshop of modernity' which could be seen 'pulsing with works' on the screens of the cinema.

It seems that the attention newsreels gave to images of urban modernisation in this type of serialised report built up over the years can be borne out by the words Mussolini spoke when opening the new Piazza della Vittoria in Brescia, in November 1932.[13] Also in this case, the single news item referring to that city takes up a whole newsreel in which one of Mussolini's most important speeches is recorded; one that remained hidden to historians under the camouflaging title of just one of so many similar openings. The scene retains a taste of authenticity, which was gradually lost from the speeches made in subsequent years from the balcony by an increasingly isolated, abstract Mussolini. A huge crowd invades a square and its voice is recorded live, overriding and interrupting that of the *Duce,* who modulates his tone according to the meaning of what he is about to say. All the other participants in so meaningful an enterprise press around him, satisfied and smiling. Mussolini tackles the focus of his subject in one speech which, though at times modified in relation to interruptions from the crowd, does not lack a confidential mention of personal memories linked to the city, almost as if to establish a relationship of personal trust with 'the public': 'Four years ago, the Podestà of Brescia submitted me the plans for the redevelopment of your city. He promised that he would carry this out, I promised that I would come here to open it. So you can see that I keep my promises'. This declaration, pronounced in the tones of one offering complicity, had been preceded by one delivered in the manner of a solemn declaration: 'People of the city of the ten days, ...I have come here amongst you first of all to take the temperature of your loyalty, and I find with much ... (interrupted by ovation) ... and I find that it is fervent and steadfast, of which I never had any doubt'.

The city and its modern transformation were in effect the object of a political exchange: loyalty to the party and the 'Fascist revolution' for the promise of modernisation of the country. The themes were ones in which everyone could believe, even those who, for geographical and social reasons, were miles from having easy access to the promised innovations. This is certainly one of the reasons, possibly the most important, why when the images of the 'awakening' of the metropolis appeared on cinema screens five years later, they had the certain effect of being the answer to something awaited and already known. Rome is alive and vital. 'On the outskirts the enormous movement of food supplies for more than a million inhabitants has begun and the freshest of foodstuffs flow into the general markets that stock thousands and thousands of outlets in the various suburbs. ... The central dairy provides for the distribution of 170,000 litres of pasteurised milk, the most complete basic breakfast food. ... The factory siren signalling the start of work echoes around the hundred chimneys that give Mussolini's Rome its industrial imprint'.

As is known, Rome has never had an industrial character, and it is a surprise that this should have been given so much emphasis in a message delivered by one who had politically always shown a fear of the hidden dangers behind the concentrations of workers and of capital that are an inherent part of industrialised production. But one ought not to be confounded by words. In a film, especially if particularly short and insistent, words have an extremely marginal role in establishing links in the memory processes. What count are the images, the overall effect, the emotional involvement, which the music and editing are able to produce in the audience. Something that is carried out with great mastery in this case. After the first narrative sequences dedicated to the work of the street cleaners, the speed with which the subsequent frames follow on to describe the movement of hands shifting crates of milk bottles and trays of fruit, or the imperative glove of the traffic policeman imposing order at an intersection, seems intent on representing one thing only – a great city is an infinite assembly of hands at work, co-ordinated and organised by a single, central mind. The centre of the city is no longer a physical place, a square or a building. The centre of the modernised Italian city of the twentieth century, 'the heart of the Urbe, is in the large, severe room (in Palazzo Venezia) opening onto the forum of the empire, where the *Duce* at his desk provides the example, and forges the destiny and fortunes of the homeland'. Who could ever be taken in by such rhetoric if all this were not the final result of a strategy primed and set in motion much earlier?

A 1932 newsreel dedicated to the achievements made in Valdagno by the Marzotto family, an important Veneto textile-producing family, is certainly one of the most significant precedents to consider in comprehending this image 'trap'. Different versions of this film exist in the archives; one first silent version with subtitles, and a subsequent one with sound track.[14] But why was so much space given to propaganda about the initiatives of a family immersed in the tradition of 'paternalistic' entrepreneurs, heirs to the archaic identity of the previous century's industry? What could be hidden in the evident recognition of entrepreneurs dealing in one of the manufacturing sectors most firmly rooted in the collective memory as a font of worker exploitation (the loom), without any consideration for the age and sex of those employed in these jobs?

The film immediately focuses on images illustrating the new planning scheme for the town where every angle seems to have been considered, starting with the factory. New, freshly constructed buildings are set aside as apartments for the office staff, and an entire area is devoted to other, more modest, buildings for the workers, of which even the interiors and furnishings are shown. What is most striking though are the shots taken inside the common dining room, in the doctor's rooms, at the school gates, in the mountain and seaside holiday places for children and at the summer camps for families. Completing the 'urban' picture are the farming areas providing for local consumption needs and, finally, sporting facilities. A last frame following the sequences of sports matches shows a group of young athletes standing on one another's shoulders to form a human pyramid. Valdagno, then, is an example of what the regime in 1932 no longer dared to promise, but showed what had by then entered into the European conception of urban life: work, home, health, education and leisure time as elements competing to mark out the rights and duties that help define the identity of the modern citizen of the industrial metropolis. Different promises, that of Mussolini in Brescia and that of the Marzottos in Valdagno, sounded like accomplished facts in 1937 Rome.

The theme of the new suburbs had timidly entered into the rhetoric of the newsreels at a significant time and place. The year was 1928, ten years after the victorious end of the 'Great War'; the place Bolzano, an area 'conquered by the homeland' and to be Italianised, where the completion of a heavy monumental triumphal arch was being celebrated with an official opening by Turati, the party secretary. Images of the opening of the new power station in Bolzano and of buildings allocated to the employees of public offices are included in the same newsreel. The architecture is still that of the suburban houses built at the turn of the century, but this is what is needed to offer and instil elements of solid identification among families which, in those years, were confused and full of longings for the past. In Rome in the same months, a new housing estate for disabled returned servicemen was opened, and the enlarged, renewed 'garden city' of Garbatella is shown. This was designed in 1920 for the State Housing Institute by the architects Giavannoni and Piacentini (who were later the two most authoritative voices in the period between the wars) and enlarged with a new plan in 1927.[15] The last pictures of the newsreel are dedicated to children at the primary school which is part of the modern facilities in the area. The leap from these first representations and those which in 1935 illustrated the new suburbs built on the outskirts of the capital – 'all styles are represented, even if "twentieth-century rationale" prevails' – is enormous, but made briskly and surely.[16] The most original part of the new city, a 'necessary' compromise between the results of modern European architectural research and the tradition of a confused 'national style' was by then formed, that which had definitively leapt the ancient walls and opened up a new prospect to the suburbs. Nothing new for Europe, but convincing staging, by the *Duce*, for the Italian audience.

The various parts of the city are specialised, the *Duce* visits and then inaugurates that which has been produced on the building sites of the 'university city'[17], the 'sports city', the 'cinema city', 'Cinecitta'.[18] Everything seems to be an ever grander and more important part of an organisation controlled in its smallest detail. In Forlì a rubbish collection system is presented as being fully operational, which certainly can't have been cheap for the 'set' designers.[19] A long line of rubbish men on bicycles spreads along the streets of the city, replacing the full bins left outside the doors of the houses with clean, washed bins, just out of the automated plant that acts as management and collection centre. The project was developed by FIAT industries, in imitation of similar projects tried out for some years in Germany, and was constructed on a trial basis in Forlì (provincial town so dear to Mussolini). Not even the cameraman seems to believe such efficiency, and can't resist the temptation to pull faces at the rubber lids on the new bins, which respond so quickly to a press of the bemused gentleman's foot on the pedal.

Organisation has by now become a real idol. The traffic light at the intersection is an authentic rhetorical symbol, on a level with the extended hand of the traffic policemen on their central platforms, directing traffic that is in no way inferior to that of today. Cars, pedestrians, buses (new ones, personally tested by Mussolini in 1928), trucks and trams alternately cross over in a perfect mass musical movement. In *Roma. Risveglio di una metropoli*, sequences already seen which illustrate all this are composed into a mosaic where all the tesserae go spontaneously to their right places, quite naturally. The cinematographic lesson made by Walter Rutmann in 1927 with his 'Symphony of a big city', seems by now an accomplished fact.[20] *Il ventre della città* (*The heart of the city*), a film by Di Cocco of 1931 undeservedly set aside,[21] effectively translated that poetry to Italy, showing how much is consumed daily by a city to feed all its mouths, in terms of animals lined up at the municipal slaughter house ready to be butchered, of bread fresh from the oven, of bottles of milk in their metal crates, of cabbages lined up in boxes, of rows of eggs in their trays. The quantities are astounding, but everything seems to move without hindrance, and to find its place as if this had already been arranged. Destiny seems to have assumed a common sense for all. It is the Rome of Mussolini. A city in prototype form, subsequently built on a widespread scale and which continued to function, though at less hectic rhythms, for many decades to come. It jammed up, perhaps definitively, only a few years ago.

Notes

1   The myth has deep and conscious roots. In 1936 P.M. Bardi wrote an article entitled *Attrazione di Roma* in which he recounted what effect his photographs of 'Mussolini's Rome' had on the friends he met on a journey 'towards Leningrad'. 'They were all architects, each one... distrustful of the 'dictatorship'... Little by little each one came round to the opinion that a Mussolini is needed in every country 'to put things right'. 'The other morning our friend Ezra Pound wired us to say that he was leaving at ten. – Before leaving one must go and see Via dell'Impero again'. 'A friend of ours from New York gave our name to a writer sent over by a big publisher in that city, charged with compiling a new guide to Rome. – I no longer recognise Rome. After ten years everything has to be redone from scratch -'. See Bardi, P.M., *Attrazione di Roma*, No. 1 March 1936, pp. 37-41, now in Bolzoni, F. (ed.), *Un anno di cinema italiano. La teoria e la pratica*, Venice, Edizioni de – La Biennale di Venezia -, 1976, pp. 141-43.

2   The architect was Sacconi, who then committed suicide due to the heavy criticism drawn down on him by that monument and by the new Palace of Justice. The initial competition for the design of the monument took place in 1882, the second in 1884. See Tobia, B., *Una patria per gli italiani. Spazi, itinerari, monumenti nell'Italia unita*, Bari, Laterza, 1991 and AA.VV., *Roma capitale, 1870-1911. Architettura e urbanistica. Uso e trasformazione della città storica*, Venice, Marsilio, 1984.

3   This essay also derives from comparisons (not explicit in the text) between Italian films on the transformation of the city and other similar ones regarding Germany and Great Britain from the same years. The documentaries I refer to were compared for the first time at an international conference entitled: 'Films for modern living', organised by myself in association with Elizabeth Lebas at the Venice University Institute of Architecture in January 1990.

4   The demolition of old buildings for the construction of the present wide urban street took place in the first decade of this century. Town planning authorities of the time confronted each other for many years in a close taking-up of positions between those supporting the reasons for modernisation and those supporting preservation of the historical patrimony. See Giovannoni, G., *Vecchie città ed edilizia nuova*, Turin, 1931.

5   On the circumstances of architecture and town planning between the wars, see Ciucci, G., *Gli architetti e il fascismo*, Turin, Einaudi, 1989.

6   The archive is that of the Istituto Luce, set up in 1925 as an off-shoot of the Fascist Government's Ministry of Press and Propaganda, which began producing newsreels and documentaries on matters of major political and social interest in 1927. The Istituto Luce remained active until the 1960s as a public body charged with carrying out more or less that same functions. It is now a public company managing access to the important historic archive in which the films and photographs produced between the 1920s and 60s are kept.

7   Luce newsreel No. 1212 of January 1937; b&w., sound, length 2'45".

8   Newsreels were shown compulsorily before the day's scheduled screening.

9   From the commentary text.

10   See Mumford, L., *The Culture of Cities*, New York, 1938.

11   See Mumford, L., *The Story of Utopias*, New York, 1922.

12   There is a more comprehensive reading of these materials in Ciacci, L., Quando si parla di città, immagini e paradossi per realtà che cambiano di significato, in *Urbanistica*, No. 103, 1994, pp. 31-45.

13   The plan for the new piazza was by the architect Marcello Piacentini, foremost interpreter of the official architecture of the regime in those years. On Piacentini's ideas regarding the need to define a national

style, see Pisani, M. (ed.), *Marcello Piacentini. Architettura moderna*, Venice, Marsilio,1996 and De Seta, C. (ed.), *Pagano. Architettura e città durante il fascismo*, Bari, Laterza, 1976.

14 Newsreel No. 1017 of October 1932: *Valdagno. Abitazioni e servizi construiti dai Marzotto*.

15 See Fraticelli, V., *Roma 1914-1929. La città e gli architetti tra la guerra e il fascismo*, Rome, Officina,1982, pp. 191-229.

16 The news item 'Nuovi quartieri a Roma' (New districts in Rome) in newsreel No. 751 of March 1935 was dedicated to this.

17 From newsreel No.756 of 1935.

18 News of the laying of the first stone is in newsreel No. 829 of 1936.

19 The system is illustrated in the news item: 'Forlì. Come si rinnova una città (Forlì. How to renew a city), in newsreel No. 1002 of 1936.

20 The reference is to *Berlin, die Symphonie einer Grossstadt*, the film shot in Berlin by Walter Ruttmann in 1927. Subsequently, in 1932, Ruttmann, made *Acciaio*, a film shot in Italy in the Terni steelworks for Emilio Cecchi's CINES and based on a text by Pirandello, which Mussolini had commissioned to represent the world of work. See Camerini, C. (ed.), *Acciaio. Un film degli anni trenta*, Turin, ERI, 1990.

21 Francesco Di Cocco, a painter who later moved to the USA, made this single short film (only 13′ long) in 1932 for CINES, at a time when this production house had received important public financing and was placed under the direction of Emilio Cecchi. Curiously, in a publication dedicated entirely to CINES there is no mention of the film apart from a single photograph shown with only the title of the film. See Redi, R. (ed.), La *Cines. Storia di una casa di produzione*, Rome, CNC, 1991.

Antonioni: Space, Place, Sexuality

David Forgacs

Of directors working in mainstream cinema, as opposed to experimental or avant-garde film-makers, Antonioni must be reckoned one of the most relentlessly abstract in his treatment of space. Probably the only contemporary who comes close to him in this respect is Tarkovsky. It is hard to imagine a more formalistic sequence in a film made for commercial distribution than the repeated shots, from different angles and in slow-motion, of a house exploding near the end of *Zabriskie Point* (1970), followed by the protracted dance of consumer goods through the air to the music of Pink Floyd, or the very slow tracking shot towards and through a hotel window at the end of *The Passenger* (1975), a shot reminiscent of Michael Snow's experimental film *Wavelength* (1967), which consists of a very slow zoom, lasting 54 minutes, towards the far wall of a long room. Many shots in earlier films by Antonioni are, like these, people-less for all or part of the time, as the presence of human figures is replaced by that of landscape (*L'avventura*, 1960) or architecture (*L'eclisse*, 1962). In a shot breakdown of *L'eclisse*, Michele Mancini and Giuseppe Perrella (1986, pp. 25-39) found no fewer than 161 shots without any people in them.

And yet at the same time all Antonioni's features are in some way about sexuality and they give prominence also to shots of women's bodies, often of a voyeuristic type. Their plots are about heterosexual relationships in crisis, adultery and sexual jealousy, desire transferred from one character to another, blocked or unconsummated. Indeed, one may say that precisely because of their very abstractness, their 'de-dramatised' quality (finely discussed by Cuccu, 1973, Chapter 3), their lack of a conventional narrative pace or clear plot resolution, they foreground what Laura Mulvey called the '*to-be-looked-at-ness*'of the woman's body (1975, p.11), though the manner in which it is looked at is different both from that of the Hollywood narrative cinema Mulvey was describing and the avant-garde cinema she was advocating. Antonioni's films repeatedly show the body of a beautiful actress (Lucia Bosé, Alida Valli, Monica Vitti, Daniela Silverio, Sophie Marceau, Irène Jacob) against a wall, framed within a doorway or window, reflected in a mirror or in glass, shot from the back, from above or below on a stairwell, lying on a bed or a couch; with her bare arms, shoulders, neck or throat in close up. These shots, because they are not obviously subordinated or functional to narrative, become similar to still photographs and allude to common forms of representation in commodity culture, like fashion photographs, pin-ups, and advertising. In *Blow Up* (1966) this relationship to still photography and fashion photography is explicitly thematised and explored.

I want to propose a way of relating these two aspects of Antonioni's cinema – space and sexuality – to one another. By 'space' I mean two things: the three-dimensional

101

space, natural or built, which lies before the camera (i.e. profilmic space) and the space of the two-dimensional film image, bounded by the frame. These two kinds of space are made constantly to interact with one another by camera movements, reframing and transitions from shot to shot. By sexuality I am referring both to the content of their plots and to their peculiar economy of displaying and looking, in which a female body is offered up to erotic contemplation but the looker's erotic gaze is arrested or troubled. There are, to be sure, eroticised shots of men too in several of the films – Massimo Girotti in *Cronaca di un amore* (1950), Marcello Mastroianni in *La notte* (1961), Alain Delon in *L'eclisse*, David Hemmings in *Blow Up*, Mark Frechette in *Zabriskie Point* – but it is only the woman who troubles the gaze in this way. I shall argue that the woman's body in Antonioni's films sometimes provides a point of anchorage for abstract space as it turns 'space' into 'place' and reconnects it to narrative and representation and at others times stands in an oblique relationship to space, halts the flow of narrative, and a typically modernist disjunction is then produced between the body and the space around it.

I suggest that the joining together of space and sexuality in the films needs to be both historicised and subjected to critical scrutiny. Antonioni's cinema, particularly that of the early 1960s, emerged from a specific moment in Italian society, in artistic culture and the history of sexuality and representation and it made a distinctive intervention into that moment. The tendency of many critics to interpret his films humanistically and transhistorically, as films about alienation or people in general, rather than about sexed and gendered bodies with a specific location in terms of class and race (the latter most notably in *La notte*, *L'eclisse* and *The Passenger*), has meant that this crucial point has been missed or glossed over. A typical manoeuvre of these critics is first to acknowledge that the sexed and gendered body has a concrete and particular function in the films but then to argue that the woman in fact stands for a universal (i.e. non-gender-specific and timeless) condition: 'The woman in Antonioni's films is the emblematic character ... of a sensitivity which the director perceives, intuits, in a large part of the human condition' (Micheli, 1967, p. 9) 'Antonioni's women are the only ones to understand that the search [for escape or self-discovery] is essential' (Chatman, 1985, p. 64). This generalising manoeuvre needs to be resisted.

Space and Place

Let me first expand upon those different meanings of space and illustrate how they work in the films, particularly those of the early 1960s. Profilmic space may be further subdivided into mathematical space – the space of solid geometry, including the 'empty' spaces between solid objects and the 'filled' spaces defined by their mass – and social space. The concept of mathematical space, according to Henri Lefebvre and others, emerged only in post-Cartesian philosophy and science. Modern physics, which is informed by it, sees space not just as a category with which, like time, people order the world (as in Aristotelian metaphysics), but as independent of thought, *res extensa* as opposed to *res cogitans*. Social space on the other hand is produced by particular societies and is typically structured by oppositions in which social and economic distinctions are manifested as physical separations – administrative city centre/residential urban area; expensive dwellings/slums; city/country; core/periphery. As Lefebvre puts it (1974, p. 31):

> every society – and hence every mode of production with its subvariants (i.e. all those societies which exemplify the general concept) – produces a space, its own space. [...] the ancient city had its own spatial practice: it forged its own – appropriated – space. Whence the need for a study of that space which is able to apprehend it as such, in its genesis and its form, with its own specific time or times (the rhythm of daily life), and its particular centres and polycentrism (agora, temple, stadium, etc.).

Architecture provides the articulation, the 'coupling', between mathematical or physical space and social space since every building occupies and restructures, outside and inside, a little bit of physical space and at the same time contributes to the production of social space, that is to say the mapping of the structures of social and economic life onto the physical world. When this happens, when mathematical or physical space is reorganised as social space, or simply when people inhabit a space or might be thought of as visiting it, then it becomes, so the philosopher Edward Casey has argued, a place. For Casey, mathematical 'space' turns into 'place' as soon as people are in it or can imagine a body occupying it. 'It is a striking fact, on which we do not often enough reflect, that while we can conceive of entirely empty spaces and times – radical vacua in which no bodies (in space) or events (in time) exist – such spatiotemporal voids are themselves placelike in so far as they could be, in principle, occupied by bodies and events.' (Casey, 1993, p. 13).

Space and place, in the sense both of landscape and of built environment, possess considerable importance in Antonioni's films but this does not mean that those films are always stably located in particular places in a geographical sense. Some are, some are not. The early short documentaries have a strong sense of geographical place; indeed, one may say that they are as much films about places as about people: the river and its banks in *Gente del Po* (1943-7), the streets of Rome in *N.U.* (1948). On the other hand the features, particularly those of the early 1960s, tend to generalise the places within them or mix different locations. For instance, the stock exchange where Antonioni researched *L'eclisse* was that of Italy's main commercial city, Milan, not Rome, where it is located in the film but where in reality share trading is of little significance. EUR (Esposizione Universale Roma), the suburb where most of the action takes place, functions as an abstract, generically modern space, in distinction both to the historic city centre and the older residential districts which are hardly seen in the film. EUR and the transport links between it and central Rome was built between 1934 and 1942 as a model new town to host the 1942 Expo (cancelled because of the war) and by 1960 it had become a thriving but characterless commercial district and middle-class suburb. Similarly, Antonioni insisted that *Blow-Up* was not specifically 'about' London. 'Places are important', he told Alberto Moravia in an an interview of 1968 as he began work on *Zabriskie Point*. 'But Blow-Up's story could have happened anywhere. *Zabriskie Point*, instead, is a film about America.' (Antonioni, 1996, p. 298).

Throughout his career, moreover, but most particularly in the films of the early

1960s, Antonioni's way of dealing with physical locations was essentially to expand their importance relative to the role they had in conventional narrative films and even in some cases to reverse the priority operating in those films whereby people were assumed to be more important than places. This was done by a deliberate breaking of the standard rule of continuity scripting and editing (as laid down in manuals like John Howard Lawson's *Theory and Technique of Screenwriting*) that a shot of a place had to be justified by its function in the plot and/or by the presence of a character in it. According to this, shots of places without people suggested that those places were waiting to be occupied by somebody, like empty stage sets before a character enters. Once a character moved out of frame the shot became 'empty' again and a transition to another shot was required. This convention about space was simultaneously a convention about time. A shot without a character in it was dead time (*temps mort*), a drag on narrative flow and a source of anxiety for the viewer, which is why editors had to cut as soon as a character left the frame. This kind of cinema was anthropomorphic in the simple sense that it could not tolerate for long the absence of a human body. This seems to be consistent with Casey's views about space and place, namely that place is defined by the presence, or even just the thinkable presence, of humans; without this presence it is frighteningly vacuous and threatens to turn back into abstract empty space.

It is often said that the first of Antonioni's films really to challenge these conventions was *L'avventura*. When Anna (Lea Massari) disappears on a small island (Lisca Bianca in the Lipari Islands) about 20 minutes into the story her companions in the boating party begin a search, which occupies a further 30 minutes of film time. On several occasions during this sequence the camera frames rocks, sea or sky with no people, creating a sense of tension between the landscape and the human figures. The first-time viewer expects the camera to discover Anna, or perhaps her corpse. Yet for all its narrative audacity, which puzzled many viewers and stretched their patience, this sequence in many ways still belongs within the dominant conventions; it bends the rules but does not break them. In fact in nearly all the island shots one or more characters either enters or exits from the frame, or the camera moves so as to bring them into frame. The only exceptions are two shots of a storm brewing over the sea and these are motivated as subjective shots from the point of view of Corrado (James Addams). Several of these camera movements contribute to a sense of spatial disorientation because they suddenly reveal characters in extreme close up or standing in a group that had been situated just outside the edge of the frame. It is as if the camera were scanning the island for Anna or traces of Anna but repeatedly comes back to the searchers. In other words the whole sequence is governed by the narrative of the search. Moreover, Anna's disappearance produces narrative which fills the remainder of the film since it generates the further quest round Sicily and determines the itinerary followed by the other main characters – Sandro (Gabriele Ferzetti) and Claudia (Monica Vitti). At the same time, the missing Anna haunts the sexual relationship which develops between these two: Sandro was Anna's lover and Claudia her best friend, so Anna remains the unseen corner of a love triangle and a source of guilt to the other two. (For a good detailed analysis of these and other aspects of the film, see Nowell-Smith, 1997.)

In *La notte* and even more radically in *L'eclisse*, Antonioni moved further from the mainstream conventions governing filmic space. In the closing sequence of the latter, a montage of street scenes in Rome lasting between five and a half and seven minutes, depending on which print one sees (the producers, Robert and Raymond Hakim, had it shortened after a hostile audience reaction at Cannes in 1962: see Cowie, 1963, p.45), there is no dialogue and none of the main characters appear. Place stops being a setting or a support, functional to and subordinate to the telling of a story, and becomes in itself the object of the spectator's attention. There is no dialogue, only pieces of diegetic sound – a sprinkler, water running from a punctured rain-barrel into a drain, a bus, children shouting – and snatches of Giovanni Fusco's atonal music played on piano, woodwind and brass. Although several of the shots contain people – a man driving a pony-trap, a nurse pushing a pram, people waiting for the bus, getting off the bus, standing on a balcony, a man turning off the sprinkler – most do not. Above all, the main characters – Vittoria (Monica Vitti) and Piero (Alain Delon) – do not reappear, despite having promised to meet at this spot this evening and the next day and the day after that. At the end of the sequence night has fallen and the last shot is a close-up of a glaring street-lamp followed by the end title.

The sequence in this way has a much more ambiguous relationship to narrative than anything either in *L'avventura* or in *La notte*. On the one hand there has been enough of a narrative up to this point for expectations about the two main characters to have been set up and to be sustained through a viewing of the final sequence, or a first viewing at any rate. The first-time viewer may expect Vittoria and Piero to come onto the scene at every cut from shot to shot, yet this expectation is repeatedly deferred and is ultimately thwarted when the end title appears. The whole sequence, in this respect, is marked by the absence of the main characters, who continue thereby to govern the narrative and the way the film is viewed. On the other hand, this very absence forces the viewer's attention to be drawn away from narrative itself to the inanimate objects and locations. The streets, rain-barrel, sprinkler, leaves and buildings become presences and not just signs of the absence of the two main characters. In fact, when one watches the film attentively or repeatedly one sees that several of the objects and places are associated with the characters; for instance, the rain-barrel into which Vittoria had first thrown a piece of paper and then on a separate occasion had dipped her hand. However, other places and objects are shown here for the first time. In other words the sequence is both attached to the preceding narrative and autonomous from it (for an excellent discussion of this sequence, and of the uses of buildings in films and photographs more generally, see Wiblin, 1997).

Il deserto rosso (1964), Antonioni's first film in colour, may have been less radical in this respect than *L'eclisse*, since it did not disengage place from narrative or autonomise the physical environment. Yet the film was distinctive in a different way since, more than any other of his films before or since, it relates place integrally to character and subjectivity. The film was in fact an experiment in making the exterior surroundings both manifest and condition the interiority of a character. The manipulation of colours, achieved by various means (colour filters, under- and over-exposure, use of telephoto lenses and out-of-focus shots to increase grain and mix colours, spray-painting parts of the landscape as well as buildings), was intended as a way of externalising the neurosis of Giuliana (Monica Vitti). *Il deserto rosso* also develops an implicit discourse about colours, place and gender: Giuliana, unlike her husband Ugo (Carlo Chionetti) is alienated from the noisy industrial plant outside Ravenna with its bright red buildings and yellow smoke. She is unhappy and physically uncomfortable in the hard white and blue hi-tech interior of the family apartment, which looks out through long rectangular windows over the docks. Even her son's toys, a robot and a microscope, belong to the male world of industry and science. She wants to decorate her shop in cooler colours, in blues and greens. When she believes her son to be ill she tells him a story about a young girl who lives on an island and swims in the clear water by pink sand and water-sculpted rocks. This is the only sequence in the film where the colour values have not been altered. It sets up (feminine) nature and natural landscape (the rocks, she says, were 'like flesh') against (masculine) industry and man-made environments. This implied gendering of place has parallels in several of the other films, for instance the opposition between towns and natural landscapes in *L'avventura* (Rome, Noto, Taormina versus the sea and rock of Lisca Bianca) or in *Zabriskie Point* (Los Angeles versus Death Valley). In *L'eclisse* the stock exchange is a fast, masculine, time-bound place, and the women who play it, like Vittoria's mother (Lilla Brignone), have an addiction to it with which Vittoria cannot identify; as she says to Pietro, she cannot understand how he can live like that; she herself wants to live to a different time rhythm but this also means living in different places where she is neither estranged nor constrained by others.

The Space of the Frame

It is in the nature of film, as of still photography, both to flatten three-dimensional profilmic space into two dimensions (i.e. to take out depth both behind the 'surface' of the image and between the image and the viewer) and to crop it on four sides. One of the best critical discussions of this aspect of film space remains that of Noël Burch in *Theory of Film Practice*, originally published in 1969 as *Praxis du cinéma*. Burch distinguishes screen space (the space of the frame) from off-screen space and subdivides the latter into six 'segments': the space outside the four sides of the frame (above, below, left, right), the space 'behind' the frame (for instance beyond a door or wall or building, if these form a backdrop to the set) and the space in front of the frame, in other words the space behind the camera in filming and occupied by the spectator during screening (Burch, 1973, p. 17). Stephen Heath, in his essay 'Narrative Space' of 1976, developed Burch's arguments in a psychoanalytic and Marxist direction, emphasising the way that the cinema of 'classical continuity' worked to 'contain' and 'regularise' off-screen space, to erase the work of the apparatus of cinema, and to construct a reassuringly stable but fictitious subject-position for the spectator (Heath, 1981, p. 45). Both of these discussions are pertinent to Antonioni. Even more relevant are the writings on film by the Russian Formalist, Boris Kazanskij, and the Soviet semiotician Yurij Lotman.

In 'The Nature of Cinema', first published in the volume *Poetika kino* in 1927, Kazanskij argued that among the arts film came closest to architecture. 'Architecture shapes not surfaces and masses, as do painting and sculpture, but rather "space". More precisely, it organises surfaces and masses (or their relationships) into space, and thus earns the right to be called a separate art.' (Kazanskij, 1981, p. 105). As well as being a space-shaping art, cinema was like architecture in two further respects: first, in both of them 'the principal and even the only creative content ... is to be found in conception and composition, of course with respect to the corresponding manner of subsequent execution'; second, both arts were 'cumbersome, and in proportion to this, *abstract*. Cinema must accumulate masses of aesthetically indifferent material and apply a complex technology in order to make visible even a minimal aesthetically significant element; likewise, architecture requires a tremendous mass of structural material and technological effort in order to obtain as a result the desired form' (1981, p. 106). The first of these claims may be true in a quantitative sense – more time is generally spent on preproduction than on shooting and postproduction – and may even apply in an aesthetic sense for certain directors (Hitchcock for instance, famously, though perhaps disingenuously, once remarked that for him most of the work on a film was complete before it went into production), but others, including Antonioni, have said almost the opposite, namely that the main creative work takes place in the filming itself. As he wrote in the introduction to the collected screenplays of his films made between 1955 and 1964: 'A film which has not been printed on celluloid does not exist' (Antonioni, 1964: xviii). However, Kazanskij's second claim is of considerable interest, and may certainly be applied to Antonioni, whose films bear many traces of that 'cumbersome' and 'abstract' process of making non-aesthetic space aesthetically significant.

In dealing with Antonioni one needs, however, to take Kazanskij's argument a stage further, since his films do not just *parallel* architecture in their aesthetic character; they (particularly *La notte*, *L'eclisse* and *Il deserto rosso*) are also films about architecture and its relationship to the human figure. In the filming of architecture its organisation of space is restructured, changed by a second-order system of spatial arrangement: the flattening of three dimensions to two, the reduction of colour (in the films before *Il deserto rosso*) to the monochromatic scale, the effects of movement within the space created by elaborate camera blocking and and edits which break and recompose space. There is a conscious and stylised use of 'conventional' signs (in Lotman's terms, i.e. Peircean symbols) such as pans, dollies, cuts and reframes, which disturb the givenness of the 'iconic' signs (shots of things); in this case, these are already architectural. Almost any sequence inside or outside a building in Antonioni's films would do to illustrate this, but the opening of *L'eclisse* (discussed below) is perhaps the most paradigmatic case.

As for Lotman, in his *Semiotics of Cinema*, first published in Russian in 1973, he brilliantly captured the importance of the frame as one of the constitutive features of filmic signification. Whereas Burch and Heath both emphasise the relationship between on-screen and off-screen space, the dialectic of presence and absence, the visible and the hidden, Lotman is more concerned with the way the image works inside the frame itself. His point is that the frame is a physical limit but not an artistic limitation; on the contrary, the boundaries of the frame are a 'particular constructive category of artistic space in cinema' (Lotman, 1976, p. 28). They produce 'a complex artistic sense of totality', both because of the 'alternation of depth levels' which fill the frame (from front to back, as it were) and because the images inside the frame seem constantly to push against its edges, attempting 'actively to break it up, to surge beyond its boundaries' (1976, pp. 30, 83). Antonioni does often use the frame (as in the island sequence of *L'avventura*) to suggest off-screen space, the possibility of someone or something hovering just outside its limits. However, he is equally, if not more, concerned with the different kinds of 'pressure' created within the frame – when it is filled with objects or emptied, when three-dimensional depth and 'planes of action' are replaced by flatness and surface, when a human figure is positioned at its extreme edges or in extreme close up or long shot.

Built Space and Bodies

Let me now bring the discussion of space to bear on that of sexuality. Consider two sequences with Monica Vitti, one from *Il deserto rosso* and one from *L'eclisse*. The first begins sixteen minutes into the film and lasts about one minute. Just before it starts, Giuliana has woken from a nightmare and has gone into her son's room to turn off his robot toy which he has left switched on and which has been scuttling back and forward as he sleeps. She comes out onto the landing. White walls (but shot with a red filter which gives them a pink tinge) are broken up by blue tubular steel rails and banisters. There is a hard cradle-shaped wooden chair on the landing. Giuliana is filmed from behind as she starts to go downstairs. She stops suddenly, draws back and clutches her dressing-gown. A cut to a frontal medium shot shows her staring off left as if she had seen something or thought of something. In the next shot she is back up on the landing. She strokes her arms as if cold, reaches inside her dressing-gown, takes a thermometer from her armpit and examines it under the light. She flops into the chair with her legs apart, reads the thermometer again, rubs her arms, runs her hands across her breasts then lets them drop upturned into her lap. At this point Ugo comes out of the bedroom, looks at the thermometer reading and tells her it is normal. He kneels down, pulls her dressing-gown up one thigh and strokes her other leg.

There are two striking things about this sequence. One is that built space does not simply frame or set off the body of the character but enters into a tense, even hostile, relationship with it. The viewer can feel that it is almost as if Giuliana shudders and shivers because of what is physically around her (hence, perhaps, her startled look 'into empty space') as much as because of what is happening inside her. The script, by Antonioni and Tonino Guerra, says at this point: 'she suddenly stops, clutches the iron banister and her eyes widen as if she is frightened by the dark invading the ground floor' (Antonioni, 1978, p. 55). In any case, this distinction between 'inside' and 'outside' loses meaning in the film since we only have access to Giuliana's mind through what her body externalises in the form of gesture, movement and facial expression. The other striking thing is the way that a look of desire is both invited (by Giuliana's apparently narcissistic, self-absorbed relationship to her own body) and refused, by the signs she gives of suffering, sickness and tiredness. This conflict between invitation and rebuttal is sharply highlighted at the moment when Ugo raises her dressing-gown and caresses her leg: she momentarily resists then relaxes. In fact, the same conflict is repeated not just in the continuation of this scene, where Ugo continues to try to arouse Giuliana and she repeats the pattern of resisting and acquiescing, but throughout the film. From the opening shot of Giuliana in her dark green coat eating a sandwich by the heaps of industrial waste to the shot of her being stared at by Corrado (Richard Harris) in the shop to Corrado's gauche attempt to seduce her in his hotel room near the end, Giuliana attracts two type of look both from other characters within the story and from the spectator. In this way her bodily presence in the film turns on the conflict between her outward physical beauty and her inner sickness, between her objectification as a sexed body to be desired and her subjectivity as a mind in crisis.

There is, I believe, a clear connection and an interaction between the two aspects of the sequence on the landing and stairs: the estranging effect of hard, cold built space can be offset, even momentarily neutralised, by the reassuring appearance of a human figure, which is also the sexed and sexual body of a woman. However, the built space risks overwhelming her again, since it is itself one of the causes of her neurosis, and any attempt to sexualise her risks being rebutted. This is overlaid on the discourse about the gendering of place in the film (as discussed above): the hi-tech house is part of that masculine technocratic rationality from which Giuliana imagines a regressive escape both to childhood (she is, in fantasy, the girl in her story) and to 'nature'. However, sex and gender remain, I suggest, separate strands of this thematic, and what is of central importance is the sense of ever-present threat exerted by the physical environment on the woman's body. As Antonioni stated in an interview with Jean-Luc Godard soon after the film was released (Godard, 1964) his aim in *Il deserto rosso* was 'completely different' (*tout autre*) from that in the preceding films. 'Before, it was the relations between characters which interested me. Here, the central character is also confronted with the social environment (*milieu social*), and this makes me deal with my story in a completely different way' (p. 10).

The sequence from *L'eclisse* is the opening of the film and it illustrates this difference well. It lasts two and a half minutes and runs after the title credits to when the dialogue starts (the opening scene as a whole, in Riccardo's flat, lasts ten minutes). The sequence establishes the tension *between* the two characters, Riccardo (Francisco Rabal), whom we see first, and Vittoria, yet it does so as much by the framing and compression of their bodies and inanimate objects within the shots and by their interaction with the room and these objects as by their interaction with each other. Neither of them speaks and they only look at one another for part of the time. Unlike the shots of Vitti as Giuliana in *Il deserto rosso*, which are mainly long shots of her whole body, several of the shots of her as Vittoria may be described as both fetishistic and voyeuristic. This is in the sense that they cut her up into separate body parts and look at her from an angle where she cannot see she is being looked at. She is filmed from the back; her long fingers hold the empty picture frame, move an ashtray, stroke the rim of a small vase; her legs are seen reflected in a highly-polished floor between the legs of the table; she curls up on a sofa with her back to the camera. However, these shots differ from the voyeuristic and fetishistic looks in the genres of classic Hollywood such as noir or westerns, the looks discussed by Mulvey, in that they are not cued, authorised, or owned by a particular male character. Riccardo is sometimes looking towards Vittoria but it is not clear that he sees her in these shots, apart perhaps from that of the legs under the table, and in several of them, because of their angle, he cannot be seeing her.

Once again there is a very particular kind of relationship between built space and the sexed body. In this case too the dense emotional atmosphere, so heavy with tension, is generated by the way the space of the frame is filled and by the absence of dialogue or any other form of communication between the characters. Time is, as it were, stretched out by this absence and by the close attention to space. Even after Riccardo and Vittoria begin their laconic dialogue, the sequence is still sustained largely by the visuals. Vittoria opens a curtain to look out of the window but it is as if it is yet another barrier: a pane of glass closes a room to the outside which can be seen through it, and outside there is just more built space, with the strange mushroom shape of a water tower that fixes this place and haunts the film. She looks in the mirror, but it reflects back both the face and the interior of the room and she recoils in horror. Meanwhile Riccardo sits slumped in an armchair, staring catatonically. He is like 'part of the furniture'.

I want, finally, to bring this back to the politics of modernity and modernism. The films produce a dislodging or unsettling of a comfortable relationship between bodies and space: the body – and in particular the body of the woman – is frequently positioned at an extreme edge of the frame, or is filmed from behind, or above, or below. Bodies and built space are in a relationship of mutual tension, even antagonism sometimes, as the building or parts of the building (a pillar, stairwell, window or window frame) hems in the figure, or leaves it isolated, or blocks it. Similarly, the use of empty spaces, or as we might say, with Casey, of places waiting to be occupied by a body, also creates a sense of tension, of mutual estrangement between the place and the body. This effect is similar, I think, to that which Walter Benjamin attributed in his 1931 essay on photography to Eugène Atget's pictures of Paris and to surrealist photography: the shots of people-less streets produced a '*salutary* estrangement between man and his surroundings' because they destroyed aura, removed (bourgeois) intimacy, the illusion of a mutually reinforcing and unproblematic relationship between people and places, and thus gave 'free play to the politically educated eye' (Benjamin, 1979, p. 251). This is true also of Antonioni's filming of built space and human bodies too – and for the same reason. Antonioni also belongs to that moment of high modernism in which the body is imagined as displaced, unfixed from a secure relationship with place. Surroundings become strange. There is a terror of the vacuum as replete or humanised place threatens to turn back not only into empty place but, still further, into abstract, mathematical space.

But the politics of this is more complicated than Benjamin assumed, since the whole operation is also gendered and sexed. It is the objectified body of the woman that freezes and disables narrativity and is offered up to contemplation. In both the sequences I have discussed, as well as in many others in these and other films, the clinical, dissecting nature of the implied spectatorial gaze is sadistic, and it reflects Antonioni's characteristic way of directing actors by controlling their every gesture and position, their interaction with space, withholding an explanation of his own intentions, monopolising knowledge of the characters and leaving nothing either to the actors' own imagination or to chance (see on this in particular his 'Riflessioni sull'attore' of 1961, reproduced in Antonioni, 1994, pp. 47–9). After putting Monica Vitti in both cases into a situation of extreme tension, like a controlled experiment, he allows her some release, but only some, in the evolution of the narrative. This dialectic between control and release is characteristic of all the films of the early 1960s and is at once the source of extraordinary visual power and their most problematic limitation.

References

Antonioni, M., *Il deserto rosso*, di Carlo, C. (ed.), 2nd edition, Bologna. Cappelli, 1978.

Antonioni, M., *Fare un film è per me vivere. Scritti sul cinema*, di Carlo, C. & Tinazzi, G. (eds.), Venice, Marsilio, 1994.

Antonioni, M., *The Architecture of Vision: Writings and Interviews on Cinema*, di Carlo, C. & Tinazzi, G. (eds.), New York, Marsilio, 1996.

Benjamin, W., 'A Small History of Photography' (1931) in *One-Way Street and Other Writings*, London, NLB, 1979.

Burch, N., *Theory of Film Practice* (1969), London, Secker and Warburg, 1973.

Casey, E. S., *Getting Back into Place: Toward a Renewed Understanding of the Place-World*, Bloomington and Indianapolis, Indiana University Press, 1993.

Cowie, P., *Antonioni, Bergman, Resnais*, London, Tantivy, 1963.

Godard, J.-L., 'La nuit, l'éclipse, l'aurore. Entretien avec Michelangelo Antonioni', *Cahiers du Cinéma*, 160 (November 1964), pp. 8-17.

Heath, S., 'Narrative Space' (1976), in *Questions of Cinema* (London and Basingstoke, Macmillan, 1981).

Kazanskij, B., 'The Nature of Cinema' (1927), in *Russian Formalist Film Theory*, Eagle, H. (ed.), (Michigan Slavic Materials, no. 19, Ann Arbor, 1981).

Lefebvre, H., *The Production of Space* (1974), trans. D. Nicholson-Smith, Oxford, Basil Blackwell, 1991.

Lotman, J., *Semiotics of Cinema* (1973), trans. M. E. Suino, Michigan Slavic Contributions, no. 5, Ann Arbor, University of Michigan, 1976.

Mancini, M. and Perrella, G. (eds.), *Michelangelo Antonioni, architettura della visione*, Catania, ALEF, 1986.

Micheli, S., 'Il personaggio femminile nei film di Antonioni', *Bianco e Nero*, 28: 1 (1967), pp. 1-9.

Mulvey, L., 'Visual Pleasure and Narrative Cinema', in *Screen*, 16: 3 (Autumn 1975), pp. 5-17.

Nowell-Smith, G., *L'avventura*, London, BFI, 1997.

Wiblin, I. 'The Space Between: Photography, Architecture and the Presence of Absence', in Penz, F. and Thomas. M. (eds.), *Cinema and Architecture: Méliès, Mallet-Stevens, Multimedia* (London, BFI, 1997), pp. 104-12.

Is Pasolini an Urban Film-maker?

Myrto Konstantarakos

In Italy today, shanty towns, deprived and derelict locations at the outskirt of cities, are often characterised as 'Pasolinian'. This is due to Pier Paolo Pasolini being the first poet, novelist, playwright, film director, essayist and columnist, as he was all of these, to portray these locations.

In the Italian cultural tradition, Rome is less central than, for example, Paris in French literature and film. This is due to Italy's past and its relatively young existence as a country with Rome as capital. Regionalism is strongly reflected in literature and cinema, even more so after the Second World War, at the end of the Fascist regime that had so strongly objected to any notion of regionalism. Writers and film-makers all set their narratives in different locations in Italy, or elsewhere, without being in any way concerned with Rome. Moreover, it is probably because Pasolini was one of only a few artists interested in the *Roma popolare* (a term for which there seems to be no English translation) that his name came to be associated with it.

My analysis here will not be concerned with the referent Rome but with Pasolini's symbolic representations and various manifestations of the discursive category which is Rome. This interest stems from a broader one in the representation of the city in film: my purpose is not to study the city as background but the way that it has been textualised, alluded to or explored, and how it has been constructed – how it has been used as a *topos* or a topic. This paper will look at the representation of Rome from the angle of spatial contrasts: centre versus periphery, movement versus immobility, inside versus outside, and speed versus slowness. However, we shall see that, beyond these oppositions, Pasolini favours spaces of liminality that best symbolise his position in society both as homosexual and intellectual.

1. Rome

Although he had previously had experience of living in cities, Pasolini's first significant encounter with a metropolis happened in the Italian capital in 1950. He was not born or raised there. As a child, he lived in the many towns in the North of Italy to where his father's career took the family. He then studied in Bologna and took refuge in Casarsa – his mother's village in the region of Friuli – during the war. All his recollections of youthful happiness are situated there in the countryside. His move to Rome was not through choice; charged with obscene behaviour, he was dismissed from the school where he had been teaching (and was expelled from the Communist Party for the same reason).

Pasolini's stay in Rome started rather badly: he could not find work and lived far from his mother who was a maid in a house. He was so desperate, and missed Friuli so much that he was unable to write for several months. When he was finally able to write again both the Friulan and Roman experiences coexisted in his work:[1] the short stories he wrote in 1950 and 1951 are set either in Friuli or in Rome with no significant difference either in style or plot, and sometimes the same narrative is adapted to suit both backgrounds.[2] In the collection of poems *Roma 1950. Diario*, the narrator recalls Casarsa while closeted in his room in Rome, but then slowly opens the window on to the streets of the city.[3] By moving from the silent and dark womb of the room to the noisy and sunny Roman street, Pasolini had been born again. He still longed for Friuli, but Rome helped him to alleviate his suffering. Slowly, Rome was seducing him.

Young males played an important role in this reconciliation to his new environment, for he discovered that both locations had attractive *ragazzi* in common, although the Roman experience was even more intense from this point of view. His exploration of the city is therefore driven by desire and his vision of Rome is charged with erotic self-indulgence and displacement of his desire for juveniles. He seems to describe places instead of characters and uses space as a form of circumlocution to talk about people. When the question: 'Which is Rome's sex?' was put to him in an interview, he responded, 'Well, I would give it neither female nor male sex, but the special sex which is that of the young males'. He was also asked which age seemed to him best to represent the capital, and he replied: 'Adolescence'. Finally, when asked what Rome resembled, he answered that it had 'the appearance of a typical young male from the periphery: i.e. olive skin, black eyes, robust body'.[4] For Pasolini, the boys *are* Rome; therefore, to possess the *ragazzi* is tantamount to possessing Rome.

2. Borgata

In his first few short stories on the Italian capital, Pasolini depicted Trastevere and Testaccio, celebrated by poets such as Trilussa, as the *popolare* areas of the town, but he soon realised that the poorest part of the population actually resided in the periphery of the city, called the *borgate*, and this is where he set his films.[5] This is the peripheral, suburban part of town Pasolini got to know since it was the only place he could afford accommodation at the beginning of his stay in the capital, in Ponte Mammolo, eight kilometres from the centre. He was working as a school teacher in another *borgata* which made commuting from one to the other extremely long and tiring. However, even when he got a better job and was able to move to a more fashionable district, Pasolini did not stop making trips to the *borgata* for this was where he met young males.[6]

The *borgate* were built between 1924 and 1940 to house and control poor families expelled from the centre by the urban policy of the Fascist regime that destroyed old and intricate working-class districts in order to replace them with broad avenues. The war and the internal migration from southern Italy brought to the *borgate* a second wave of inhabitants who built illegal dwellings, *baracche abusive*. Most of the periphery was made up of slums; only later were council houses built by the Fascist government with the overt aim of keeping the poorest parts of the population out of the centre of the city.[7] The majority of the characters in Pasolini's Roman prose and early films (*Accattone*, 1961; *Uccellacci e uccellini*, 1966 and *La terra vista dalla luna*, 1967) live in the first type of dwelling, but his character Mamma Roma's highest aspiration is to move into the second, a move of which she is very proud.

As the margins of the city, the outside, the *borgata* can be said to be the main character of the Roman short stories, novels and films. The dregs of society live amongst the rubbish of the city: the space of the *borgata* is shapeless, composed of building works, rubbish tips and ruins, for the capital had not yet been entirely rebuilt since the war. However, its depiction in later works is not dissimilar even though the *borgate*'s facilities were improved.

Those who live at the margins of the city are at the margins of society. The inhabitants of the *borgate* do not belong to the world of artisans and small shop-keepers in the way that those from the working-class district of Testaccio do, for instance. If they have a job, it is as a labourer or builder, but the majority of Pasolini's characters do not work: women are prostitutes, men are pimps or thieves. They belong to the underworld, the *lumpenproletariat* that gets by on petty crime. Accattone is neither able to work nor to steal; he can only be a pimp. To Stella's suggestion that he might find a job, he reacts violently: 'What for? To give my blood to others? Nobody drinks my blood! Work! Only animals work!'[8] And when finally he does make an attempt at working to prevent Stella from becoming a prostitute, the film-script refers to him as *schiavo*, 'slave'. If Pasolini's love for Charlie Chaplin manifests itself in the speeding up of the image found in *La ricotta* (1963), for example, it does so in the choice of the character of the tramp in the same film too.

In the 1950s, within the tradition of Neorealism, Pasolini is not concerned with wealthy characters, but with the underclass of working or unemployed persons – vagabonds, beggars, criminals, prostitutes, thieves. However, more than the Neorealists, he portrays the *classes dangereuses*, the lower depths of society, presenting thereby an alternative version of the world. Marxist scholars much criticised Pasolini's preference for the underworld rather than for the factory workers. The inhabitants of the *borgate* are outside the city and outside the capitalist circulation of money. Sam Rohdie argues that the point is precisely this: 'It was not the world of the exploited, but rather a world inhabited by those despised by capitalism, those useless to it and at its geographical and social periphery: the pimp, the whore, the savage'.[9] Hence they have their sacredness. Pasolini's chosen characters are as outside productive capitalist society as poets, hence as Pasolini himself. The revolutionary value of these films cannot therefore be formulated in 'traditional' Marxist terms: Pasolini believed that, by their mere existence, poetry and art scandalise, hence their revolutionary strength.[10] The artist needs the establishment in order to exist and to create, but always stays in the 'margins', questioning the power of the centre.

3. Motion

Because of the stark division between centre and outskirts, the *ragazzi* are forced to move between one and the other. The Roman films are articulated around the *ragazzi*'s journeys from the *borgata* to the city centre and back and between suburbs: they sleep and work (when they work) in the periphery, and they enjoy themselves in the city. The space they haunt is presented as a kind of urban jungle. They retaliate against their social ostracisation by stealing, and rebel against the power of the centre by breaking its rules. Hostile to the authority and the power represented by the centre, on the one hand they take advantage of the economic possibilities offered by it, while on the other they prefer to stay on the margins of the city and refuse it.

Most of the films are concerned with male characters' walks. The young male characters are rarely immobile in Pasolini's works, but the aim seems to be secondary to the motion. An often very hungry title character Accattone goes back and forth in the *borgata* under the sun and Pasolini describes *Uccellacci e uccellini* as a journey.[11] However, one must ask whether the movement of the males is a negative one. Are they constantly on the move because they have no place of their own to stop? There is no doubt that their wandering is the sign of their spatial *malaise* and neurosis: the inhabitants of the slums, like Pasolini, are rootless and lack identity. However, my contention is that the youths assert their freedom by not staying still and by their purposeless wandering. The direction of their movement is of no relevance: by ignoring the division between centre and periphery young males transgress the boundaries of the city, and by wandering in the city they violate bourgeois immobility – the *status quo* of urban representation against bourgeois sedentarity.

4. Speed

These slow and painful walks recall the *Via Crucis*, thereby comparing the young male characters to Christ, even in other films than *Il Vangelo secondo Matteo* (1964).

Although slowness is connotated positively, a rapid mode of transport is desired by the characters, for example by Ettore in *Mamma Roma* (1962). Circulation is at the very heart of the modern conception of the city and, as Walter Benjamin and others remind us, speed signifies modernity, the modern experience of the city. Pasolini was fascinated by speed and bought a fast car, an Alfa Romeo, straight after his first literary success, the collection of poems *Le Ceneri di Gramsci* in 1957. In this, Pasolini himself might have been a victim of the American celebration of the car, particularly glamourised by cinema. Was this a case of Pasolini falling into the trap of advertising he so often denounced? The car is certainly a consumer item alongside the washing machines and televisions Pasolini disapproved of. However, if he chose to have an automobile in his life, he constantly emphasised in his works the disadvantages of a fast mode of transport: speeding cars kill, turning the American myth of the car as provider of freedom upside down. Cars driven by customers injure prostitutes physically and psychologically in *Accattone*. When bad weather disrupted the shooting, Pasolini looked for an alternative ending. Instead of dying by swimming in the river after lunch, Accattone steals a motorcycle and has an accident with it.[12] In *Mamma Roma*, the new motorcycle bought by Ettore's mother gets him into trouble too – trouble from which he will eventually die.[13]

Although Pasolini's prose and films are not about his incursions into Rome as a *flâneur*, his practice as one (at night in search of young males) is reflected in the whole of his work when depicting his characters' trips on foot. Like Baudelaire, Pasolini stages the poet/city relation as an amorous encounter. The *flâneur* is male and stands outside the capitalist circulation of money and work of the city: his is an indolent

Pasolini with a small boy on the set of La ricotta   *(© Archivio Fondo Pier Paolo Pasolini)*

protest or, as Christopher Prendergast puts it, a 'resistance to the rationalised city of economic modernity'.[14] The poet wandering slowly in the city expresses his condition of exile and uprootedness. Indeed, if the characters in the Rome narratives are in exile in Rome, so is their author.

Rapid transport is reprehensible because it abolishes the distance between the suburbs and the centre. Centre and periphery are so far apart that the time needed to go from one to the other has to be long and painful and fast vehicles cancel out this essential social distance; provoking the levelling effect Pasolini called *omologazione*. One should argue that spatial exclusion is necessary to the survival of this *sottoproletariato*: when the *ragazzi* gain easy access to the bourgeois space thanks to rapid transport, and the periphery is absorbed by the centre, their 'culture' and values disappear. Pasolini's characters belong outdoors in the *borgata*, in the countryside. Movement is therefore fundamental in Pasolini's poetic world: slow movement is a guarantee of the alienation of city centre from periphery; speed abolishes this otherness and perverts its significance.

5. Nature

The slow walks so crucial to Pasolini can only take place on the road and along rivers:

it is by rivers and on beaches that he can see the *ragazzi* bathe. By the rivers, the youths enjoy themselves, playing cards and soccer and singing while dressing and undressing. Their swimming in the rivers gives Pasolini opportunities to see them with no clothes on and to expose their bodies, like at the beginning of *Accattone*. Moreover, like streets, rivers are places of love, but they are also sites of escape from the exhausting rhythms of the city within the city. By strolling along the rivers, close to the water, one is transported into a different world. Countryside can emerge in the very heart of the city. Like streets, rivers bring out the 'country' side of the town. The river is nature in the city. Moreover, grass grows on riverbanks. Representing an Edenesque image of the parks or of the gardens, green grass stands for the peasant world of Friuli; but also, like rivers, it is the manifestation of nature in the city.[15] Therefore the urban places Pasolini most describes are in fact 'rural' ones – roads, riverbanks, gardens and parks with a strong emphasis on grass. If we saw that the *borgata* is the countryside in the city, these *topoi* bring the characters, the film-maker and the spectator back to nature even in the very centre of the metropolis and introduce (with all the sexual connotations that this word implies) nature within an urban environment.

Pasolini's symbolics of space need to be thought about in terms of a Rousseauist paradigm. Like Rousseau, he believes we never lose our 'natural' side and we can cultivate it, as Rousseau did, by walking in the countryside and socialising with peasants. The impact with the metropolis is so strong that Pasolini takes refuge in a smaller unit, similar to that in which he used to live up to that point in Friuli. In Rome, he looks for the familiar 'village' within the city – the suburb, which Raymond Williams calls 'the knowable community'.[16] Only then can he recreate the social web he needs to exist, function and be happy.

We have seen how, from 1950, the representation of space in the cinematic production of Pasolini is characterised by a stark division between the centre and periphery of the city. This stark division between the two places does mirror this particular urban topography and historical physicality, but is also part of a private conception of urban space as inner/outer. The *borgata* is the indeterminate and perhaps unnameable place 'over there', where lives a population at the edge of the city's acknowledged spaces. Writing on 'The Environs de Paris', T. J. Clark argues that in 19th-century French literature and paintings, the suburb is 'recognised to be a specific form of life: not the countryside, not the city, not a degenerate form of either,'[17] but in-between. If there is a powerful view that the suburbs represent the site of modernism, they are also the territory for self-projection and mirroring identity. The possibility of knowledge of the city corresponds for Pasolini to the displacement of the desire for the city's inhabitants: through his descriptions, he constructs a complex and ambivalent erotics of urban space. The questions of identity are here twofold: of the city, but also of the self. Pasolini loses, and finds again, his mental stability and sense of identity through the reiterated descriptions of the city.

Confronted with dichotomies, he opts for neither extreme but stays ostensibly 'in-between'. In his Rome works, his characters belong to the subproletariat, between the working class and the bourgeoisie; or even between the working class and the peasantry. They are neither children nor adults, but adolescents. In spatial terms,

Pasolini and adolescents play football on the set of La ricotta

Pasolini sets his prose works and films between the city and the countryside – in the *borgata*. In temporal terms, between day and night, he favours dawn and dusk; between winter and summer, spring and autumn are his favourite seasons. Through the representation of liminality in space, he expresses his social and sexual position in society: Maurizio Viano argues that Pasolini belongs to the oppressed group, the intellectuals, of the dominant class in the same way as, being homosexual, he belongs to the 'dominated faction of the dominant sex'.[18] By choosing liminality, Pasolini was able to talk about politics and homosexuality in the prejudiced context of Italy at the time. Within an urban environment, wherever he is, Pasolini concentrates on places in which the boundaries between city and countryside are blurred. Pasolini directs his gaze to the periphery wherever he is, even when this term does not make much sense in the country where he finds himself. The same opposition between city and countryside is to be found in works set in 'Third World' locations like Africa and India.[19] Like Marco Polo describing to Kublai Khan the cities of his empire in Italo Calvino's *Le città invisibili*, all Pasolini's cities are a variation of the same.[20]

The landscape he obsessively constructs is in many ways very similar to the one of his Friulan works, as the countryside of Friuli 'by now is a region of my soul and, even if I do not go back there, it is in me'.[21] Pasolini kept trying to match Friuli's landscapes (the region of his mother which had become the landscape of his 'self') with the ones of his environment, even when this happened to be an urban one. All of his locations bring us back to a single one, situated in the past.[22] He sets his narrative among the

118

indeterminacy of the Roman suburbs, outside the limits of the authorities of the centre. The *ban-lieue*, being outside the 'ban' of the authorities – the *polis*, the city – it allows for natural elements to invade its urban space.[23] As a place of liminality between city and countryside, the shapelessness of the *borgata* is an indicator of its natural and primitive character.

In her comparison of Freud's hysterics and Jasper's nostalgics, Elizabeth Bronfen emphasises 'that both are illnesses of the imagination. To be more precise, while hysterics suffer from too lively an imagination, nostalgics seem to suffer from their imaginations not being flexible enough to encompass a change in geography.'[24] Therefore, 'the nostalgic suffers from pleasurable memories she would like to reenact, but which she cannot because she has been displaced from the one site promising such a satisfying fulfilment' (1998, p. 272). Like Pasolini with Friuli, 'the nostalgic produces idealisations of a lost homeland to compensate for a sense of not belonging' (1998, p. 264). The nostalgic somatises the loss of a familiar geography by 'staging a battle against the unfamiliar social space' (1998, p. 277); in this case, Rome. However, by working on criminal young girls, Jasper comes to realise that nostalgics are in fact idealising what was far from being a happy family situation and by their actions make any return home impossible, 'as though the acute danger to their psychic survival had from the start not been the absence but rather the unbearable presence of too much home, the chaotic proximity connected with this social maternal space' (1998, p. 278). This is how Jasper justified their crimes: 'Now prevented forever from returning home from their exile, they can sustain the precarious fantasy of inactness without running the risk of fatal implosion. For within psychoanalytic terms, not the loss, but rather the extraordinary attraction of the home is what threatens the subject' (1998, p. 278). If the too-maternal Friuli was perceived as dangerous for Pasolini's psyche, its reenactment in Rome (or anywhere else) was conversely safe enough.

In *chaos* – in the countryside – man goes back to being himself, returning to his nature: nature and chaos are the state from which human beings originate and to which they return. Traditionally, these have been given feminine attributes: we are born from women and women are closely linked to all rites surrounding death.[25] The fascination for Pasolini of natural places, even within the city, might therefore be the translation of the love for his mother, of his inability to detach himself from her. If Gaston Bachelard posits that nature is tantamount to a creature who gives haven, protection and nurture,[26] and Pasolini's urban environment is 'natural', we can therefore draw the conclusion that, in his work, the city is female and mother – hence the title of his second film, *Mamma Roma*. By revealing the 'natural' elements of the urban environment, Pasolini recreates a maternal environment, without the risks associated with Friuli.

Countryside outside the city, city in the countryside, the Roman *borgata* is neither one nor the other.[27] Urban space is won by man against natural elements.[28] The *borgata* is space won from nature but nature still survives in rivers, dirty grass or dry bushes; further, nature can reclaim its space at any moment, like in the case of floods in his novel *Una vita violenta* (1959). The periphery becomes then the representation of the unstable chaos dominated by the elements.

A band plays in La ricotta   *(© Archivio Fondo Pier Paolo Pasolini)*

In conclusion, if Pasolini is chiefly known for his 'discovery' of urban deprivation, first in Rome, then in the Third World, and for their depiction in poetry, novels, short stories and films, it seems on reflection, however, that the urban places he most describes introduce natural elements into the city.[29] We can therefore go as far as to suggest that, although Pasolini purported to denounce the living conditions of the poor, the representation of space was in fact paramount for him and he only selected urban places according to their 'natural' qualities. Moreover, Zygmunt Baranski has long since unveiled Pasolini's pretences to popular culture: he argues that 'In Pasolini, *cultura* normally means 'high' culture, namely, the élite intellectual and artistic traditions which have been carefully constructed over many centuries'.[30] Pasolini showed extreme elitism in art. Both in his own production and in his judgement of others, he expresses a nostalgia for a humanist bourgeoisie that allowed room for popular culture to survive, in an (as Rohdie puts it) 'attempt to reconcile an old popular culture and an old bourgeois culture against the popular of the present' (1995, p. 180). I therefore agree with David Ward and Sam Rohdie who argue that 'Pasolini's work was more a passionate regret for a lost humanism than it was a lament for lost primitivism' (1995, p. 183).[31] Pasolini expresses his discomfort in spatial terms: the intellectual is outside society, excluded from the centres of power, as his characters are outside the city centres: 'Expelled as traitor from the centre of the *bourgeoisie* and an external witness of the working class, where is the intellectual, why and how does he exist?'[32] In fact, the past Pasolini longs for is the past when the intellectual still had prestige, a role to play in society and, ultimately, power.

Notes

1 See Baranski, Z. G., 'Notes Towards a Reconstruction: Pasolini and Rome 1950-51', *The Italianist*, Reading University, 5 (1985), pp. 138-49.

2 Such as *La rondinella del Pacher* rewritten later to suit the Roman dialogues of *Ragazzi di vita* ('La rondinella del Pacher', *Il quotidiano*, 3.9.1950, then in Pasolini, P. P., *Un paese di temporali e di primule*, Naldini, N. (ed.), Parma, Ugo Guanda, 1993, p. 168).

3 *Roma 1950. Diario*, Costanzo, M. & Scheiwiller, V. (eds.), Milan, All'insegna del pesce d'oro, 'Lunario', 1960 [1953].

4 'Quant'eri bella Roma', interview by Luigi Sommaruga, *Il Messaggero*, Rome, 9.6.1973; then in Pasolini, P. P., *Storie della città di Dio: racconti e cronache romane, 1950-1966*, Siti, W. (ed.), pp. 161-68, Turin, Einaudi, 1995, pp. 162-63.

5 Trilussa's real name was Carlo Alberto Salustri, born in Rome 26 October 1871. See *Tutte le poesie*, Pancrazi, P. (ed.), Rome, Mondadori, 1951.

6 Pasolini lived in Piazza Costaguti, at the Portico d'Ottavia at first; then in the periphery near the jail of Rebibbia, in Ponte Mammolo. In 1959, he moved to Monteverde, via Fontenaina, in the same building where the family Bertolucci was living. He then settled in 1963 in the affluent district of Eur.

7 David Forgacs depicts how 'The first *borgate* had been created in the late 1920s with the Fascist 'gutting' (*sventramento*) of the inner cities. The old houses between the Coliseum and Piazza Venezia were demolished to make way for the Via dell'Impero (now Via dei Fori Imperiali). The residents, mostly families of artisans and tradespeople, were rehoused on the peripheries with few or no amenities and poor communications into the city centre. The next generation of *borgate* were post-war; in some cases they were just clusters of shacks (*baraccamenti*), in others they were apartment blocks built by speculators without planning permission.' (Forgacs, D., *Italian Culture in the Industrial Era 1880-1980*, Manchester, Manchester University Press, 1990, p. 12)

8 *Accattone*, in Pasolini, P. P., *Alì dagli occhi azzurri*, Milan, Garzanti, (1965) 1989, p. 332.

9 Rohdie, S., *The Passion of Pasolini*, London, British Film Institute, 1995, p. 35.

10 See his interview by a young German actress in 1972, *S.P.Q.R.*, directed by Volker Koch.

11 Communicato stampa n.131, Cinema Ritz, Milan, 4 May 1966, then in Pasolini, P. P., Betti, L. & Gulinucci, M. (eds.), *Le regole di un'illusione: i film, il cinema, Rome*, Associazione 'Fondo Pier Paolo Pasolini', 1991, p. 406.

12 'Il 4 ottobre 1960', *Il Giorno*, Milan, 16.10.1960.

13 Interestingly, the car in Jean-Luc Godard's *Le Mépris* is of the same make as Pasolini's Alfa Romeo; ironically Pasolini was killed by his own car driven by a *ragazzo* who was attracted by the speed of the machine.

14 Prendergast, C., *Paris and the 19 Century*, Oxford-Cambridge, Mass., Blackwell, 1992, p. 201.

15 Green grass recalls the deepest levels of Pasolini's memory: when shooting *Edipo re*, he is happy to find the setting which corresponds almost exactly to the one in which his mother used to take him. (Pasolini, 'Edipo re', interview by J.A. Fieschi, *Cahiers du cinéma*, Paris, 195 (November 1967)) He recalls being happy as a baby on the grass: 'A blanket on the grass. The baby boy happy in the sun. His small eyes are open: he is not hungry, he is not thirsty, and he enjoys the peace of that time of day' (Pasolini, P. P., *Edipo re*, Milan, Garzanti, 1967, p. 47, then in *Le regole*, p. 159) In the first scene of *Edipo Re*, echoing Pasolini's memory, the baby is left alone on the grass, in the sun and we only hear women laughing. He is then

breastfed by his mother in the field. The film ends in the same field of vivid colours, where Oedipus, now blind, concludes: 'life ends where it begins'. Hence grass comes to summarise life as a whole.

16 'Thus it is still often said, under the pressure of urban and metropolitan experience, and as a direct and even conventional contrast, that a country community, most typically a village, is an epitome of direct relationships: of face-to-face contacts within which we can find and value the real substance of personal relationships. Certainly this immediate aspect of its difference from the city or the suburb is important; it is smaller scale; people are more easily identified and connected within it; the structure of the community is in many ways more visible.' (Williams, R., *The Country and the City*, London, Chatto and Windus, 1973, pp. 165-66)

17 Clark, T. J., *The Painting of Modern Life: Paris in the Art of Manet and his Followers*, London, Thames and Hudson, 1984, p. 147.

18 Viano, M., *A Certain Realism: Making Use of Pasolini's Film Theory and Practice*, Berkeley – Los Angeles - London, University of California Press, 1993, p. 75.

19 He speaks of 'this avenue of the periphery (if periphery and centre have meaning for Indian cities).' (Pasolini, P. P., *L'odore dell'India*, Milan, Longanesi, 1962, p. 59)

20 Calvino, I., *Le città invisibili*, Turin, Einaudi, 1972.

21 'Parole buone', *Dialoghi con Pasolini*, n.34, 23.8.162, then in Pasolini, P. P., *I dialoghi*, Falaschi, G. (ed.), Rome, Editori Riuniti, 1992, p. 285.

22 Rohdie takes this memory beyond the 'real' place: 'His India is like his Naples which is like his Yemen, his Harlem, his Calabria, his Rome *borgate*, the Sassi di Matera, the alleys of Palermo. They evoke earlier descriptions and memories of the Paradise he lost in Friuli which blurred with another maternal paradise, even further back,' (1995, p. 57) which I would call the maternal womb. For a discussion of Pasolini's treatment of time, see Gordon, R., 'Being and Film-Time in Pasolini's Cinema', in 'Cinema and Ideology', Rodgers, E. (ed.), *Strathclyde Modern Languages Series, New Series*, 1 (1996), pp. 3-16.

23 At the beginning of Part II of *Petrolio*, the novel Pasolini was writing when he was killed, therefore unfinished and only published by Garzanti in 1992, Carlo goes through a savanna that degenerates into a waste land before becoming a city.

24 Bronfen, E., *The Knotted Subject: Hysteria and its Discontents*, Princeton, New Jersey, Princeton University Press, 1998, p. 274.

25 See the work of Badinter, E., *L'Un est l'Autre*, Paris, Odile Jacob, 1986 on Western female representations and death throughout the ages, in particular p. 175.

26 'Sentimentally, nature is a "projection" of the mother.' (Bachelard, G., *L'Eau et les rêves: essais sur l'imagination de la matière*, Paris, José Corti, 1942, p. 156)

27 Chapter II of De Nardis' study on Pasolini's *borgata* is entitled: 'La città si sgretola', 'The city crumbles' (Nardis, L. de, *Roma di Belli e di Pasolini*, Rome, Bulzoni Editore, 1977).

28 In a similar comment made at a time when he knew Pasolini (and indeed he told him the story that gave its name to *Alì dagli occhi azzurri*), Jean-Paul Sartre describes nature around Venice as being contaminated by the city in Sartre, J.-P., *La reine Albemarle ou le dernier touriste*, Paris, NRF Gallimard, 1991, p. 80.

29 It might be interesting to recall that, as a university student, after losing his dissertation, *tesi di laurea*, on painting, Pasolini chose to write another one on Giovanni Pascoli, known for his rural themes.

30 Baranski, Z., 'Pasolini: Culture, Croce, Gramsci' in Baranski, Z. & Lumley, R. (eds.) *Culture and Conflict in Post-War Italy: Essays on Mass and Popular Culture*, pp. 139-59 (London, Macmillan, 1990), p. 141.

31 See also Ward, D, *A Poetics of Resistance: Narrative and the Writings of Pier Paolo Pasolini*, London, Associated University Press – Madison-Teanech, Fairleigh Dickinson University Press, 1995.

32 'Dov'è l'intellettuale?' *Dialoghi con Pasolini*, n.33, 13.8.1968, then in *I dialoghi*, p. 462. The following article in the same issue of *Vie nuove* starts with the same questions and attempts to answer them: 'Less than a decade ago, the answer would have been quick and simple: "the intellectual is a spiritual guide of the aristocracy of the working class and also of the educated middle classes." He was all in all an authority, an authority of the opposition [...] Italy was still a poor (*paleocapitalistico*) country and the scholar could easily embody, like still today in poor and uncultured countries, the "national" role of the guide, the prophet.' (Pasolini, P. P., 'Il caso di un intellettuale', *Dialoghi con Pasolini*, n.33, 13.8.1968, then in *I dialoghi*, p. 462)

Transformations of the Urban Landscape in Spanish *Film Noir*

Alberto Mira

1. Cities of Imagination: good and evil in *noir* city

Urban landscapes have a special relevance in the films known as *film noir*.[1] The *noir* look soon became as distinctive as those of the western or the screwball comedy. It presented an easily recognisable gallery of characters (the faithful friend, the clumsy henchman, the villain, the gangster moll, and of course, the hardened, cynical detective) and a particular set of props (trenchcoats, hats, cigarettes and guns). But most importantly, it created new approaches to the representation of the city, which became a landscape of the imagination, as legendary as that of the western. Empty offices in labyrinthine buildings after working hours, darkened streets with threatening corners, the abrupt light of a street lamp, run-down suburbs, back alleys and wet pavements, all evoked in narratives by Raymond Chandler, Dashiell Hammet and other masters of detective fiction, received striking visual treatment especially thanks to the work of cinematographers such as Harold Rosson, Nicholas Musuraka, Elwood Bredell, James Wong Howe or Sid Hicox.[2] Even the earliest examples of *noir* thrillers are concerned specifically with urban characters and lifestyles (*Underworld*, 1927) as if the city, rather than a set of characters or plot conventions, was the defining characteristic of this kind of film: it is only in large cities that human nature becomes degraded enough for the stories of betrayal and corruption (with which *noir* is concerned) to be staged. *Noir* has actually been described by David Bordwell (1985) as an attitude of 'nonconformity' within classical American film, rather than a 'genre'. A social reading of the genre would propose that *noir* is the result for social unfairness arising in the modern city. Consequently, key titles will often articulate a symbolic opposition city-countryside. Following this formulation, urban spaces stand for a pessimistic view of human nature and the countryside offers a possibility for redemption, normally represented in terms of 'otherness'. The country works as the legendary point of destination for the characters once they finish their last criminal operation. This is a recurring image that runs through the golden age of the genre during the late 1940s (John Huston's *The Asphalt Jungle*, 1950; Jacques Tourneur's *Out of the Past*, 1947) to some of its more recent, neoclassical manifestations (for instance, in the controversial original ending to *Blade Runner*, 1982, rejected by Ridley Scott in the latter '…Director's Cut'). In the moving last image of John Huston's film, Sterling

Hayden, the hardboiled criminal with a soul, who has been wounded, crawls out of his car into the countryside, near the horses he always missed.

The narrative in *Out of the Past* (a.k.a. *Build my Gallows High*) turns around the opposition between, on the one hand, a peaceful rural community which offers the protagonist, Robert Mitchum (an ex-detective with a weakness for dangerous women) the possibility of integration into the community through marriage and, on the other hand, the ruthless, ambitious, obsessive urban characters played by Jane Greer and Kirk Douglas. In both films, the pastoral is the elusive landscape of childhood, drenched in sunlight, which the protagonists long for and want to inhabit, but which will ultimately be denied to them. The city represents harsh, hopeless reality and reflects on a pessimistic view of the human condition that has been linked to existentialism.[3] Harold Rosson's camerawork for *The Asphalt Jungle* is a perfect example of how a physical landscape is visualised to seem imaginary, even nightmarish: arches, bridges, puddles, sharp corners, beams of light, create a dangerous world that may conceal unpunished crime, but also holds threat. Cinematography thus visualises the city as hell.

The *noir* aesthetic, as reflected in these classic instances, can be accounted for according to two different reading approaches. One of them, which we could designate as the 'metaphorical' interpretation, places images in the realm of the symbolic: the image stands for abstract notions about human condition. The second is what we could call a 'metonymic' reading: the image points toward a concrete reference, the city as represented stands for the actual urban landscape and the process of meaning works following classical referentiality. This second approach makes *noir* a socially relevant genre that illustrates real social problems of political corruption and capitalist oppression. Metaphorically, murky landscapes point toward a metaphysics of the human condition; metonymically, on the contrary, they are a comment on social structures that encourage human beings to behave as the characters. As a consequence, there is space for ambiguity (both moral and social) in the reading of *film noir*: it does give a pessimistic version of human nature, but it also questions the stability of human social structures.

In the context of post-war Spanish culture such tension between metaphor and metonymy, that could lead to an uncertainty in the meaning of *film noir*, was politically problematic. National-catholic ideology attempted to draw a clear, unmistakable line between 'good' and 'evil', so that no ambiguity was possible. Actions which fitted into national-catholic discourse were 'good'. 'Evil', on the other hand, was identified with sin and with political dissidence (again distinctions between both of these were consciously blurred). Furthermore, given that the government explicitly identified with those principles which Franco helped to impose, there was an ideological need to make clear that a majority of 'good', peace-loving Spanish citizens were living in a 'good', peace-loving country. Children's school-books even explained that Spain was God's favourite country, which (they continued) accounted for the nice weather conditions and the triumph of Franco. Any film that presented corruption and lent itself to a metaphorical reading as introduced above gave cause for concern. Films such as *Gilda* (1946) had a controversial reception and were salvaged by the censors and produced violent responses from audiences.[4] Yet, as long as the action took place outside Spanish territory, it could always be argued that such moral corruption was characteristic of the Americans and other foreigners, and therefore did not say anything about Franco's Spain. In practical terms, this made home-grown *film noir* nearly impossible in the 1940s. Representation of corruption was too close for comfort: placing hotbeds of corruption in actual Spanish cities would give strength to readings (both metaphorical and socially relevant) which would easily be used as a critique on the political situation.

Actually, nothing resembling this tradition appears in Spanish cinema until the 1950s as the country starts very slowly to leave the isolation which was the outcome of Civil War and Fascism at the beginning of the decade, and the process will not be completed until the late 1960s. Apart from the tight control to which the arts were subjected, there were also industrial reasons why the *noir* models were not imitated during the 1940s. By 1950, there was a new sense of an industry quickly growing.[5] This meant an awareness that the cinematic models that dominated for a decade had become obsolete: industrial film production, no matter how weak, needs to take audiences into account and offer them novelty and excitement, a sense of surprise which was mostly impossible within the range of representation officially encouraged. Classic American genres had the kind of prestige among audiences that Spanish film-makers felt they needed to exploit. At that moment, urban landscapes were little more than mere backgrounds to romantic comedies. The city was never dealt with as a topic. This was almost to be expected: by the end of the 1940s, urban expansion was still slow in Spain. Most of the population still lived in the countryside. The city was ideologically constructed on film as the place for sophistication and luxury, in sharp contrast with actual urban life during the period. Damaged by war and a long, impoverished post-war period, Spanish cities were far from glamourous. Lacking in the most basic conveniences, inhabited by loners and dismembered families, a poor population barely managed to survive among the ruins. Cinematic representation of this state of things runs counter to official propaganda on the situation in the country. If acknowledged at all, poverty had to be reinscribed in the frame of christian charity and the essential 'goodness' of the 'innocent' poor, who would receive reward from their eartly sufferings.[6] On the other hand, the countryside was home to the kind of social identities favoured by the regime: the essence of Spanish national identity could be found in the microcosmos of the Andalusian *cortijo*, or large country house, where even servants sang happily apparently proud of their social position and even made friends with the wealthy landowners in a perfect picture of social harmony. It is precisely the comment on the problem of rural exodus that will provide a perfect excuse for the introduction of *film noir* under Francoism that didn't clash with the prevailing ideology.

Surcos (1950), directed by José Antonio Nieves Conde, was the film that came to change the situation and offered an alternative in the representation of the city. It tells the story of a country family who travel to Madrid in order to make a living. They take rooms with a relative and go their separate ways seeking a job. What they do find is not always legal and sometimes not even proper. They will end up leaving the city in order to return to the country, where life is harder but dignified. There are two elements which made *Surcos* possible, thereby opening up new possibilities for the representation of the city in Spanish cinema. On the one hand, Nieves Conde was a member of the Falange, one of the ideological underpinnings of Francoism. It must be remembered, that Francoism, in itself, was the result of a military uprising, and the winners imposed a national catholic creed, but it was far from a revolutionary movement with clear intellectual roots such as the one that triumphed, say, in Russia in 1917. Falange intellectuals had a vision of society which sometimes strikingly (and embarrassingly) coincided with the one held by thinkers from the extreme left: society is described as a beehive in which everyone has a task to perform in order to contribute to the common endeavour; hopefully, in an ideal society, there should be no privileges. Falange can be regarded as an anti-elitist, populist doctrine that supported an elitist, oppressive right-wing regime. As a consequence, Falange intellectuals showed a concern for the social that could not be opposed by the regime.

At the end of the 1940s, immigration to the large cities increased to become a social problem. There was a general situation of economic crisis and hunger, and large cities represented opportunities to find a job and get ahead.[7] Within Falange discourse, this move into large cities was mostly regarded as a mistake as it upset the balance and created masses of unemployed people who had to survive in the margins of the law. This is exactly the story Nieves Conde wanted to tell; Madrid is not necessarily the solution to peasants' problems, and a new set of problems arises when people risk starting a new life somewhere they are not acquainted with. Families are destroyed and their members feel pushed into a life of crime or frivolity. In the film, the father starts losing authority when he is unable to find a stable job, the daughter starts as a maid to the lover of a theatrical impresario and will end up in show business, where she will run the risk of becoming prostituted; the younger son will be fired from his job as a delivery boy when his merchandise is stolen. The older son, impatient to make easy money, becomes entangled into a life of crime and leaves home to live, outside wedlock, with a fallen woman.

The second element that made *Surcos* possible (incidentally enabling a critical discourse on the city taken up by later *noir* film-makers) was the influence of neorealism as an aesthetic. Neorealism produced a number of urban narratives in which the city was far more than mere background, becoming something like a character. Neorealist directors such as Rossellini or de Sica shot their films in the actual streets and cities were represented in all their misery (*Bicycle Thieves*, 1948) and devastation (*Germany, Year Zero*, 1947; *Roma, città aperta*, 1946). The explicit framework was conservative and christian-humanist, which was attractive for Falangist film-makers, giving them the opportunity to contain the representation of life in large cities lest it could be read as a critique of the regime.[8] Even so, *Surcos* was not a comfortable film for the authorities. In acknowledging the existence of the underworld, of an impoverished class that would resort to crime in order to survive, the film implied that all was not well with the new state of things and the film faced the difficult task of striking a balance between social critique and propaganda. The Francoist media had been giving a triumphalist version of the situation for over a decade, never dealing with the problems in Spanish society. Manicheism was one thing (one could depict communists and other outlaws as evil), but the general situation was one of triumph and the times were glorious.

The film crosses into *noir* territory in one of its plot strands, concerning the older son, who becomes part of a gang of criminals. Several elements in this section are striking for the times: the 'bad' character is not a communist, nor anything essentially evil, but a normal young man who has to resort to theft in order to move on. The audience is asked to be involved with the character's situation rather than just dismiss it as wrong or sinful: they can disapprove of his behaviour, but in the narrative context, the character does not seem to have a choice once he (mistakenly) arrives in the city.

The film uses images of the city symbolically to good effect. On the one hand, following Falangist notions of society as a well-ordered beehive, Nieves Conde shoots Madrid as a place where everything works: buses move swiftly, in straight paths in front of the camera, buildings and lampposts form a grid of intersecting lines that give the impression of a peaceful place. Urban landscape is the picture of balance and social well-being.[9] On the other hand, the *noir* plot gives us shots of darkened streets and empty roads where the underworld can do their work; there is a sense of threat and displacement, as if we were having a glimpse into the darker side of the system. This is relevant in a metaphorical reading: provided the characters are in the wrong place, the world is bound to look dark to them. The lighting rejects the expressionist mode in favour of neorealism: it was important that the city was recognisably a real, concrete place, that it referred directly to Madrid and not to some landscape of the imagination. In order to maximise this effect Nieves Conde chose, unusually for the times, to shoot on location.

Surcos is at the crossroads between neorealism and *film noir*. As in the former, the city is presented as a social landscape, the result of a particular state of the nation. It is also represented as a problem: those who come to the city in pursuit of false dreams, therefore becoming displaced from the place where they belong, can be swallowed up into the darker corners of society. It is true that the city can be corrupting, but only for those who do not fit into its structures. The film was intended as a warning for the masses of people moving into a potentially degrading new world. It starts with the image of furrows under the sky, a reference to hard work, but also aimed to mystify life in the country. The clash between the city and the countryside is therefore not clearly resolved in favour of either (as it is in classic *noir*), in an 'essential' way, but for the family whose story it tells, life in the city leads to frustration, corruption, failure, crime and death.

2. Francoist *Noir:* peaceful streets

As we see, some elements of *film noir* did find their way into Spanish film in the 1950s, even if a high price had to be paid and *noir* narratives lost their transgressive potential and their existential pessimism on the human condition once they were adapted to fit the censors' demands. One of the central aspects of the genre, whatever the moral meaning of particular films, whatever their narrative closure, is precisely that the system is far from perfect, that evil does exist and that, in a more or less permanent way, it can affect ordinary people.

Surcos made new approaches to the representation of the city easier, and even opened up the possibility of a Spanish *film noir*. As it has been pointed out elsewhere (Heredero, 1993), it was certainly a very narrow possibility. A degree of moral ambiguity is one of the most interesting features of *film noir* as a genre. The line separating good from evil, crime from law, can be crossed and the opposition between these becomes less absolute. A character may not 'be' evil, but become entangled in a life of crime. And some characters can be criminals but appear as respectable pillars of society, as it happens with the Louis Calhern and Kirk Douglas characters in, repectively, *The Asphalt Jungle* and *Out of the Past*. Such ambiguity would have been intolerable to the Spanish authorities at the time: the state which was born after the Civil War could not be questioned explicitly. There was some degree of dissidence, but it should not be allowed expression. By the end of the decade, artists, including film-makers, had learned to circumvent the demands of the censors through coded language, through the use of literary works and seeking complicity with audiences. Until then, there was a pressure to avoid any ambiguity in the representation of society. This was specially strong in the case of *film noir*. The narrative needed a clearly moralistic outcome which left no doubt as to where the limits between good and evil lay; writers had to make sure that those who transgressed got their due. In case this was not enough, *film noir* of the 1950s is explicitly used in support of the police as an institution. Films such as *Brigada criminal* (1950) opened with a text that pinned the narrative down as a mere illustration of the hard work the police does as an institution. The notion of corrupt policemen was officially an oxymoron in the world created in these films: policemen in Spain were brave, clever, unambiguously good and unhesitant in the support of the law. Literature and historical research, as well as individual experience testified to the contrary, but it was a view that could not be expressed in popular art.

Apartado de correos 1001 (1950) constitutes one of the purest examples of early *film noir* in Spain and a clear illustration of ideological pressures shaping the genre and in particular the representation of the city. The titles are preceded by a prologue that shows a series of images of Barcelona, where the film will take place, and at the same time we hear a voiceover framing the narrative. This prologue is perfectly extra-diegetic, and its function is to define the perspective from which the text that follows is to be read. The images represent a busy Spanish city at daytime, where everything seems to be running smoothly. We are shown famous sights and the streets have an air of everyday normality, cars fill the roads and tramways move along reinforcing the notion of order and stressing the presence of public service. There is nothing 'arty' about this overture, the visual style is closer to that of the touristic documentary than to *film noir*; there are no characters and it is pervaded by a detached, objective look. The (male) voiceover is clear and authoritative, as in a newsreel, and also seems to stand outside the narrative while being aware of it. Basically, it tells the audience that this is a film that attempts to bring actual facts before them, and that the images they'll see have been shot in the same streets where they happen in fiction. Finally (as in

Brigada criminal), the commentator praises the police force as a group of individuals who will defend people's right to peace and quiet from those who want to disturb it. The prologue is thus foreclosing the narrative even before it starts unraveling.

The plot follows a police investigation into a murder committed in the streets. The victim is a young man who has become caught in a scam through a fake newspaper advertisement. He comes from a small country town, which is represented as a site of a certain pre-lapsarian innocence: the light music accompanying a postman in the first sequence, as well as the fact that the young man is introduced in a shot with his father and they are seen rearing chicks, all emphasise this country idyll. As a consequence of this, the city acquires more potentially dangerous connotations: it is the place for crime, even cold-blooded murder, but in Franco's Spain criminals are always caught, peace is rarely broken and quickly re-established when it is (it will take the police three days to solve this murder case). What is more, in Franco's Spain violence and crime can only exist as an extremely marginal activity, not as a symptom for the state of things. As soon as the young man is shot (about five minutes into the narrative), the voiceover comes back to insist on the efficiency of the police as we are offered in quick succession a series of images that show how the investigation gets swiftly under way. It is important to realise how strong the pressure of official discourse between the film and reality was: in the early 1950s, crime and corruption were rife in the Spanish state, according to all reliable sources. This was indeed a very good reason to pretend that it did not exist or, at worst, that it was under control. Given that police corruption was a convention of classic *film noir*, its absence in Spanish *film noir* could be read as an attempt to give credibility to the official version.

The main narrative has two distinct genre strands: on the one hand, that of *film noir* in the washed-out Spanish version; on the other, that of documentary film. From *film noir*, the film-makers take a few stock characters and plot elements, most notably the rookie agent on his first serious mission placed alongside a more experienced cop, as well as a girl who could or could not be involved with the criminals. Yet, a condition seems to be that they lack any psychological or even typological depth (the dummy-like performances given by the actors Conrado San Martín and Manuel de Juan did not help): in this way, the policemen seem like pieces in a well-oiled machine. We are also offered a climactic chase inside a funhouse reminiscent of a similar one in Welles's *The Lady from Shanghai* (1948), as well as a small range of gestures (the cop smoking as he waits for the suspect surrounded by cigarette butts) and situations (close following of the woman on a tramway) that remind audiences that they are in *noir* territory while also stating that this world is substantially different from the state of corruption present in a film like *The Asphalt Jungle*.

In the representation of urban landscape, *Apartado de correos 1001* follows the conventions of documentary. Whereas the city in classic *film noir* tends to come alive at night, its Spanish counterpart exists mostly in the daylight. Once more, this can be read as an attempt to construct a space close to the experience of the audience. Insistence on shooting on location and in public buildings is part of the same strategy. On the one hand, the truthfulness of the film's point (that you cannot get away from the Spanish police, that they are the guardians of public welfare) is stressed, on the other hand the

Francoist city is presented as an efficient, safe, well-organised mechanism. As in *Surcos*, public transport moves along swiftly, it seems reliable and it is never overcrowded; pedestrians are always cooperative and helpful; people in cafés are always nice; streets are clean and often lined with trees; and of course everybody in the police station works in accordance with 'scientific' methods.

Apartado de correos 1001 illustrates the ideological project of early Spanish *film noir*. The tension between metaphor and metonymy in the representation of the city is kept in a stable balance. On the one hand, the city represented, we are told, stands for actual cities in which spectators live. But also this particular version of urban life is made to stand for the success of the Francoist state where *film noir* is impossible, simply because there aren't enough crooks and dark alleys.

As the 1950s progressed, new approaches to the representation of the city were attempted, but the good image of the State had to be safeguarded, mostly through narrative closure (disclaimers, unlikely moralistic endings). As one could expect, *noir* and a negative version of urban life were incompatible, as if these two aspects reinforced each other. But the city did appear associated with crime and marginality in religious films and social melodramas. Whenever marginal characters or petty criminals appeared, their treatment was mediated through national-catholic discourse.[10] In a film like *Cerca de la ciudad* (1952), petty crime is the result of lack of charity, and the figure of a priest is introduced to articulate the film's point and to guide the audience's perspective. When, in the early 1960s, a critical cinema started to appear (of very limited results given the watchful eye of the censor), films about crime were sometimes chosen to make a comment of the less attractive aspects of Spanish society. Carlos Saura's *Los golfos* (1959), for instance, features the rabble of impoverished suburbs, in the middle of waste urban landscapes never shown in *Apartado de correos 1001* or *Brigada criminal*. Also, it refuses catholic discourse to account for the protagonists' criminal behaviour. These characters are the consequence of a particular state of things that is somehow related to the ideology that ran the state (of course this was often left unsaid, it was audiences 'in the know' who had to draw their own conclusions, a typical strategy of critical cinema under Franco). But it was close to impossible to make this kind of statements too explicitly.

3. Escape from Reality: re-readings of the *noir* city in post-Franco film

The death of Franco brought about the end of censorship and consequently a new hope for Spanish film-makers. In principle, almost anything could now be portrayed in film. However, this does not necessarily mean that the relationship between the cinematic signifier and referential reality (whether social, political or historical) was straightforward and that a new transparence had been achieved. It is true that there was not a monolithic ideology shaping (or attempting to shape) images and narratives, according to restrictive patterns, in every film; and shooting on location (thereby encouraging a sense of reality) had become commonplace; however, new pressures soon started to create a new set of conventions. On the one hand there seemed to be a need to bring back the repressed. Everything that had been forbidden or under control under Franco was now brought to the foreground in film. Sex was, as expected, one of the issues audiences were expecting to see on screen and it was also something that film-makers seemed eager to explore. But so were extreme violence and historical narratives (Spanish history as a text had been a site of conflict during Francoism, and revisionist accounts were immediately reflected in films of the period). On the other hand, a new discourse on national identity arose in the late 1970s that insisted on Spain's libertarian tradition and valued freedom above everything else. In Spanish cinema of the early transition we also find a strong critical component (often, it is true, diluted in mere parody). Given that, as we have seen, any discourse explicitly questioning the *status quo* was forbidden under Franco, film-makers felt that constant denunciation of corruption is not just a right but a duty: the ugliest, most uncomfortable aspects of Spanish society were brought to the screen in the work of film-makers such as Eloy de la Iglesia, who – in a series of films from the late 1970s – explored controversial issues such as drug addiction, terrorism, the police state, party politics, homosexuality and street violence.[11]

Sex, violence and corruption are central to *film noir*, and maybe that is why the genre goes through something of a renaissance in Spain from the 1980s onwards. Thrillers were popular enough among audiences (an important aspect in a period of unrest in Spanish film industry) and they could deal with history: *Si te dicen que caí* (1989), for instance, can be read as *film noir* set in post-war Barcelona (at the same time, *noir* imagery became a way to represent the dark years of early Francoism in films like *Madregilda*, 1993). They featured strong doses of sex and graphic violence. Many of Eloy de la Iglesia's films of the period can be read as very personal thrillers in which most classic conventions are rejected and there is a strong emphasis on metonymical narration with a socially relevant message. Cities and character types in Eloy de la Iglesia's *Navajeros* (1980), *El pico* (1983) and *Colegas* (1982) were very close to those actually inhabiting the streets of Madrid or Bilbao and thus diverged from classic *noir* stereotypes, even if the plot situations as well as the moral ambiguity presented are remiscent of Hollywood thrillers. His is an urgent cinema which through often shocking images attempts to remind audiences of the social reality around them. Cities in his films are made up of hostile places, derelict estates and abandoned building sites, rooftops, dumps and shanty dwellings, showing a different side of Spanish reality. Eloy de la Iglesia eschews the metaphorical in order to portray reality as it was felt by young working class people. Very few other film-makers followed suit, and this sense of urgency will be almost absent in other urban thrillers of the period. Purer instances of classic *noir* (José Luis Garci's *El crack*, 1980) managed faithful reinscriptions of the city as a damp labyrinth and the moral ambiguity running through the genre was stretched to the point of plain cynicism. *film noir* made a comeback as pastiche.

The city in new *noir* has been appropriated by a different rhetoric, but still at this point we find that a metonymic or social reading of urban landscape is discouraged by narratives and images – Eloy de la Iglesia's attempts to encourage this reading were dismissed or even mocked by the critics. There are two instances of Spanish *film noir* in the 1990s that can illustrate how the new political situation produced new visions of the city and the conditions in which they are represented in post-modern *film noir*. Pilar

Miró's *Beltenebros* (1991) capitalises on the postmodern *noir* revival, whereas Enrique Urbizu's *Todo por la pasta* (1991) attempts a neo-*noir* look with a post-modern twist.

Beltenebros (*Prince of Darkness*) is a rather faithful adaptation of a novel by Antonio Muñoz Molina. Directed by Pilar Miró, it bears all the marks of a quality international production: literary pedigree, an international cast (Terence Stamp, Patsy Kensit, Geraldine James and John McEnnery together with José Luis Gómez and Simón Andreu), and expensive sets for a narrative that takes place in two distinct eras – 1946 and 1962). The film tells the story of Darman (Stamp), a republican agent who is sent on two separate occasions to Spain in order to eliminate a mole within the party who might be a traitor responsible for the decimation of the underground anti-Franco movement. On the first occasion, he kills the wrong man (after falling in love with his wife), and the ghost of this murder will haunt him for years. He is ordered to go back to Spain sixteen years later, in order to kill another traitor, and he complies reluctantly; during his mission, the present and the past will clash in the figure of a fascinating strip-teaser who works in a shoddy cabaret.

Following Muñoz Molina's descriptions, Madrid is imagined by Miró as a grey mausoleum. The sun hardly enters this world of eternal gloom, wrapped in a shroud nightly darkness or thick clouds. Huge buildings dwarf characters, something stressed by recurrent shots from below. People appear trapped against the ceiling and walls become oppresive. A limited colour palette featuring cold grey-blue hues, in which red seems to be limited to the lips of the strip-teaser adds to the effect of a monochrome reality. The city is represented as abandoned cinemas and warehouses, seedy nightclubs and dark streets where the glaring light of street lamps makes blackness even more threatening.

Pilar Miró and his cinematographer Javier Aguirresarrobe thus convey a metaphorical landscape which represents the oppressiveness of Franco's regime, the hopelessness of a period that was known as 'a time of silence'. Firmly rooted in *noir* conventions, corruption seems to inhabit a territory safely locked in a stylish past. This is not, it must be added, a necessary feature for any film that does not deal with a recent present. Historical reconstruction can be projected into the present and historical film can be made to enter debates on contemporary issues (an obvious recent example would be Derek Jarman's *Edward II*). However, in *Beltenebros*, every visual element, characters and events are clearly recognisable as twice removed from contemporary reality: first, because they are clearly framed in a set of circumstances that bear no relationship to contemporary Spanish issues (by 1991 Francoism was felt to be a thing of the past); secondly, and maybe even more important, because careful insistence in the *noir* look and narratives convey a sense of imagined world closer to that of thrillers such as Carol Reed's *The Third Man* (1949) than to the corruption and uncertainties of a socialist Spain. The film itself explicitly encourages a reading that will place it into the realm of fiction. The post-modern source novel deploys a series of mirror images that articulate the narrative: sentimental novels, old films (most notably *Gilda*) and duplicated events and characters (two missions, two women) ensure that audiences keep making connections among a rich intertextual tapestry that will also discourage a contemporary reading, trapping meaning into language and preventing them from becoming historically relevant for post-Francoist conditions. In the end, post-modern writing perpetuates the Francoist silence on the city by other means.

The second example is still more striking in its refusal to refer to contemporary reality. If the city in *Beltenebros* escapes the actual through historical distance and emphasis on classic genre conditions, *Todo por la pasta* seems to follow a diametrically different direction. Set in the present and shot on actual location, it makes an effort to revise convention and *noir* style in order to adapt it to reflect a recognisable urban landscape. Yet, a different set of strategies will once again prevent a metonymical, socially concerned reading.

The film opens with a shot of a motorway at dusk. A tracking shot on a car drives us on toward a city as night comes during the credits, and we hear a hammering, feverish score remiscent of Bernard Herrman's work with Hitchcock. The city is Bilbao, and we are quickly plunged into its streets, for a slice of nightlife. The camera stops at the door of a seedy nightclub (a poster advertising a 'Sado-show' is by the door) and swiftly crosses its door, leading us down a narrow staircase into the bar. On the stage, a sex act is taking place. The masochistic woman acting in the show, Azucena (María Barranco), will be one of the film's protagonists. The film's first sequence (very subtly edited to evoke a single long shot) therefore places the ensuing narrative firmly within the city: what follows is to be regarded as one among many possible stories that may happen at any moment in the busy, dirty, dangerous post-modern city. The main character is presented as part of these conditions and appears in a violent, sex-laden atmosphere. But at the same time, the film's strategy is also revealed as playful: Azucena does not seem to have her mind on her work, her screams of pain are pathetically tame (she will be told off later on) and the final effect is comic rather than shocking. Pain and sordidness are immediately revealed as show-business, a performance for people in search of cheap thrills. This tension between explicit violence and performance will be a productive strategy throughout the film.

Representation of the city follows this pattern. The landmarks of Urbizu's city are red light districts, porn cinemas, a crumbling estate, murky offices, a blood-splattered police station and an abandoned warehouse. All of these are tackled with relish by the director. Excess seems to be the main guideline for the depiction of urban life. In visual style, we are not that far from Eloy de la Iglesia's dirty realism. Yet, instead of a return to social reality, achieved through narrative earnestness, Urbizu's city is presented with baroque extravagance, emphasising language against actuality. Its ultimate reference is a textuality full of post-modern excess.

As in *The Asphalt Jungle* or *The Killing*, the narrative is sparked by a heist gone wrong. The loot was to pay for the murder of a politician who might investigate city corruption and the operation had been instigated by the police. Police inspectors, small-time crooks, young delinquents and other characters will risk their lives in order to obtain a share of the money. Anything goes in this mad chase: betrayal, violence and cold-blooded murder are revealed as the only forces in a world devoid of sentiment.

This can be transposed to the way in which the post-modern city is imagined. Of course *Todo por la pasta* does not have a serious statement to make about either contemporary life or about the post-modern city. On the contrary, the post-modern city is taken for granted, as a starting point. Whereas Francoist representations policed the relationship between the cinematic city and its real counterpart (so that, among other things, they were as dissimilar as possible), *Todo por la pasta* uses the myth for fun. The narrative still makes use of the opposition of city/countryside, which are described in similar terms to those proposed in *Surcos* and in the classic *noir* models such as *Out of the Past*: the country is still the place for honest work, for somewhat innocent people. When an old people's home (where Verónica – who will become Azucena's friend and ruthless competitor in getting the money – works) appears for the first time, the lounge music in the background provides a stark contrast with the aggressive soundtrack under the credits. However, innocence is impossible in the city, especially among the very poor. At some point, the film seems to hint at a 'sociological' view of the urban spaces: when Verónica (Kitti Manver) poses as a social worker in order to find out about the money's whereabouts, she visits a rundown housing estate. As elsewhere in the film, representation of this particular urban space emphasises degradation: dampness and gritty writing adorn the walls and the windows hardly have any panes. The flat Verónica visits is also a brothel inhabited by threatening types. Following the conventions of the national-catholic representation of urban spaces (as in *Surcos* or *Cerca de la ciudad*), this should lead the audience to feel concern or even pity for the residents of the area. It is then that, in a post-modern coup that has an element of Buñuel, the film turns convention on its head, showing how these people not only can fend for themselves but are really dangerous. The decrepit old lady who looks as she can barely move, but still brandishes a kitchen knife against Verónica, on realising that she may be not quite the social worker she pretends to be, constitutes an image at once comic and chilling. Here, Urbizu seems to eschew any sentimentality in the treatment of the poor for a cynical and grotesque treatment devoid of any social responsibility.

Like *Beltenebros* and other classic *noirs*, *Todo por la pasta* closes with an escape into the country. Azucena finally meets Verónica, who has managed to get hold of the loot by seducing the adolescent son of one of the corrupt policemen, who knows where it is hidden. The three of them establish some kind of libidinal utopia (including homoerotic feelings between the women) and run away, leaving the city behind in a road very similar to the one opening the narrative. Again, the opposition between the city and the country is symbolically resolved in favour of the latter: the city in post-modern *noir* is not even the organic, well-provided place of Francoism; it stinks and becomes almost uninhabitable. But in its visual overkill, *Todo por la pasta* finally makes the city too removed from human experience; in its narrative cynicism, the film discourages any constructive comment on contemporary problems. Urbizu presents a moral landscape in which there are no positive features, an urban nightmare for which no solution can be envisioned. Post-modern irony also keeps undermining any reading that can approach urban squalor as a problem. Narrative drive and the shock of dirty realism is all that is left.

Both *Beltenebros* and *Todo por la pasta* reflect the new ethos of post-modern representation of the city that may give us some insight into the interconnections between politics and cinema. In the 1950s, representation was explicitly political. The city on the screen was regarded as a landscape that necessarily bore a close relationship to actual cities. It was easier to change the latter than the former, and consequently representation was shaped by ideology. Symbolic and visual constructions of urban landscapes were therefore 'conservative', in that they were made to support the regime's ends. There is always a certain indeterminacy in representation and meaning cannot be pinned down completely. But it was clear that every effort was being made to erase ambiguity. Recent reinterpretations of the *noir* thriller are post-modern in upsetting this use of cinema as a part of an ideological programme. Urban landscapes are offered to us in all their grittiness, but somehow they are not 'our' urban landscapes. Far from using the impact of representation of the city to support a 'progressive' programme (one of the fears of Francoist censors), its function is merely narrative. Madrid and Bilbao are explicitly cities of the imagination, and excess in representation is possible because the connection with real cities never really comes true. In this way, *Beltenebros* refuses any comment on contemporary corruption and *Todo por la pasta* creates a world in which any politically relevant discourse is absent and narrative thrills are the only law.

Notes

1   On *noir* status as genre, see Bordwell, D., Staiger, J. and Thompson, K., *The Classical Hollywood Cinema. Film Style and Mode of Production to 1960*, London, Routledge, 1985, p.75.

2   See Krutnik, F., 'Something More than Night: Tales in the *Noir* City', in Clark, David B. *The Cinematic City* (London, Routledge, 1997).

3   See Christopher, N., *Somewhere in the Night:* film noir *and the American City*, New York, Free Press, 1997.

4   Gubern, R., *La censura: Función política y ordenamiento jurídico bajo el franquismo (1936-1975)*, Barcelona, Península, 1981.

5   See Heredero, C.F., *Las huellas del tiempo: Cine español 1951-1961*, Filmoteca de la Generalitat Valenciana, Valencia, 1993.

6   See Cueto, R. (ed.) *Los desarraigados en el cine español*, Gijón, Festival de cine de Gijón, 1998.

7   On the ideology that determined representations of urban immigration, see Gubern, R., 'Notas para una historia de la censura cinematográfica en España' in Gubern, R. and Font, D., *Un cine para el cadalso* (Barcelona, Euros, 1975).

8   This is discussed by Heredero (1993).

9   In doing this, there is a rejection of 'neorealist' aesthetics that were being tried elsewhere in Spanish cinema, see Sánchez Biosca, V., 'Fotografía y puesta en escena en el film español de los años 1940-1950' in Llinás, F. (ed.), *Directores de fotografía del cine español* (Madrid, Filmoteca Española, 1989).

10 See Martínez Bretón, J. A., *Influencia de la iglesia católica en la cinematografía española (1951-1962)*, Madrid, Harofarma, 1987.

11 See Aguilar, C. (et al.), *Conocer a Eloy de la Iglesia*, Filmoteca Vasca, San Sebastián, 1997.

References

Aguilar, C. (et al.), *Conocer a Eloy de la Iglesia*, San Sebastián, Filmoteca Vasca, 1997.

Benet, V. J., 'Notas sobre el cine policiaco español' in Hurtado, J. A. & Picó, F. M., *Escritos sobre el cine español, 1973-1987*, Valencia, Filmoteca de la Generalitat valenciana, 1989.

Bordwell, D., Staiger, J., Thompson, D., *The Classical Hollywood Cinema. Film Style and Mode of Production to 1960*, London, Routledge, 1985.

Christopher, N., *Somewhere in the Night:* film noir *and the American City*, New York, Free Press, 1997.

Clark, D. B., *The Cinematic City*, London, Routledge, 1997.

Cueto, R. (ed.), *Los desarraigados en el cine español*, Gijón, Festival Internacional de Cine de Gijón, 1998.

Gubern, R. et al., *Historia del cine español*, Madrid, Cátedra, 1995.

Gubern, R., *La censura. Función política y ordenamiento jurídico bajo el franquismo (1936-1975)*, Barcelona, Península, 1981.

Gubern, R., 'Notas para una historia de la censura cinematográfica en España' in Gubern, R. and Font, D., *Un cine para el cadalso*, Barcelona, Euros, 1975.

Heredero, C. F., *Las huellas del tiempo. Cine español 1951-1961*, Valencia, Filmoteca de la Generalitat valenciana, 1993.

Krutnik, F., *In a Lonely Street:* film noir, *Genre, Masculinity*, London, Routledge, 1991

Martínez Bretón, J. A., *Influencia de la Iglesia católica en la cinematografía española (1951-1962)*, Madrid, Harofarma, 1987

Monterde, J. E., 'Zavattini en España', in *Ciao, Za. Zavattini en España*, Valencia, Filmoteca de la Generalitat Valenciana, 1991.

Sánchez Biosca, V., 'Fotografía y puesta en escena en el film español de los años 1940-1950', in Llinás, F., *Directores de fotografía del cine español*, Madrid, Filmoteca Española, 1989.

The Clinic, the Street and the Garden: Municipal Film-making in Britain Between the Wars

Elizabeth Lebas

Introduction: Films for Modern Living

Film historians are familiar with the films of the British Documentary Movement. Recent re-appraisals of their makers' philosophy have questioned what Brian Winston has termed 'the creative treatment of actuality', showing its intellectual and narrative origins and its particular engagement with notions of evidence and mimesis.[1] From the point of view of film history, much is known about the aesthetic influences upon films of the Movement, their contemporary relations to the State and the film industry and their contribution to later documentary film and television. In turn, comparatively less has been written not by the film historian, but by the geographer and the architectural historian about their part in the reconfiguration of the national territory and national reconstruction in the 1930s and in post-war Britain.[2] This essay proposes to consider particular non-commercial films of social reform made prior to the appearance of a national documentary cinema. It suggests that these films offered a visual vocabulary for the re-imaging of worn urban spaces into spaces for a modern everyday life and as such prepared the ground for a reforming discourse on the whole of the national territory. It relates to a local cinematographic activity in the 1920s and 1930s amongst charitable societies, working men's societies, professional bodies, political organisations and in particular, municipalities.[3] Many of these films were commissioned and produced by national non-governmental institutions such as the Co-operative Society, the Central Council for Health Education, the British Red Cross Society and the Conservative Association and shown locally, but apart from films made by municipalities themselves, were not also produced locally.[4] Local authorities would however come to play a role in later documentary film-making.[5]

Characterised as films of education and persuasion, although rarely mentioned by film historians, municipal films have yet to be the subject of a full study.[6] This essay proposes therefore to introduce some of these films with the understanding that it cannot offer a comprehensive survey or analysis and only a suggestion of their worth. Of comparative rarity, usually made anonymously or by amateurs, difficult to identify from other footage in local and national archives, often of stark visual and technical simplicity, they pose a number of challenges to the researcher.

These are films in which instruction, repetition and the mundane were one. Usually between 75 and 1,500 metres in length, at first they may only divulge acts of repetitious efficiency or sequences of flowerbeds in bloom. If later film-makers wanted a claim on the 'real' without mechanical reproduction, the claim to the 'real' of the near future 'in the present' for these films is precisely that of mechanical reproduction (Winston, 1995, p. 9).[7] As 'silent' films, if they have any scenario at all, are moral tales, their address being in the second person. These are not films for national distribution in which the first person plural of the documentary film voiceover complicity addresses the class-united 'nation'. Films made by municipalities were financed by the elected, made by their officers and shown to their constituents. The spaces shown in them are the very tensions between these political constructs, as well as their resolutions. They are difficult therefore to apprehend without knowledge of the immediate physical, social and political contexts of their making and showing. And yet these municipal films altogether offer a haunting glance at urban life at the beginning of the 20th Century: without conscious effort at realism (to instruct and show how something *should* be) they show reality, not by a search for authenticity but by their very lack of artifice.

A way they can be envisaged in the widest sense is as part of the making and projection of the 'social' as a sphere of negotiation and consensus concerning rights and obligations between State and citizens following the Great War and the advent of Universal Suffrage.[8] This was a period of considerable economic restructuring and expansion of internal markets for all social classes. Legislation concerning local government, housing, education and social welfare which had been evolving since the mid-19th Century were being realised soon after the Great War as experimentations with new models and practices of social intervention and of reciprocities between State and citizens. In this, how the spaces of the making of the new collective self were represented was crucial.

Politically, if women had acquired the vote, they were also under considerable pressure from government and unions alike to withdraw from their wartime participation in the labour market into what were for many working people a new kind of family life and domestic sphere. It was women who had the main task of socialising themselves and their families into an urban life now bound by new mutual personal and collective social obligations. Central to this model partnership was being healthy. Health became a means whereby politics could be medicalised and made scientific and from this rendered social. It also sanctioned the use of new methods and technologies. In turn, messages about health were laden with political content.

The showing of moving images about health and how to achieve it within the exhausted infrastructure of the 19th-Century city, despite personal poverty, was the central purpose of municipal films and film showing. Their audience was by most of their themes – child care, hygiene, the prevention of disease – targeted at women and their children, but as they also included in the presentation of wider and more explicitly male-defined political issues such as housing and council activities, they also aimed at an audience of working men. It is difficult to know how many people saw these films over the four decades they were shown, but a previous study of the film-making activities of Bermondsey Borough Council, by far the most active municipal film-maker of the 1920s and early 1930s, estimates yearly audiences of between 15,000 and 30,000 in the 1920s and 1930s. These fell radically after the war, but in turn, the municipalities did lend and exchange their films.[9] The activities shown in the films were usually rigorously gendered. Men were the professionals, and women the recipients of body-centred instructions. When it came to the representation of the activities of the council as a whole in the public exterior spaces of the borough, men still represented official activity. There is some evidence to show that children of both sexes viewed the films but that adult men and women viewed them separately (Lebas, 1995). Tuberculosis however, united all. In a film entitled *Consumption* made by Bermondsey Borough Council in 1931, a young tubercular man is the 'hero' of the film. The representation of the married working class couple as object of a social message had yet to be fully invented.

That living and working conditions themselves were the causes of diseases like tuberculosis, rickets and diphtheria, also provided the possibility of showing the ways whereby the urban environment itself could also become 'healthy' and implicitly also raise new kinds of collective expectations.[10] Films could show both procedure and progress in ways that were practical, succinct and even entertaining.[11] In turn, by showing the actual sites and settings of procedure and progress to inhabitants who were called upon to visit them and in the case of new housing estates, actually occupy them, they played a vital role in assigning and re-designating new spaces for another way of living. Films were shown for free in town halls, clinics, schools, youth clubs, working-men's clubs, political associations, the courtyards of housing estates, public gardens and in the streets. All highly regulated spaces, but nonetheless spaces which had also been acquired by reform and sometimes struggle. Their images showed how old spaces were being re-used for collective purposes, what new kinds of spaces looked like, and sometimes where they actually were. They functioned as a means of recognition and reassurance and made symbolic links between past and present and present and future at a time when visually these links were neither fractured nor emphasised by architectural modernism. Council administrative buildings were often in neo-classical style, but when it came to the provision of health services such as tuberculosis treatment centres and maternity and child health clinics, councils had to make do with whatever premises they could find.[12]

Until the advent of the National Health Service in 1948, public health was under the aegis of local authorities and the Ministry of Health. Municipal Public Health Departments had a wide remit which besides implementing preventative measures concerning hygiene and disease, also had the duty of condemning insanitary housing. A duty which with the reorientation of housing policy in the late 1920s towards central city slum clearance and overcrowding, gave them considerable powers. These were powers which directly contributed to the clearance and regularisation of the 19th-Century industrial urban environment, but which at the same time, due to the scale of public investments required for new construction, resulted in comparative failure. Overcrowding in Britain's central cities did not really decline until after the Second

War and while the building of flats contributed a new architectural typology to the urban landscape, they could not solve the local housing problem. Nevertheless, municipal Public Health Departments were not only usually the most powerful executive arm of local councils, but they were also staffed by professionals who had a considerable legacy of urban intervention and an intimate knowledge of the bodies and living conditions of those whom they served. Public Health Departments who had produced photographic records of slums and their dwellers since the late 19th Century were the main instigators of this cinematographic activity.[13] In showing living conditions, both old and new, as council officials they were responding to two kinds of audiences: the audience which had the power to change things, the councillors, and the audience living under them, the citizens.

In turn, municipalities as a local tier of government were subject to national social and fiscal policy, yet, far more than now, they also had considerable fiscal autonomy and jealously guarded their political and geographical territory. As they were financed by the municipality and shown on non-commercial premises, municipal films may not have been subjected to the Censors and thus could play a relatively independent role in promoting a municipal culture and in enlarging the parameters of local identity.[14] Many boroughs had been created from the amalgamation of vestries only at the turn of the century and struggled to overcome parish politics and neighbourhood insularity. To do this, municipalities not only had to publicise their activities and become the holders of the future in the local and everyday sense, they also had to include and incorporate their constituents as they lived in the present. Many films were also the municipal records of achievements and events and of the settings in which these took place and were shown as propaganda, collective chronicle and celebration. The films showed the geographical location of new services and sites as they showed council officials in the performance of their professional duties, and thus could be associated together with site, authority, identity and reassurance. As films were shot locally and shown locally, viewers often could also recognise themselves in them and in this way a very complex identification between image and reality could take place. On film, ordinary life and ordinary people were incorporated into something meaningful and epic. Yet, unlike later documentary films, these were not films *about* modern living, but *for* modern living, peopled by those who could individually as well as collectively recognise themselves in settings which already existed and were defined as immediately practicable and politically attainable.

Of the local authorities who commissioned or made municipal films between the wars thirteen have been identified, although few of their films have survived.[15] Certainly, many more local authorities only showed instructional, including municipal films. Special distributors such as Community Interest Films, S.C.D. and the Central Council for Health Education existed for this purpose.[16] Local authorities never showed commercial feature films. The reasons for this were complex. Firstly, they would not compete with local commercial rate-paying cinemas. Moreover, private consumption gave viewers an individual choice to view. The claim which municipalities made on their viewers was entirely different and underlined the emergent separation between the social realm of the State and an increasingly commodified popular culture. The claim was one of time, not money and if the viewer had a right to view films without charge, he or she also often had an obligation to do so under a variety of education, infant and maternity welfare and public health acts. Behind this was also an ongoing debate within Labour about the frivolity and depoliticising nature of feature films.[17] Of the film-making local authorities identified, many had a Labour majority in strongly socialist areas and as Tim Boon has pointed out, also had almost by virtue of a combination of poverty and socialism influential Public Health Departments (Boon, 1999).

The films essentially showed images of two kinds of processes: on the one hand, how to cure and prevent disease and stay healthy, and on the other, the process of municipal engagement. Uniting them was the slogan central to Bermondsey Borough Council's entire political engagement but implicit elsewhere: 'Prevention is Better than Cure' (Lebas, 1995). With this practical philosophy underwritten by prudence and responsibility, a wide remit of intervention could be legitimated. Below, we briefly explore how the representation of three spaces controlled municipally – the street, the clinic and the public garden – expressed this philosophy and underwrote negotiations between the self and the collective, and between the collective and the popular to create new spheres of shared values. The examples used are mainly from the films made by Bermondsey Borough Council, a unique film-maker in producing 30 known films between 1923 and 1938 (Lebas, 1995).

Locating Municipal Films

Much of this film-making and film commissioning was to decline after the advent of sound in the early 1930s. Bermondsey Borough Council however attempted separate phonograph recording for a couple of films.[18] Sound required studios and introduced equipment beyond the technical and financial reach of most municipalities, although municipal films were not reliant on recorded sound. They were always shown as part of a spoken lecture and to capture their audiences could draw upon surviving pre-cinematographic cultural traditions – the lantern slide show, the scientific demonstration, the music hall, street preaching, and the postcard.[19] As during the summer months films were often shown outdoors, even the quality of sound amplification available in the largest commercial cinemas would have been inadequate.

The Film Quota introduced in 1927 to compete against American imports and to promote a national film industry, and the setting up of the Central Office of Information and in war-time, the Ministry of Information, were national political forces which also contributed to the centralisation and codification of imagery. Although much has been written about the philosophy and aesthetics of what emerged as the Documentary Film Movement as a result of this centralisation and nationalisation, little is known about the influence local non-commercial films may have had on the Movement and in turn whether films of the Documentary Movement contributed to the decline of municipal film-making. Certainly the convention of showing scenes of 'before and after' and fascination with the servicing and manufacturing processes are in evidence in both municipal and documentary films – *Oppin*, a film made by Bermondsey Borough Council in 1930 on the less than hygienic living conditions in the

Kent hop fields, shows a long sequence devoted to the preparation of hops. Moreover, opinion is divided on the popularity of documentary films. Film documentarists made claims which were not supported by evidence.[20] In any event, if municipal film-making declined irreversibly by the mid-1930s, their particular audiences did too. Glasgow Corporation was a noteworthy exception, but by the 1940s their films, like the older municipal films, were mostly for viewing by children in school.

By the late 1930s some metropolitan governments were commissioning sound films. In 1939 Realist Films released *The Londoners* directed by John Taylor and made to commemorate 50 years of the London County Council. This somewhat quirky film, part docu-drama, part 'heritage film' and part demonstration of the metropolitan government's activities, has close connections with the countless commercial newsreels and travelogues hitherto made on London. It is also similar to the many other films made by the film documentarists in this period (and during the Second World War) in which London was used as a backdrop to demonstrate new technology, or to convey the imperial message of London as 'first city of the Empire', or to exemplify the nation's courage during the Blitz, and finally, to illustrate policies of national reconstruction.[21] There is no evidence to show that this film, initially shown in commercial cinemas, was commissioned by the London County Council (LCC), nor that the LCC ever made its own films. Metropolitan London was perhaps too large and complicated to identify with other than as emblem and concept.

However, in 1939 Paul Rotha produced a film for Manchester Corporation which was released in 1947 entitled *A City Speaks: a film of Local Government in England.* It is not known why this film was released several years after the war. It is very likely that the precise geographical documentation of specific places was classified information. Certainly, wartime documentary films, even films featuring London, are not spatially detailed. The film as a whole bears close comparison with Rotha's *Land of Promise* made in 1945 and its closing caption places it firmly within the socio-political philosophy of the Documentary Movement: 'This film is dedicated by the citizens of Manchester to all those whose courage and energy will create the cities of the future.' In 1947, West Ham, the first local authority in Britain to have a Reconstruction Committee, commissioned Stanley Read, later Director of the British Film Institute, to make a film on its reconstruction activities entitled *Neighbourhood 15.* If *Neighbourhood 15* was a film of post-war reconstruction like the many others produced by the Ministry of Information, as Nicholas Bullock has noted, it was far more in the tradition of the municipal film, showing not the promises of things to come, but what the council was actually doing. As with Bermondsey's *Some Activities of Bermondsey Borough Council* (1931), this is direct filming of those actually carrying out rebuilding and here too the viewer is invited to identify directly with his or her own neighbourhood and relate its progress to the unique approach of their municipality (Bullock, 1997).

Glasgow Corporation had already commissioned Gaumont to make a film in 1922, when John Wheatley, future Minister of Health under the first Labour Government of 1924, was then Chair of its Housing Committee. The film, entitled *Glasgow's Cattle Market and Housing Programme* shows the marble staircase of the town hall, Merklands' cattle wharf, council house-building and includes sequences of gardens also used in a film commissioned from Gaumont the same year, *Parks Department*. These are the first known municipal films which shows the council's activities by showing the spaces under its control. That same year, John Maclean, as candidate for Glasgow municipal elections, had proposed the municipalisation of working-class leisure and a municipal film policy (Hogenkamp, 1989, p. 20).

In the 1930s and after the War, Glasgow Corporation continued its cinematographic activities making both silent and sound films. It is beyond the scope of this essay to give an account of the entirety of its production and evolution, but some comparisons can be suggested between it and the other committed earlier municipal film-maker of the interwar, Bermondsey Borough Council.

A silent film made in 1935, *Sadness and Gladness* relates the transformation which take place in the lives of two working-class sisters when they go on holiday at a summer camp supported by the Education Department's Committee on Necessitous Children. The scenes depicted are not unlike those of a film made by Bermondsey Borough Council in 1929, *The Shirley Schools*. Shots of poor and overcrowded streets showing ill-clad children are juxtaposed to the council's 'place in the country' where children romp in the sunshine. The difference between the two films is not only stylistic. *Sadness and Gladness* is a narrative constructed from the point of view of the children, while *The Shirley Schools* has a static pictorial quality and basically shows children doing gymnastics on a sunlit lawn to a row of assembled dignitaries. The difference is that of the changes which had taken place in national social policy in the intervening years. Bermondsey's Shirley Schools were country orphanages: as the opening caption of the film delicately states, they were 'For orphans or for children of parents, who owing to circumstances, are unable to keep them' and managed under the Poor Laws, still then in operation, by the Bermondsey Board of Guardians. While the closing scenes of *Sadness and Gladness* show the girls coming home to waiting parents and a father with a job, those of *The Shirley Schools* show an adolescent boy and girl dressed in the set of clothes provided for them leaving to fill the situations for which they have been trained for.

These two Socialist municipalities nonetheless were the only ones known who made films explicitly for children, but their tone is marked by their difference in time and while Bermondsey's *Where's There's Life, There's Soap* (1927), a film on how to practice personal hygiene, was whimsical and street-wise and delighted in transgression, treating the audience to a close-up of a smelly armpit, the 12 films produced in 1949 as part of the Glasgow Civic Films series by the Education Department were to stimulate citizenship among junior secondary school children, showed with a voiceover worthy scenes of the Corporation's museums, water supply, hospitals and parks. If Bermondsey's children sang out loud as they crowded around the cinema van, it is unlikely that Glasgow's children sitting at their school desks with their complimentary textbooks sang too.

In the meantime, as previously mentioned, government institutions and some private ones such as the British Commercial Gas Association, were commissioning documentary films. But these films were putting forward issues of national debate promoted by a National Government for national rather than local audiences. The people had acquired the practice of voting, of identifying with their municipality, of being responsible for their own health, and of behaving appropriately in spaces under the aegis of the council. By the end of the 1930s, the question of the remaking of the city as a whole, its relation to its hinterland as source of water and leisure, the problem of regional imbalance and the physical and economic reconfiguration of the entire national territory had become part of a national agenda about which the government wished to inform its citizens. The planner and the architect now replaced the doctor and the nurse as figure of authority and the medical discourse itself was evolving away from the immediacy of the body towards questions of environmental pollution and food supply.[22] In the post-war period, New Towns such as Harlow were the subject of films, some made for television, to promote New Towns policy and attract residents (Gold & Ward, 1994, 1997). Their audiences may have originated from the bombed-out central cities, but what they saw were not films *for* modern living but *about* modern living in spaces not of their making.

Nevertheless, despite the cinematographic nationalisation of the social agenda, local authorities continued to produce film footage, sometimes with sound and in colour, into the 1960s and even early 1970s. The East Anglian Film Archives carry a number of films which were made or commissioned either by Norwich City Council or given by local amateur film makers to the Council. Perhaps the last truly municipal film about council activities made for local viewing is *Proud City* (1955, 1,600 feet, sound and colour) by W.G. Kemp for Norwich City. Although not viewed, film notes suggest a simple update of Glasgow Corporation's *Glasgow's Cattle Market and Housing Programme* (1922). The cattle market, public gardens and council housing are shown, as are the police, fire and Civil Defence services, an old people's home and the local golf club.

In the 1970s and early 1980s the Greater London Council and other local authorities were to revive, now with the aid of the video, film-making activity.[23] Although supported rather than made by the council and now part of cultural rather than public health policy, these video films made by local community groups retain some of the imagery of their forebears.[24] By the early 1950s even national audiences for civic films had almost disappeared and film production had been reduced to disparate footage of municipal events, gardens and housing estates informally taken by local amateurs and councillors with their Super-8 cameras. The films had become nostalgic souvenirs of municipal rituals.

The Clinic, the Street and the Garden

In briefly considering how the municipal camera re-articulated social spaces, the spaces of the clinic, the street and the garden take on new allegorical meanings of public and private, lightness and darkness, town and country, popular celebration and government. The symbolisation of reform in the early 20th Century associated Christian imagery of the passage from darkness to light with a medical enthusiasm for radiation and light. Film became alive with light and captured the body on which the brightest light was shed.

The reform of the body was the point of departure for the reform of the entire national territory and the focus of municipal films. The camera moved closely over the working body – its bowed legs, varicose veins, knarled feet and pitted surface like a surveyor moved over wasteland, pointing to wrong, indicating remedy and warning. Always warning. The body was surveyed as a landscape, worn and derelict before its time, but still possible of reform if subject to sunshine and fresh air. If the starting point of reform was the body as wasteland, the endpoint was the body politic as pastoral landscape. In war-time and post-war reconstruction documentary films, the damaged city has replaced the damaged body, but it too can be repaired by the redemptive powers of nature. In these films, Britain, the most urban of all nations, is first and foremost 'this sceptered isle'. Its reform is firstly about its reconstitution into something imagined as it once was.

The site of this reform, and its showing, was the clinic and the solarium. The first film shown publicly by Bermondsey Borough Council was in 1922 to a group of women attending one of its 12 maternity and child health clinics. It was on venereal disease. Films about the treatment of shell shock in a clinical setting had already been made during the Great War and continued to be made during the Second World War.[25] What municipal films show is not only the interiors of clinics and their technology, but how to behave in them in order to be processed. Undressed babies are firmly sat on the knees of doctors and nurses in stark, white rooms. In a darkened room, children in loin cloths parade in an orderly fashion around a brilliant sun lamp, while naked babies wearing goggles quietly lie in cots as they are being radiated. Men offer their bared chests to the X-ray machine. The message is clear. Active consent to passive treatment is what will make you better and prevent you from dying. To disrobe and offer your body to science is the point of departure between the past and the present and what is to come.

Such scenes of a new private ceremony are repeated in scenes of public ceremony. Municipal power makes an heroic and class identification with the national body politic. By the early 1920s, films of processions and opening ceremonies were a genre firmly established by the newsreel and the amateur film-maker. A film made in 1913 by the owner of the Peckham Hippodrome for the council is a record of the Second National Alexandra Rose Day. It shows dignitaries arriving at the Town Hall to women selling artificial flowers. These appear to be the dignitaries' wives.[26] The scene is repeated – but only with the Duchesses entourage – in early 1930s footage from Bermondsey captioned 'Visit of HRH Duchess of Kent'. A 1915, Gaumont Graphic newsreel, '*Bermondsey Welcomes its Hero: Coporal Holmes, V.C.*' is echoed in a 1945 film of heart-stopping actuality made by an unknown commercial photographer, *V.E.Day Parade in Hackney*. The film shows a motorcade headed by Montgomery of all the army units, including an extremely rare shot of the Army Film Unit progressing down Cambridge Heath Road. In turn, Bermondsey historically expressed its own socialist position with *May Day March 1938*. Footage begins with a procession leaving Bermondsey with Trade Union banners and a 'Here Comes Health' float and a May Queen Float, and arriving to Hyde Park. The camera closes in on banners proclaiming 'Stop War, Vote Labour' and 'Fascist Destruction'.

The genre of the celebratory newsreel was to be taken up repeatedly by the municipalities. The opening ceremony of housing estates and civic centres became stock footage in the 1930's and followed a strict convention. There is a long shot of a seated audience of local people (possibly the new tenants) and councillors in a closed-off clean and empty street, closing in on a shot of the podium at which the Mayor, the Mayoress and other dignitaries are seated, followed by a close-up of the Mayor giving a speech and concluding with a scene of the Mayor at the door of a new dwelling giving keys to a young couple, or of dignitaries mounting the steps of the new building. This is a municipal copy of national political ritual where local worthies can be identified and embodied by the image and in which a new spatial typology can be unquestionably associated to council property.

In another type of film, the decontamination film, ritual and spatial sequencing are used to arrive at a similar outcome. *Preston Slum Clearance* (1937) by Preston Public Health Department, was made in connection with national slum clearance legislation and already has documentary features. A map of the entire clearance area is used to explain the process of implementation. The film opens with a scene of slum children carrying rubbish which closes in on two council workmen arriving to the door of a house marked with an X to signify its status as an infected premise. Scenes of the removal of the house's content and the technical process of decontamination almost identical to those of Hackney's Public Health Department's *Decontamination of the Home*, 1938, follow. The film ends with a scene of two dignitaries standing by new council housing with the Union Jack flying overhead.

Interestingly, the films of Bermondsey Borough Council do not contain abject scenes of personal dispossession or scenes of municipal notables. In *Some Activities of Bermondsey Borough Council* (1931), anonymous mattresses and undergarments are readied for the Council's shining new gas chamber by council workmen (what can't be radiated is gassed). Nor do they show local dignitaries and their wives or municipal functions. When dignitaries are filmed, it is at their work. In *Glasgow's Cattle Market and Housing Programme* the whole council is shown in session. In a Bermondsey film, *Consumption* (1932), the story of a young man's management of tuberculosis, Dr. Salter, physician and M.P. for Bermondsey, plays himself.

The street itself is the subject of new representations. It is the setting for appropriate behaviour. In a scene shown in *Consumption* and re-used in *Where's There's Life, There's Soap*, injunction against spitting in the street is shown by a young man spitting into his handkerchief. By the cinematographic process, space is enlarged into what is desired. In *Some Activities of Bermondsey Borough Council* (1931) the Council's street tree planting activities – and new garden suburb – are represented in a long panning shot which turns what is in reality a very short street into a formal avenue. What is also desired is a new kind of woman, and in *Health and Clothing* (1928) she appears, young and slim in a short simple dress striding down that very same street. This appeared to be the only 'modern' street in Bermondsey.

The contrast between the closing scene of *Health and Clothing* and footage of ordinary street life also by Bermondsey Borough Council, *Tower Bridge Road Market* (1931) is more than the tension between 'us' as we are, and 'she' as she ought to be.

While the young woman in *Health and Clothing* is filmed head on, walking towards the camera, the people in *Tower Bridge Road Market* are filmed from a first floor window, the only such angle in all the Council's films. The street and its people become spectacles of themselves.[27] But for us now, for a few moments, the faces that turn up to the camera are what we would have been and we can recognise our past selves in the municipal family album, for this was the purpose of these incidental scenes and unedited footage. During the film lectures they served as an integrating *divertissement*, a gesture to the intrinsic importance of the viewers themselves, not as they ought to be, but as they were to themselves, made heroic by the camera.

Street scenes were not, however, as frequently shown as scenes of public gardens and flower beds. The most unedited of footage, its meaning is probably the most complex and even the most allusive interpretation is beyond the scope of this essay (Lebas, forthcoming). Public parks and gardens were about far more than rest and hygiene or places where working people could observe and emulate the behaviour of their betters. In London, many, if not most public gardens were created over graveyards and thus served the double purpose of deconsecrating them and reincorporating their dead into the municipal realm. Parks and public gardens were also effective ways of exploding the secret passages of the slum and engaging in speculative gentrification. Victoria Park in London is a good example of an attempted partnership in the 1860s between the London Metropolitan Board of Works and speculators. Created to break up East End slums and to promote new middle-class neighbourhoods near the City, it came to offer a great gathering space for protest marches into the West End.The bland sunlit footage of public gardens and flowerbeds appear to deny their existence as spaces laden with death and ambiguity and contradiction, only to project images of what already exists and everybody agrees on. Public parks and gardens had existed since the mid-19th Century and as such do not show new municipal policies and achievements. What they show is the working-classes at rest in an appropriate way and the experience of calm and abundance which the council also provided for the health of its citizens. Gardens were exuberantly planted in a heavy Victorian style in stark contrast to scenes of technical progress in purpose-built interiors. That they were valued spaces to both municipality and people is obvious by the amount of footage devoted to them. Bermondsey Borough Council even made a colour film of its famous flower beds in 1938. Public gardens were about a claim to arcadian possibilities, a representation of respectability and horticultural care and prowess. They also represent what documentary and reconstruction films will later show – a sovereignty over all the different parts of the collective territory and everyday life which will be extended from the borough to the nation.

How many municipalities made films and how many of them have survived is difficult to estimate. Many films were destroyed during the Second World War and traces of their existence often exist only in the surviving minutes of municipal councils and damaged miscellaneous footage. Some films were donated to the National Film archives after the establishment of the National Health Service in 1948 and the dissolution of municipal Public Health Departments. During the course of this research, *V.E. Day Parade in Hackney* (1945) made by a local commercial photographer for Hackney Council was found in Hackney Archives. Footage from Bermondsey Borough's Public Health Department, including scenes of the 1937 May Day Parade in Hyde Park, a *sortie d'usine* and of a lecture on civil defence was found in 1992 in the basement of Peckham Library. N*eighbourhood 15* was located in a drawer in Tower Hamlets' Planning Department. Scattered among local and regional archives or in private possession, there are still finds to be made. Municipal films are first and foremost films made by a particular and historically located kind of political authority. One which both incorporated and contributed to create a form of social consensus which was to last well into the 20th Century. The films gave modern credibility and legitimacy to this local political authority and at the same time have left behind images and messages of itself as almost distant past. Municipal films are among the footage which offers the greatest veracity about the appearance of actual urban places and spaces and of ordinary people of the early 20th Century. They reach us as documents which we can neither yet quite understand or ignore but which remind us of the urgency of doing so for the making of a new political conception of place.

Notes

1   Winston, B., *Claiming the Real. The Documentary Film Revisited*, London, BFI, 1995. Sussex, E., *The Rise and Fall of the British Documentary*, Berkeley, University of Calfornia Press, 1975.

2   Bullock, N., 'Imagining the Post-War World. Architecture, Reconstruction and the British Documentary Film Movement', in Penz, F. & Thomas, M. (eds.), *Cinema and Architecture, Méliés, Mallet-Stevens, Multimedia* (London, BFI, 1997), pp. 52-61. Gold, J.R. and Ward, S.V., '"We're Going to do it Right this Time": Cinematic Representations of Urban Planning and British New Towns, 1939-1951' in Aitkens, S. C. & Zonn, L. (eds.), *Places, Power, Situation and Spectacle: a Geography of Film* (Savage, Maryland, Rowman and Littlefield, 1994), and "Of Plans and Planners. Documentary Film and the Challenge of the Urban Future, 1935-1952", in Clark, D. B. (ed.), *The Cinematic City*, London, Routledge, 1997.

3   See Hogenkamp, B., *Deadly Parallels. Films and the Left in Britain, 1929-1939*, London, Lawrence and Wishart, 1986. As Hogenkamp relates, independent and local film viewing began early in Britain and tended to be associated with the political left. In 1929 the Federation of Workers' Film Societies was established with Ralph Bond as founding member in opposition to the less radical Masses Stage and Film Guild which included among its members Labour Cabinet Ministers George Lansbury and Fenner Brockway both close to Dr. Alfred Salter, ILP MP for Bermondsey. Salter was to play a decisive role in promoting film making by Bermondsey Borough Council.

4   Hogenkamp, pp. 176-78. The Labour Party was much slower to respond to the use of films for political propaganda, forming a Joint Film Committee only in 1936 for whom Paul Rotha wrote a pamphlet entitled *Films and the Labour Party*. Nothing came of it.

5   Recent work by Boon written from the viewpoint of the production of a national discourse on public health between the wars, has significantly begun to rectify this absence. See Chapter 4, 'Medical Officers of Health as Health Film Producers' in *Films and Contestation of Public Health in Interwar Britain*, unpublished PhD thesis, University of London, 1999. It is clear that by the mid-1930's local authorities saw themselves as key players in the imagining of a national urban policy. For example, the final credits of *The Great Crusade. The Story of a Million Homes* (1936) on national slum clearance policy produced by Fred Watts for Pathe Pictures Ltd. gives thanks to J.B. Priestley and local authorities for their help with the scenario.

6   The work of Rachel Low still represents the most comprehensive empirical survey of non-commercial cinema of the period, but does not characterise locally made films as such and only mentions the films made by Bermondsey Borough Council. See for example, *The History of the British Film, 1918-1929*, (1971), *The History of the British Film, 1929-1939*, (1979), *Films of Comment and Persuasion* (1985), London, Allen and Unwin. An exception to this is Boon (1999).

7   Boon (1999) makes this very point. Acting, editing and a scenario were perceived as deflecting from the point which was being made. The 'plot' was considered self-evident. For example, a comparatively late silent film made in 1935 by the City of Birmingham Public Health Department, *Diphtheria: Prevention is Better Than Cure* (15 mins.) consists essentially of one child after another being inoculated with Diphtheria vaccine.

8   Lebas, E., Magri, S. & Topalov, C., 'Reconstruction and Popular Housing after the First World War: a comparative study of France, Great Britain, Italy and the United States', *Planning Perspectives*, 6, 1991, pp. 249-67.

9   Lebas, E., '"When Every Street Became a Cinema", The Film Work of Bermondsey Borough Council's Public Health Department, 1923-1953', *History Workshop Journal*, Issues 39, 1995, pp. 42-56.

10 As N. Pronay and D.W. Spring have shown, the expansion of the electorate from 1918 for the first time included the working-class which had fought and died during the Great War and had also acquired a new militancy and its own means of propaganda. It was therefore essential that new communications technologies, particularly film, be firmly under government control. There is no doubt that municipalities played a propaganda role. See 'Introduction' in Pronay, N., & Spring, D.W. (eds.), *Propaganda, Politics and Film, 1918-1945* (London and Basingstoke, The Macmillan Press, 1982).

11 As Dr. Connan, Chief Medical Officer of Bermondsey Borough Council and maker with Mr. Bush, Chief Adminstrative Officer and Mr. Lumley, radiographer, of the films of Bermondsey Borough Council explained with regards to his theory of the usefulness of film, 'There is a distinct advantage over the lantern slide, for instead of showing a single act, the film can demonstrate process, and thus relate cause and effect' (*Sanitary Report of the Metropolitan Borough of Bermondsey*, 1925, p. 68).

12 Lebas, E., 'The Making of a Socialist Arcadia: Arboriculture and Horticulture in Bermondsey After the First World War', *Journal of Garden History*, forthcoming 1999. One way of making these premises identifiable was for the municipality to tend front gardens and provide window boxes in a distinctive style.

13 Tagg, J., *The Burden of Representation: Essays on Photographies and Histories*, London –Basingstoke, Macmillan, 1988. Booth (1999) identifies from *The Health Education Yearbook, 1939* , five local authority Public Health Departments having made health educational films: Bermondsey, Camberwell, Holborn, Hounslow and Willesden – all London boroughs.

14 Under the 1909 *Cinematographic Act*, local authorities had the responsibility for ensuring the safety of film exhibition and although the British Board of Censors was set up in 1912, it appears that municipal films were not submitted to the Censors. Finance was a more critical issue. The films made were cheap and easily absorbed into the councils' budget. There is some evidence to show that early and expensive film stock could be filed under expenses for radiographic film. See Lebas, 1995. Gillian Rose has written on the role municipalities plays in forming new working-class identities: see Rose, G., 'Locality, Politics and Culture: poplar in the 1920s', *Environment and Planning D: Society and Space*, 1988, pp. 395-408.

15 Those identified are Aberdeen Borough Council, Birmingham Corporation, Bermondsey Borough Council, Bristol Borough Council, Camberbwell Borough Council Dagenham Borough Council, Glasgow Corporation, London Borough of Hounslow, Hereford County Council, Hackney Borough Council,

Lambeth Borough Council, London County Council, Manchester Corporation, Preston Borough Council and Willesden Borough Council.

16 Bermondsey Borough Council in fact rationalised making its own films on the grounds that rentals were too expensive. See Lebas 1995.

17 Jones, S.G., *The British Labour Movement and Film, 1918-1939*, London, Routledge and Kegan Paul, 1987.

18 Connan D. & Bush, H., *Better Than Cure: A Handbook on Public Health Propaganda*, London, Douglas, 1927.

19 Lebas, 1995 and 'Films and Film Footage in Local Authority Archives: an Experience', *The Hackney Terrier. Friends of Hackney Archives Newsletter*, nos. 20 and 21, 1990-191.

20 For example, see Swann, P., *The British Documentary Film Movement, 1926-1946*, Phd. Thesis, University of Leeds, 1979 and The Arts Enquiry, PEP, *The Factual Film*, Oxford, OUP, 1947.

21 Sorensen, C., *London on Film*, London, Museum of London Publications, 1996.

22 See Boon, T., '"The Smoke Menace": Cinema, Sponsorship and the Social Relation of Science in 1937' in Shortland, M. (ed.), *Science and Nature. Essays in the History of the Environmental Sciences* (London, British Society for the History of Science, 1993), pp. 57-88. Also by the same author, 'Agreement and Disagreement in the Making of "World of Plenty"' in Smith, D. F. (ed.), *Nutrition in Britain. Science, Scientists and Politics in the Twentieth Century* (London – New York, Routledge, 1997).

23 Prior to its dismantlement by the Conservative Government of Mrs. Thatcher in 1987, the Greater London Council was a strong promoter of local cultural production and funder of locally made and shown films, often in association with the Independent Film, Video and Photography Association which remains very active. These tended to be issues based films with poor housing, council neglect and homelessness as the main themes, but could also put forward the community's critical appraisal of the municipality's policies as *Biteback*, made in 1985 by the Alternative Strategy Project community group – a film funded by the London Borough of Tower Hamlets.

24 A slum interior with walls sweating with damp and crawling with vermin are a recurrent image of municipal slum clearance films. See for example, *Preston Slum Clearance* produced by Preston Borough Council in 1938, three years after Edward Ansty's *Housing Problems* funded by the British Commercial Gas Association. Bermondsey Borough Council's films never showed the poor in their own interiors, only close-ups of delapidated walls – not because appalling housing conditions did not exist, as Public Health Committee Minutes poignantly attest, but probably out of respect for its inhabitants. Housing films of the 1970s and 1980s made by community groups show almost identical images and became known as 'damp patch films'. However, if interwar films on slum conditions show scenes of dreadful interiors, these were almost invariably followed by a resolution – scenes of council workmen arriving to fumigate or of building sites of new council housing. In the more recent films, the detriorated housing *is* council housing and there is no municipal resolution. Owner-occupation was on its way.

25 For example, *Neuro-Psychiatry*, produced by Basil Wright in 1943.

26 Smith N., *Films and Local Studies*, unpublished manuscript of a talk given by Southwark Local Studies Archivist, circa 1990.

27 For a discussion of the fascination of ordinary street scenes in early cinema, see Gunning, T., 'Urban Spaces in Early Silent Film. From Kaleidoscope to X-Ray', Department of Comparative Studies, University of Copenhagen, 1994.

Centre, Periphery and Marginality in the Films of Alain Tanner

Lieve Spaas

In his brief study on space in cinema, Russian semiotician, Jurij Lotman, draws attention to the contradiction that exists between the confined space of cinema within the frame of the screen and the unlimited space of the world to which cinema inevitably refers. Strictly speaking, space in cinema is located within the perimeters of the screen, but a distinction must be made between the visible space on the screen and that which lies beyond the screen and is recognised as such by the viewer. Lotman argues that in cinematography, more than in other visual arts, images which fill the inner bounds of artistic space 'attempt actively to break it up, to surge beyond its boundaries'.[1] American film theoretician Noël Burch, who chose to live and work in France, also draws attention to the twofold nature of cinematographic space, that which is shown in the shot and that which the viewer knows to exist outside the shot.[2] French narratologist André Gardies makes a further distinction and differentiates between the 'here' – the space visible on the screen, the 'there' – the invisible space contiguous to that on the screen, and the 'elsewhere', – the space that is neither visible nor contiguous to the screen but is suggested by a character, or evoked through sound and dialogue.[3] For the three critics mentioned, 'space' is in the first instance textual, that is to say, a self-contained system which emerges from a specific film itself. These theoretical models have contributed considerably to developing our attentiveness to the creation of cinematic space.

My aim in this study is to set out from these critics' categories but extend them in two ways. Firstly, I shall extend the notion of space beyond the physical space on and off the screen and examine how we can infer a social space from the physical space. Both Lotman and Gardies pave the way for such an extension: Lotman stresses that space in cinematography is 'isomorphic to the unlimited space of the world' (Lotman, 1976, p. 83), whilst Gardies emphasises the cultural knowledge the spectators bring to bear when seeing a film and which will make them perceive a spatial dimension beyond the strictly filmic one. Secondly, I shall go beyond the individual film and take an 'auteur' approach, that is to say, examine space, not just in a single film, but in the entire *oeuvre* of a film-maker whose specific personal style remains discernable in his films and who, therefore, attains the status of an 'auteur' film-maker. The style may evolve, but the director's 'signature', so to speak, remains in evidence. 'Auteur' examples include famous directors such as Alfred Hitchcock, Howard Hawkes, Jean

Renoir, and Orson Welles but also less illustrious, yet well-established directors, such as Agnès Varda and Alain Tanner. It is the latter one I shall be dealing with here.

One of Switzerland's foremost film-makers, Tanner was instrumental in drawing international attention to Swiss cinema and became the dominant figure of the 'new Swiss cinema', which based itself on, and freed itself from, the celebrated Swiss tradition of documentary. It was firmly rooted in Francophone Switzerland, '*la Suisse romande*', but also showed awareness of the cultural complexity within Switzerland, which is a mosaic of four linguistic regions subdivided in twenty cantons, six semi-cantons and one federal city, Berne. Such division makes a 'national cinema' virtually impossible. Moreover, it was not until the 1960s that the art of 'cinema' was recognised in Switzerland's Federal Constitution. Tanner was subsequently instrumental in promoting fiction film and in obtaining equal status for fiction film and documentary.

Tanner's film career spans over 40 years and constitutes a kind of journey at once cinematographic, geographic and ideological. His interest in cinema prompted him to collaborate with Claude Goretta in a Ciné-Club, when he was a student of economics at the University of Geneva. The only two professions that interested him were seafaring and film-making and after his studies at Geneva, he briefly joined the merchant navy but soon returned to Geneva where he worked in journalism and wrote on film and jazz. His film-making took off in 1955 when he succeeded in finding work in the British Film Institute in London, made a documentary, *Nice Time*, in collaboration with Claude Goretta, became acquainted with the *Free Cinema* movement and met Marxist author, John Berger, who was to become a close friend and the scriptwriter of four of Tanner's films.

These experiences were to lay the foundation for Tanner's cinema of social commitment. Through *Free Cinema*, Tanner became aware of the fact that beyond the screen there is not only another space which is evoked but there is also a 'hidden' reality which traditional cinema avoids. Tanner discovered early that the socially excluded remained absent from traditional cinema and recalls that, if a worker were to be included in the visible space, he 'could only be a funny character or an assassin'.[4] From London, Tanner moved to Paris and became acquainted with the New Wave cinema which, after the political commitment of the *Free Cinema*, seemed to him to be too much like a right-wing anarchism.

One can distinguish three main phases in Tanner's *oeuvre*. The first is that of ideological commitment and social awareness, where the characters are cast in and against a social space. In the second phase, the emphasis lies on the existential position of the individual character. Finally, in the third phase, a feeling of being adrift seems to dominate and cinema itself is questioned. The stylistic coherence underlying the different phases is twofold. On the one hand, Tanner's cinema remains marked by the documentary tradition and, although he has opted for fiction films, his films reveal a refusal to 'tell' a story but emphasise the gaze of the camera. On the other hand, his films are characterised by a technique which favours the long take, the tracking shot and the inclusion of 'empty shots' where the camera lingers on the empty space after the characters have left the frame. This last characteristic may also reflect the influence of documentary film.

Tanner's films exemplify the documentary/fiction alliance: whilst freeing Swiss cinema from the 'documentary' genre decree, he remains nevertheless profoundly 'documentary' in his fiction. In this kind of film, which vacillates between fiction and documentary and aims at constructing and deconstructing the narrative, 'space' becomes the tangible expression of the endeavour to re-direct the viewers to the world they are trying to escape from. The 'elsewhere' becomes a privileged category but is to refer further to what is not shown in traditional fiction film, the socially excluded and the process of film-making itself.

The dominant spatial distinction in Tanner's films corresponds in several ways to the threefold structure suggested by Gardies – here, there, elsewhere. Firstly, Tanner's approach to space is that of a social scientist; he places himself outside the space of the film and outside society and moves, to and fro, from 'here' to 'elsewhere', in and out of Switzerland. Secondly, Tanner's representation of urban society, expressed in terms of centre, periphery and marginality may be seen as analogous to Gardies's threefold spatial structure. Finally, Tanner's native Switzerland is based on a geo-linguistic 'here' with an adjacent different geo-linguistic region,'there', beyond which lies the 'elsewhere' of another powerful country, be it France, Germany or Italy, where the main cultural nucleus of that linguistic region lies. In other words, the cultural 'centre' of each language is 'elsewhere', outside Switzerland. This three dimensionality which underlies Switzerland's cartography is tangible in Tanner's films, twelve of these are particularly relevant for his uses of space and will be referred to in this study.

The first two societies depicted in Tanner's early films are non-Swiss. The first film, *Nice Time* (1956), is set in London, whereas the second, *A City at Chandigarh* (1966), concerns the building of the Indian city in Punjab, Chandigarh. This important experience, gained through these commissioned films, undoubtedly contributed to shaping Tanner's views on Swiss society. Tanner is Swiss, but he is also a traveller who takes a critical look at his own society and is at once both native informant and anthropologist. After 1966 six major films are set in Switzerland, *Charles mort ou vif* (1969), *La Salamandre* (1971), *Le Retour d'Afrique* (1973), *Le Milieu du Monde* (1974), *Jonas qui aura 25 ans en l'an 2000* (1976), *Messidor* (1979). For his three subsequent films, Tanner leaves Switzerland. *Les Années Lumière* (1981) is set in Ireland, *Dans la ville blanche* (1983) in Portugal and *No Man's Land* (1985) at the frontier between Switzerland and France. For *La Femme de Rose Hill* (1989), Tanner returns to his native Switzerland.

The first film, *Nice Time*, is a seventeen-minute documentary on London nightlife, made in collaboration with fellow Swiss film-maker Claude Goretta. This film, part of the *Free Cinema* series, was shown at the National Film Theatre in 1957 under the general title *Look at Britain*. The Britain portrayed by the two Swiss film-makers is not a well-defined segment of society, but is made up of random individuals who happen to be in Picadilly Circus. Without providing a story, Tanner and Goretta have, however, chosen a central theme, that of Eros. The film, in black and white, opens and closes with London's well-known Eros fountain, which becomes the centre piece of the film, both formally and semantically. The camera circles around the fountain, captures the nightly visitors, who seem to repeat the camera's own circling movement. Taxis, people standing, sitting or strolling – all are apparently moved by and towards Eros. The camera captures the twofold movement of the crowd– towards the centre, at the beginning of the film, and away from it at the end. A dense crowd moves up and down – a classless and ageless group of people in Piccadilly Circus by chance and whose activities are recorded by the camera.

The film draws attention to peripheral members of society – the sailor, the prostitute, the transient in the city – all socially on the fringes of society but nevertheless central to it. Although the action of the film is limited to Piccadilly Circus, the film conveys a universal place, a square or crowded place in any city, anywhere in the Western world. Tanner and Goretta highlight the economic and social importance of the city's centre where, after regular business closing time, a new consumption nucleus is created. In an embryonic way, this first film brings out the Swiss film-makers' fascination with the centre/periphery dichotomy on a geographical as well as a social and a cinematographic level. Already in this film, space is not only an essential component, but is also endowed with a social dimension: the city becomes a metaphor of society in which transience and marginality emerge as powerful themes.

The manifest interest in social reality, already expressed in *Nice Time* through the centre and periphery dichotomy, becomes more prominent in *A City at Chandigarh* (1966). This 60-minute documentary, co-scripted with Berger, constitutes an East/West collaboration as a Western architect, Le Corbusier, is commissioned by premier Jawaharlal Nehru to build the new capital of Punjab. Two Western artists, Tanner and Berger, film the creation of this new capital and its emerging social structure. Chandigarh is an architectural masterpiece but, although he designed it for Indians to live in and had a specific view of the society that was to inhabit the city, Le Corbusier had no views on the social dimension of the building process. When Nehru went to see Le Corbusier in Paris, the architect reassured him that the city could be conceived in Paris and he wrote to him: 'We are capable of ensuring the solution to the problem here, 35 Rue de Sèvres'. Pierre Jeanneret, Le Corbusier's cousin and also an architect, was to spend more time in Chandigarh and confirms in a letter that Le Corbusier was guided by a superior logic which bore little relation to the Punjab's social reality.[5]

The dichotomy between architectural design and Punjab's social reality and forces of production emerges through the commentary by Berger that accompanies Tanner's images. This commentary extends the space beyond the images seen on the screen. It introduces the social reality which the film cannot fully render and draws attention to the tension between East and West, between the new city conceived by a Western architect and Punjab, between architectural design and social structure. As Tanner's camera shows, the city dwells on the buildings and glides along the cement curves that dominate the structures, or rests on a casement through which the mountain scenery can be seen, then on the profile of an Indian, Berger, the Marxist novelist, narrates and provides a strong socio-political element which draws attention to the building process and to the production forces which Le Corbusier ignored.

The soundtrack thus takes the viewer beyond the space of the screen and away from the centre of the new city and suggests another space, that of the builders and the gypsies excluded from the city. The geographic separation corresponds to an economic one: the people living on Chandigarh's outskirts, although economically essential to the

The Middle of the World   *(British Film Institute)*

city, earn much less than those living in it. The centre/periphery dichotomy becomes evident and emphasis is placed on the topography of the city and its hidden socio-economic structure. The only people not living in the city are those who built and are still building it. Berger places these builders, men and women, in a wider spatio-historical context by relating them to the builders of other famous historical sites. Through Brecht's poem he evokes other cities, Thebes, Babylon, Lima:

> Who built Thebes of the seven gates?
> In books you read the names of kings.
> Was it kings who carried the stones for the building?
> And Babylon, destroyed so many times
> Who built it up again?
> And in Lima, radiant with gold,
> Where did the builders go?
> On the night the great wall of China was finished
> Where did the masons go?

The camera returns to the women carrying the building materials, and the narration specifies that in the building of Chandigarh centuries were spanned. What is

156

architecturally one of the most modern cities of the world was built by men and women who had to cart each brick, each load of earth and concrete, as they were carted 4000 years ago.' Berger draws attention to the fact that all the elements visible in the city – the wool factory with its two hundred workers, the birth-control clinic, the children who all learn to read – contrast with Indian society at large, which is poor, unemployed, and illiterate. Berger takes the viewers beyond the screen and forces them to 'see' this invisible elsewhere.

For example, when Tanner's camera penetrates the small and crowded health centre where a female doctor shows contraceptive devices, Berger mentions that India's production of food is sufficient for only two-thirds of the country's entire population and that this population increases by nine million people a year. When children are shown in the primary schools of Chandigarh, Berger mentions that 70 per cent of Indians are illiterate, indicating that problems of such magnitude can clearly not be solved in Chandigarh's small health centre or teaching arenas. The contrast is not merely between finished and unfinished city, but is extended from this new capital to the Punjab and to India at large. Some 800 architects gathered at Chandigarh early in January 1999 to celebrate the 50th anniversary of the city Le Corbusier created. A newspaper article recording the event seems to echo Berger's commentary when the author refers to 'Chandigarh's seas of concrete often bereft of people' and writes: 'For the rich, Chandigarh is an oasis ... but for the poor, 100,000 people banished to distant slums, it is a different story.'[6] Le Corbusier's principle behind the planning of the city, Berger remarks, is a search for *joie de vivre* but Berger draws attention to the sharp contrast between that *joie de vivre* and the sheer exigencies of survival that underlie the building process.

For Tanner, interested in urban and social structures, this project in collaboration with Berger presented an important opportunity which sharpened the perception of urban and social space that was to become a recurrent theme in his feature films. There is no doubt that the experience of filming the work of a Western architect's struggle with his ideals and their suitability for Indian society, whilst following the analysis of this process by a committed Marxist, has been decisive in Tanner's film career.

Although Tanner's feature films, unlike the documentaries, do not take the city as their immediate object, they nevertheless maintain the city as an essential component of the narrative. The city is not just a background against which a story unfolds, but a historical, economic, and cultural determinant of a society. With the exception of *The Middle of the World*, Tanner's feature films before 1980 are all set in Geneva. In each one of them, the main characters seem at odds with society and feel ill at ease in Geneva's social climate. In the first Geneva film, *Charles Dead or Alive* (1969) the main character, Charles Dé, a successful businessman, suffers a mental breakdown on the very day of the centenary of the family's business, a Geneva watch factory. The city is shown to have provided Charles with a self-image which, at the age of 50, fails to coincide with the image Charles discovers in the reflecting space of the his bathroom mirror. The identification Charles made with his city shifts to his own image to which he no longer relates. He, the owner of a watch factory, suddenly perceives how he has been fashioned by Geneva and its paternalistic system and feels compelled to reject the approbatory gaze he receives from the factory and the city. This identity crisis makes him abandon his family and professional position. His journey away from watch manufacturing, from family, from conventionality and from paternalism takes on geographic and linguistic characteristics. As he goes through various stages he moves from centre to periphery and each time takes a different name. From Charles Dé he becomes Mr Schwartz, then Carlo, completing in this way a mental journey through Switzerland's three linguistic regions.

He finally falls in with a young couple, Paul and Adeline, who live on the periphery of the city and of society, having rejected all conventions and material wealth. As Charles drives them home, they stop at one of the couple's favourite places to gaze at a site which shows no resemblance to the postcard Geneva tourists know. Instead, they praise the suburbs and satellite towns and add to the vilification of the city by pushing Charles's car into the ravine. Adeline also relates a dream she had in which the entire centre of the city was transformed; the quay of the lake had changed into a mining port, the boats had turned black, parks had become steelworks and, at night, flames from the factory chimney illuminated the lake while noises of all kinds roared above it. Through this Geneva dream, an aesthetics of ugliness is produced in which industries belch out polluted flames over the city. This is a far cry from the watch factory abandoned by Charles and from the city that prides itself upon its order and cleanliness, its wealth gained through international bureaucracy and banking. Reminiscent of Chandigarh, where the city excluded the builders and the gypsies, Geneva, the successful model of Western capitalism, keeps hidden its poverty and social sores. Jim Leach draws attention to the analogy that exists between such urban cleansing and traditional film editing which 'effaces all traces of the work'.[7] Aesthetically and socially, Tanner extends screen space and shows or implies the 'elsewhere' which artists and urban planners prefer to ignore and expel.

In *La Salamandre* (1971), the emphasis is again placed on social marginality and on exclusion. In this film too the alienation of the individual is set against the background of Geneva's 'perfect' social space, but here the main character, Rosemonde, unlike Charles, is an outsider from the beginning. The last of a large family that has to live on the produce of a small-holding in the countryside, she goes to live with an uncle in the city, earning her keep as domestic help to relieve the financial burden of the family. City life is not what Rosemonde might have expected. The pleasures usually associated with the city make way for the tedium of living with a retired uncle in a small flat.

The film starts when a journalist and an author, Pierre and Paul, are commissioned by Swiss television to write a script about a shooting incident in which the niece injured her uncle and which made newspaper headlines. As they research their subject, they learn how society charges Rosemonde with numerous failings and untidiness but these accusations are offset by the camera as it lingers on the rubbish in the street which has accumulated because of a strike and films the rent supervisor who steps in dog excrement. The normally 'hidden' side of the social space erupts now and then in the 'here' of the screen. Pierre and Paul, unable to complete the script, become in effect characters in a script in which, like Rosemonde herself, they are portrayed as misfits in society, literally confined to its edges. Rosemonde lives for a while over the border in

France; Paul, in order to avoid expensive housing, lives in a kind of 'no man's land near the border' while Pierre dreams of Brazil and leaves Switzerland for France at the end of the film. The camera thus transforms the microcosm of Rosemonde, Pierre and Paul into a macrocosm of society with Geneva as its focus.

The malaise of the individual in Geneva's social space is also prominent in *Return from Africa* (1973). The film presents a Geneva couple, Vincent and Françoise, who have to leave their condemned flat. Prompted by the prospect of bourgeois life in dreary Geneva, they plan to leave for Africa. However, their journey never takes place and, too embarrassed to tell their friends, they opt for self-imposed exile in a condemned, although not unattractive flat. Having sold most of their belongings, they are reduced to a rudimentary lifestyle and their self-imposed exile assumes the characteristics of a journey to Africa – the dream of primitive Algeria becomes a fake primitivism in the heart of Geneva. The 'return' to Geneva, to Western society, is slow and the desire comes long before the actual return. Like the couple, the viewers have become trapped in the condemned flat. As Vincent and François finally 'return' from their simulated journey and end their self-exile the camera shows the expulsion from Switzerland of Emilio, a friend-immigrant worker.

As in the other Geneva films, the Geneva Vincent returns to is seen as industrialised, polluted and congested with high-rise buildings, banks, offices and parking lots from which immigrants are expelled or where individuals feel ill at ease. Moreover, the centre ejects its inhabitants, buildings are demolished and high rentals force people to live in crowded flats or away from the centre. The many tracking shots accompanying the people to or from work render the distance between work and residence tangible for the spectators. As people seek to leave the city because of its inhuman nature, opportunists, wishing to secure maximum profit, speculate on this need and create new centres away from the city where the land becomes overpriced. This is especially the case in Tanner's last Geneva film, *Jonah who will be 25 in the year 2000* (1976), where a wealthy banker speculates on the creation of new centre away from the old centre and, in so doing, extends the boundaries of the city and creates a periphery of the periphery.

Jonah emphasises the periphery-centre dichotomy in a powerful way. Eight characters, whose names all begin with the letters 'MA', recalling the May 1968 events, meet by chance in Geneva's periphery where two of the eight characters run a small organic farm. The farm is on the fringe of the city and the capitalist system, since its ecological concerns are at odds with economic profit. Each character rebels against an aspect of capitalist society, advocates a specific philosophical principle, attacks a social injustice, or holds a definite opinion on ecological or educational matters. They are all marginal people, ill-integrated in their society, employed in work which offers little if any profit. The child Jonah, born on the farm, represents an ideology born of a set of ideologies that are historically and topographically determined.

The two central narrative events, the encounter of the eight characters and the birth of Jonah, take place on the farm away from the geographic and capitalist centre, Geneva. This narrative de-centring mirrors the social structure: these marginal characters are peripheral in Swiss society. Through two of the characters, Marie and Marguerite, the theme of immigrant labour recurs and adds a further insight into

Jonah Who Will Be 25 in the Year 2000   *(British Film Institute)*

Geneva's social periphery. Two categories of immigrant workers are shown, the 'frontier worker' and the 'seasonal worker'. Marie, the 'frontier worker', is allowed to work in Switzerland but must return to France, her home country, every night. Marguerite, the woman who runs the small farm with her husband, extends sexual favours to nearby 'seasonal workers' who, unlike the frontier workers, are allowed to reside in Switzerland but may not bring in their families. The film shows a few brief shots of the shabby barracks provided for these seasonal workers, obliged to leave their wives and children abroad.

Charles, La Salamandre, Return from Africa and *Jonah* constitute Tanner's 'little Genevan theatre'. The term 'theatre' inevitably suggests a confined space for, unlike cinema, theatre has strong spatial limitations. The characters in these films feel confined and ill at ease in the social space they inhabit. Many come from elsewhere and remain ill-adjusted in a country that exploits immigrant labour, frowns upon marginality and 'otherness'. Tanner has assigned filmic space to the marginal, who are denied a proper space in Swiss society and has taken Geneva as a microcosm to demonstrate how capitalist economy has ordered urban space and how, in turn, society itself has become structured on the model of this capitalist urban architecture. Tanner's films reveal a relentless effort to extend filmic space and to render manifest the elsewhere and the

160

hidden, to include the peripheral and the marginal in the 'here' of the narrative and the screen.

In two films, one preceding and one following *Jonah who will be 25 in the year 2000*, space is still Swiss but not Geneva. The 1974 film, *The Middle of the World*, co-scripted with Berger, is located in 'the Middle of the world', somewhere in the Swiss countryside; it is also the name of a restaurant where one of the first meetings between the two main protagonists, Adriana an Italian waitress, and Paul, a local candidate for the forthcoming elections, takes place. The 'Middle' becomes a metaphor for the entire film and for the society in the film. In the 'Middle', the world is divided in two: one side for the 'rich', one side for the 'poor' as it is in the restaurant where he invites her to the 'rich' side. For Paul, the 'Middle' is geographic, economic, political (North and South come together); for Adriana, the 'Middle' is invisible, personal, related to the body. While he is a life-long resident of the Middle, she passes through it. Seen at the start of the film travelling in a train towards the Middle, at the end of the film she awaits the train which will distance her from it. Whereas Adriana refuses to stay in the Middle, Paul contains it and is contained by it. She is the foreigner, he is the 'local' who treats the Italian immigrant waitress to tourist Swiss presents, a musical cow, a watch, a camera. His middle-of-the-road politics are reduced to 'solving problems' and his conquest of Adriana is conducted like an electoral campaign which, like the election, will fail. But Adriana, who came from a politically committed Italian background, has, unconsciously or subversively defeated and turned down this Middle of the world candidate. She leaves the Middle and opts for her immigrant status: at the end of the film, she is seen working in a factory in German-speaking Switzerland.

1976 marks the end of the collaboration with Berger, and with this the ideological strand in Tanner's films fades. The corpus of the four Tanner-Berger films are marked by a Marxist view of society and history and emphasise the analogy between filmic, urban and social space. The films displayed a concern with the extension of space into the social sphere and with the insertion of those elements which shed light on social structures and which reveal the similarity between the threefold division of space – here, there and elsewhere – and that of urban society's demarcation of centre/periphery and marginality. After this period, the struggle with space becomes more personal, existential and, above all, cinematographic. The emphasis on marginality and on the 'elsewhere' remain but, at the same time, the construction of cinematographic space and the spectators' visual perception of space come to the foreground.

In 1978, Tanner made an experimental 8mm video film which focuses on cinematographic space. The 30-minute film, *Temps mort,* records the images of a return journey by car and by train between Geneva and Berne. In order to capture the images of the journey, Tanner attached the camera to the window of his car and recorded a number of three-minute cassettes. In the editing process, he selected and juxtaposed various three-minute segments. Seeing the recordings of roads, cafes and landscapes was a discovery for Tanner, who then added a commentary giving his ideas on film, on television, on the image, on empty space, on roads and on duration and time. This is a real 'journey-film', where the camera itself becomes the traveller. The experiment elicits a comparison between film-making and travelling. If, up to 1976, the characters in

Tanner's films seemed to be fleeing from something or wishing to escape to an elsewhere, in *Temps mort*, the ever-moving images themselves seem engaged in a flight or an escape. This video-recording of a Swiss journey also brought out the salience of the contrast between the fullness and the emptiness on the screen.

It is not astonishing, then, that Tanner's subsequent film, *Messidor* (1979) is a kind of road movie in which space becomes the very material the film is made of. The film opens with a long aerial shot of the Swiss countryside accompanied by one of Schubert's *Winterreise Lieder*. The soundtrack records not only the voice of the female singer but also the roaring of the helicopter from which the beautiful Swiss lakes and mountains are filmed. Slowly, the camera reveals a multitude of cars and roads cutting through the landscape until the roads become more and more numerous and form an intricate web. The camera cuts to a young girl standing on a platform, a train moving in the background and a road sign saying 'city centre'.

Before the viewers glimpse the two main characters, they have travelled, so to speak, across Switzerland. Space itself seems to have assumed the status of a character in close relationship to two girls who are about to hitch-hike, one because she has lost her train ticket, the other because she wishes to escape the noise of the city. The geography of Switzerland structures the narrative: the direction of the story is an arbitrary itinerary along the Swiss roads on which the girls set out. They meet as a car stops and picks them both up. What was to be a return home for one girl and a few days away for the other, becomes an endless, hopeless and ill-defined journey on roads that lead nowhere and present little or no safety.

During this random journey, a picture of a self-righteous Swiss society emerges from the comments made by the drivers and other people met by chance: 'We people with jobs pay for the three-quarters of the population' or 'Abroad a catastrophe would happen'. Whilst offering paternalistic advice for the girls' safety, the male drivers try to take sexual advantage of them. Moreover, the 'catastrophe', a violent attempted rape, does happen, not abroad as one driver prophesied, but by Swiss drivers in Switzerland. What was a random adventure becomes, after the attempted rape, a deliberate wandering along the Swiss roads that begins to resemble a 'cops and robbers' movie, a journey to a non-space that must last as long as possible as the film blends the ill-defined existential search of the two girls with a cinematographic rendering of space.

Tanner's subsequent three films are all set outside Switzerland. *Light Years Away* (1981) in Ireland, *In the White City* (1983) in Portugal and *No Man's Land* (1985) in an area between the French and the Swiss border in the Jura region. The spatial metaphor pervades all three films as the characters remain engaged in a journey towards an ill-defined destination. Although *Light Years Away* is set in Ireland, the two protagonists seem to live in a kind of nowhere, in exile from society, both physically and socially. In *In the White City*, the mechanic-sailor deserts his ship on a stopover in Lisbon, and undertakes a journey of descent within himself. In *No Man's Land*, the spatial symbolism is explicit through the choice of a real 'no man's land' which becomes the location for the fraudulent activities of several people living on one or the other side of the border.

A theme of transience underlies these post-1976 films. Space no longer functions as a metaphor for society but becomes so visually pervasive that doubt is cast on the earlier metaphoric use. The sea in *In The White City*, the Irish mountains and skies in *Light Years Away* and the frontiers in *No Man's Land*, are themselves the essence of the films, structuring the characters and the narrative without the ideological overtones that prevailed earlier – in fact, throwing into question the very use previously made of space. Rather than being an appropriate image for social structures, space becomes the fabric of the narrative itself: the characters no longer live in a particular space but enact space and interiorise it. Whereas the characters in many earlier films lived on the periphery of a specific city, in these two films the spatial focus is on the wild beauty of Ireland, on the immensity of the sea or on an ephemeral no man's land and more emphasis is placed on the relationship between the characters and the space around them.

In *Light Years Away*, Yoshka, an eccentric character who at first lives by himself near his car cemetery in a kind of nowhere, is later joined by Jonah, a young man whom he met in a bar. The relationship between the two moves through various stages: from master/slave to master/pupil and finally to father/son, at which stage Jonah is deemed worthy to learn of Yoshka's dream of flying and his plans to realise this dream. When Yoshka finally enacts his dream and attempts to fly 'light years away', he is tragically thrown back to earth, his eyes pecked out by an eagle. As the vast space of nature and sky fill the screen, the Icarus dream comes to an end: the limits of space and gravity bring the dreamer back from utopia and the film-maker back to the perimeters of the screen.

In *In the White City*, the main character, Paul, sailor-mechanic and amateur film-maker, is also called back from his dreamed 'elsewhere' to the reality of his abandoned 'here'. The film opens with a wide view of a ship in a misty sea; it then cuts to Paul in the noisy and hot engine-room of the ship when it is about to enter the harbour of Lisbon. Paul, who loves the sea but who spends eight hours a day in an engine-room, has become alienated from the sea. Paradoxically, then, the notion of journey begins with the stopover in Lisbon, where he decides to desert the ship. The apparent infinity of the sea on which he lives has, in fact, limited his vision spatially as may be seen in his filming activities. With his 8mm camera, Paul takes views of the sea and has himself filmed standing on deck in front of the sea, smiling clumsily into the camera. He walks into the city, holding the camera in front of him, and captures his own moving image in unselective tracking shots, unable to see what he is actually filming. Later he will film Rosa, a woman met in Lisbon, and try to capture her body in extreme close up shots, attempting even to penetrate into her mouth so as to fill the entire screen with the blurred close-up of the mouth's orifice.

The 8mm films, juxtaposing the unedited clips of the open sea, of Paul walking or occupying the screen in front of the sea and of the close-ups of Rosa's body, are sent to the wife in Basle who projects them onto the wall of her living room, unable to make sense of these de-contextualised clips. The desperate attempt of the sailor film-maker to undertake a journey of descent within himself, to find a 'white city' where silence and solitude are white, to do away with space through immobility is translated into filmic space through the 8mm clips which, shot in Lisbon and projected in Basle, on the one hand, illustrate the endeavour to transcend space through the magnified close-up of an orifice or the extended wide angle shot of an infinite horizon and, on the other hand, address the spectators' visual perception of space. However, the struggle with space and images will yield to that of space and words when Paul, having sold his 8mm camera, is seen writing what the voiceover will convey – that the sea is the only 'country' he loves.

In *No Man's Land,* Tanner turns to a place of pastures and forests between the French and the Swiss border. This space, which apparently does not belong to anyone – a real no-man's land – is carefully patrolled by French and Swiss customs officials. Located in the Jura region, it is perhaps more a state of mind than a geographical reality. In search of adventure and love, the no-man's land, devoid of ideologies, offers the four main characters a fertile space to dream of an elsewhere where they hope to be able to materialise their dreams: for Paul who dreams of flying, it is Canada; for Madeleine who wants to sing, it is Paris; for Jean, who loves animals, it is the countryside, and for Mali, the frontier worker who aspires to return to her home country, it is Algeria. No-man's land becomes a place of mobility as inhabitants of the adjacent communities seek to communicate or to engage in fraudulent activities. Tracking shots abound in the film and are never substituted by a zoom, instead, they make the no-man's land a place of tangible activity and movement.

Most of the films by Tanner since 1987 seem to be motivated by a search for a new meaning and have been less well received by both the critics and the public. However, the one which draws attention to space in a powerful way and echoes many of Tanner's earlier ideological and aesthetic considerations is his 1989 film, *The Woman of Rose Hill*, for which Tanner returns to his native Switzerland. 'It does not look like the Switzerland we know from chocolate boxes,' one woman told him at the London film festival. 'No,' Tanner replied, 'I am not paid by the tourist bureau.' Indeed, a tourist Switzerland it is not, even though the classical Tannerian takes and slow tracking shots give spatial prominence to the Swiss countryside when he fills the screen with undulating golden fields or windswept tree tops.

These light-drenched, windswept or mist-shrouded takes are the background against which the social drama unfolds, the drama of a the 'woman from Rose Hill' a mail-order black bride. She comes to Switzerland from a far-off island in the Indian Ocean, having seen a much younger version in a photograph of Marcel, the ageing unattractive farmer-husband she is to meet in the Vaudois. Tanner films the lonely woman walking along misty roads, or takes her in close-up off centre, leaving space for the snow-covered countryside. Inside the house, the image of the overpowering husband's mother, literally projecting her shadow onto the wall, captures the threat of this silent presence. Julie's pregnancy by Jean, a man to whom she feels emotionally close, complicates matters since conformism, paternal authority and social laws will intervene and bring about Julie's expulsion: she will be expelled, *manu militari*, from her '*fausse terre d'accueil*'.

Lotman drew attention to the painters and the film-makers' relentless effort to break up space and to make it surge beyond its boundaries. Lotman, like the other critics mentioned here, explore this 'beyond' principle and examines how the invisible enters the spectators' field of perception. The 'boundaries' of the screen constitute the main parameter for a discussion of what can be classified as 'here', 'there' and 'elsewhere'.

The study of Tanner's *oeuvre* has led to a reinterpretation of these categories and revealed that the strategies surrounding the representation of space are manifold: there is an attempt to extend space but there is also a manipulative striving to blot out an undesirable and unsightly elsewhere. Tanner has revealed these strategies in two ways. Firstly, he has translated the notion of the screen's boundaries into that of political 'frontiers', in particular those of Switzerland. Immigrants abound in Tanner's films and their status varies according to the convenience of their Swiss employers. But the analogy operates in both ways: filmic space reflects political structures and, in turn, these structures exemplify the manipulation of space by the film-maker. This view casts a different light on the 'extension' of the boundaries and unmasks the exclusion/ inclusion that dictates the film-maker's decision in the same way as political frontiers are erected and immigration laws drawn up. Secondly, besides the ideological commitment which characterises the analogy between the boundaries of the screen and the socio-political frontiers, there is also an emphasis on the non-ideological personal quest of the individual who attempts to transcend the boundaries of space and undertakes an ill-defined journey within the self or to an imagined elsewhere. Such was the case for the girls in Messidor, for Yoshka who wanted to fly, for Paul whose beloved country was the sea. In each of these these films, the film-maker's quest to experiment with fullness and emptiness becomes more tangible.

Space then in Tanner's films is a search, a search for what lies beyond the perimeter of the screen and which traditional cinema keeps hidden. It is also the foundation of the individual's quest for an elsewhere which ultimately lies 'here' within the self. If, in the first case the inclusion/exclusion opposition operates, in the second, the visible/invisible criterion prevails. In both cases the film-maker has to confront the endless struggle with space which underlies any form of representation.

Notes

1. Lotman, J., 'The Struggle with Space,' *The Semiotics of Cinema*, Ann Arbor, Michigan Slavic Contributions, 1976, pp. 81-83.
2. Burch N., 'Nana ou les deux espaces,' *Une Praxis du cinéma*, Paris, Gallimard, 1986, pp. 39-58.
3. Gardies, A., 'L'Espace,' *Le Récit filmique*, Paris, Hachette, 1993, pp. 69-83.
4. Dimitriu, C., *Tanner*, Paris, Editions Henri Veyrier, 1995, p. 98.
5. Petit, J. *Le Corbusier par lui-même*, Genève, Rousseau éditeur, 1970, pp. 103-4.
6. Goldenberg, C., 'Chaos creeps up on Idia's "city of the future",' *The Guardian*, 12 January 1999, p. 12.
7. Leach, J. *A Possible Cinema: The Films of Alain Tanner*, Metuchen- London, The Scarecrow Press, 1984, p.56.

Acknowledgement

I wish to thank Gloria Cigman and Trista Selous for their comments and support.

Between the Two: Dimensions of Space in Finnish Cinema

Jukka Sihvonen

Connecting People[1]

Films, just like other products of art and culture can be seen as reconstructing and recycling characteristics which belong to one's national heritage and collective unconscious. Films construct and modify everyday life by offering people in different geographical locations but within a shared linguistic field an opportunity to reflect upon their own community adherence; if not along the course of time, at least retrospectively. Therefore the notion of 'community' is rarely a one-way street leading from cultural artefacts to individual modes of behaviour.

In Finland community in this sense means a herd; a tribe and tribalism. Stories about the forest people transform into stories about the village people transforming further into stories about the city people.[2] The tangible context changes but the sense of tribalism pertains. What we have here is a small, rather tightly organised and uniform group of people (even visually) with their own peculiar language on the Uralic end of the Uralic-Altaic language group. Today it is a culture of synthetic jogging suits and sneakers; beer bars and curved sausages; Russian tourists and phone-sex ads; ice-hockey arenas and bank machines. The most visible change in the geographical landscape of Finland during the past ten or twenty years has been the mushrooming of telecommunication masts, antennas and satellite dishes. One can hardly find anywhere in the world that has as many mobile telephones per head of population as there are in Finland: every other Finn has a cell phone. It is clearly the number one nation in the world regarding Internet connections. This tribe seemingly wants to be connected. However, at the same time it wants to be left alone.

If there is one basic underlying characteristic of Finnish culture, it might be this kind of peculiar if not paradoxical form of duality and contradiction: there is a willingness to be connected with high technology which, at the same time, allows one to be left alone. Because the connection is virtual rather than tangible, technological rather than face-to-face, it creates 'another space' for the participants transforming them into simultaneous observers. From this perspective the history of independent Finland (officially from 1917 onwards) could be seen as reconstructing the basic ideals of what has been called the Romantic Enlightenment, which elsewhere was fading away, if not even earlier, at least after the First World War and during the 1920s.[3] This notion refers to an attempt to be an enlightened observer and a romantic participant

166

simultaneously. The aim is to maintain a distance that allows one to research, examine, analyse and study the reality, but also, to throw oneself into the stream of life. The idea is to experience virtually, with the fullest emotions; if not actually in everyday reality, at least in the imagination. Implied is a belief that this paradoxical intertwining can become possible through technological progress, and because it cannot in the end, it is also a sole source of a widely felt collective anxiety and depression climaxed for example in the so-called 'arctic hysteria'. This syndrome is a strange combination of mental disorders caused by an overdose (during the summer) or lack (in the wintertime) of natural light 'consumed' together with excessive drinking of alcohol.

A parallel perspective to this kind of mental landscape is derived from a more clearly defined Romantic contradiction:

> (...) the individuated self's dependency on, even fusion with, this totality (an all-inclusive totality other and greater than the self), invariably figured in maternal terms, is the very condition of absolute free individuality; or to reverse the terms, the absolute, ungrounded agency of the self is seen to derive from the dissolution of the self into a larger whole.[4]

The construction of contradictions, however, does not end here. Instead, as Gerald Izenberg notes, since the individuality of the creative self is understood as *absolute* in Romanticism, therefore the contradiction is doubled: human individuality is also held to be superior to, even the very source of, the overarching totality to which it submits itself.

I will read Finnish cinema as a multi-levelled stack of different but concurrent contradictions, the basis of which is the relationship between an absolute individual and an overarching totality (hence 'Between the Two Spaces . . .' being referred to in the title). Through these contradictions and conflicts Finnish cinema has gained its peculiarly paradoxical characteristics which in many ways refer to the position 'in-between'. From this perspective contemporary Finnish cinema exemplifies the transformation and transportation of these polarities and their representations into the realm of more or less nostalgic memories. Today Finnish cinema exists only in this kind of imperfect tense.[5]

Conflicts and Connections

In pursuing something that later came to be called 'a national cinema', two distinct and sometimes competing points of view had already found expression in production and distribution during the 1930s in Finland. One branch of the film community wanted Finnish cinema to follow broader influences and international trends by using the themes and fashions of modern European and American films. This group embodied the belief in *contact*. The other group placed more faith in Finnish topics arguing that wider success could be gained only by domestic profits and more local acceptance. Seemingly this group embodied the belief in *inherence*. In its own way, these divergent paths can be seen in the two major production companies, Suomi-Filmi (Su-Fi) and Oy Suomen Filmiteollisuus Ab (SF) both established right before the mid-1930s. The former tried to follow international trends by focusing on modern, urban stories. SF concentrated more on agrarian topics and adaptations of national themes which had been borrowed from national literature published earlier. Naturally this duality is not clear-cut, perhaps just a question of emphasis, but nevertheless, it exemplifies a dual construction which was clutched for a long time afterwards.[6]

One of the first significant events of Finnish cinema, even before it was talked about as fundamentally 'national', was Erkki Karu's film *Nummisuutarit* (*The Village Cobblers*, 1923). The story is actually a play by Aleksis Kivi, the national poet of Finland. It has been filmed twice since the early 1920s: a sound film in 1938 directed by Wilho Ilmari, and a colour film in 1957 by Valentin Vaala. In Karu's early adaptation (which still is widely considered as the best of the three), the basic two elements of Finnish cinema (and Finnish culture by and large), forest and alcohol, are given one of their first cinematic embodiments. The famous sequence in which the drunken protagonist, Esko, wrestles with trees in the forest is one of the key scenes of Finnish cinema because it highlights how the frustrated anxiety of the Finnish man is dealt with – as it often is even in real life – in relation to wood. This element with its variations (forest, trees, wood, lumber, logs, logrolling, paper industry, etc.) is the basic recurring element of Finnish cinema.

In addition to various ways in which the First and the Second World Wars affected Finnish film culture, they also left a permanent mark on the landscape of themes and topics discussed in several films. Most of all, the presence of war has been seen as a source of national and collective trauma. As a traditional and concurrent topic in Finnish films, war serves yet again a dual purpose: on the one hand almost as documentary realism, and on the other as harmless entertainment. Examples related to the connection between war and entertainment belong to the rich tradition of Finnish military farces from the late 1930s, 1950s and early 1990s. In this genre the army serves as the backdrop for various comic situations in and through which it is possible to speak about contradictions with innocent humour and harmless gags. In the realistic war films the spirit of national defense (linked with the fantasised threats against independence) has always had its place as part of the ideology of consolidation. *Tuntematon sotilas* (*The Unknown Soldier*), directed by Edvin Laine in 1955, produced by SF and based on an immensely popular book by Väinö Linna, is one of the most successful Finnish films both on domestic and international screens. Rauni Mollberg directed a remake of this story in 1985; Pekka Parikka recycled similar motifs in *Talvisota* (*The Winter War*, 1989), and Olli Saarela's new film, *Rukajärven tie* (*On the Road to Rukajärvi*, 1999) is yet another war movie. Even the internationally (in)famous contemporary Finnish-born film director, Renny Harlin, has expressed his dream to direct yet another movie about The Winter War (1939-1940).

Conforming to the literary ways of expressing the development of Finnish culture, Finnish cinema can be seen to follow similar scenic stages – forest, marsh, field, village, city. Correspondingly, these scenic stages are linked to one another through connecting channels which in many ways embody the in-betweenness of Finnish films – rapids, lakes, rivers, roads, railways, streets, seas. There are many cinematic stories about each of these scenic elements which are part of the Finnish landscape. Furthermore, they have strongly modified the images Finns have collectively about themselves, their national landscape and mentality. These scenic elements, the 'connectors', are tangible signs of the way in which Finnish cinema has constantly emphasised the relationship and the location in-between.

One can begin from the forest: in *Nummisuutarit*, trees spin wildly around in the eyes of the drunken protagonist, who has been betrayed in his marriage plans. In Valentin Vaala's *Vihreä kulta* (*Green Gold*, 1939) based on Hella Wuolijoki's book, the forest symbolises prosperity and industrialisation, but also exploitation and pollution. In 1956, William Markus directed for SF a film simply entitled *Metsä* (*The Forest*), though not released until four years later as *Lumisten metsien tyttö* (*The Girl from Snowy Forests*). The story builds around a clash between civilised values represented by the teacher and the harsh life and its brutalities in the Finnish outback, meanwhile being a love story over the class-lines between the teacher and the girl living in the forest. In Risto Jarva's film *Jäniksen vuosi* (*The Year of the Hare*, 1977), again based on a popular novel published earlier, the forest is given yet another meaning, this time as a hiding place. A journalist becomes fed up with the fierce rhythm of modern life and finds a new relationship with nature when running into a baby hare injured in a car accident. In many lumberjack and logrolling films the forest constitutes a milieu for the work described in the stories. Through logrolling, via the rapids and rivers, the emphasis shifts from the forest more towards the village.

Mikko Niskanen's film *Käpy selän alla* (*Skin, skin* 1966), an important breakthrough towards new filmic expression in Finland, uses the forest with an ironic touch: the literal translation of its Finnish title is 'A pinecone under the back'. Here we have an expansive scenery, mythically so loaded and pregnant with meaning, shrunk to a small object, the cone. Simultaneously it signifies how much the presence of old values meant for the young city students whose camping trip to the countryside the film is about. Together with Rauni Mollberg, Niskanen in most of his other films is more interested in representations of the countryside. This is clearly suggested in his major work, the realistic epic and true story *Kahdeksan surmanluotia* (*Eight Deadly Shots*, 1972). The dreariness of the remote countryside drives the protagonist Pasi (the director himself in the role) to a desperately insane act: he shoots the four policemen who have come to arrest him because of unpaid taxes.

In an agrarian culture, the countryside with its fields, farmhouses and mansions constructs the surroundings for the familiar (and familial) tales of love and money. In the Niskavuori films, based on Hella Wuolijoki's plays, a good overview of this tradition can be gained over almost half a century of film production by several companies and directors; the first one is Vaala's *Niskavuoren naiset* (*The Women of Niskavuori*, 1938) and the last one (so far) Matti Kassila's *Niskavuori* (1984). The central scape in these films is the Niskavuori mansion in southern Finland, its ownership, relations to the political and cultural life in general, and so forth. The women in these stories are exceptionally strong and powerful both in terms of love and wealth. One might argue that the mansion is characteristically ruled by matriarchal principles. However, in the films this aspect often becomes blurred. The discrepancy between love and labour is described by the fact that power can belong to the women only at the expense of love. The origins of disappointment are triggered by the actions of men.

Their smallness is emphasised further by relating them to larger (and socially more important) issues such as the permanence of the estate and the clan.

In more recent films the countryside has become a site of anxiety from where one wants to or has to escape, or a space one is only travelling through. Films reflect in this way the broader cultural changes that occurred in Finland during the 1960s and 1970s: serious rural depopulation and rapid urbanisation. This meant that more and more people moved to southern Finland, to or near Helsinki, thereby stretching further another domestic conflict between the North and the South.

Barns and Villages

Dreams of love and freedom, two basic dreams of Finnish cinema, are set in one scenic environment such as the countryside, but during different periods they are interpreted in slightly different ways. A concrete example could be the image of a hay shed (or the like) as one of the fundamental chronotopes of eroticism in Finnish films. In Särkkä's film *Kulkurin valssi* (*The Vagabond's Waltz*, 1941) there is a scene in which a gypsy woman (Rosinka, played by Regina Linnanheimo) rests on a haystack and whispers to the male protagonist, the vagabond (Tauno Palo) with suggesting gestures: 'Are you afraid of me?' In Mika Kaurismäki's *Rosso* (1985) there is a scene filmed on the plainlands of Finland. Deserted sheds are scattered around the flooded and flat landscape. The protagonist, an Italian hit man, has to spend a cold and wet night in one of those sheds with only his dreams to keep him company. From the openly erotic steam and passion of *Kulkurin valssi* we have arrived at another world: in this one the urban foreigner of *Rosso* is an alien without friends, language, or residence. Temporarily the distance from Rosinka's eroticism to Rosso's loss of love and freedom is about 40 years but thematically they exist side by side.

Kulkurin valssi was a tremendous success during the war years. Within a short period of time more than one million Finns (about a quarter of the entire population at that time) had seen the film. The songs from the film were memorised and played endlessly on the radio. The refrain of the title song tells quite a bit about the elementary fantasies of Finnish cinema:

> *I'd rather dance on the country road*
> *together with the humming of trees.*
> *Please come with me my little girl,*
> *to dance the vagabond's waltz!*

Kulkurin valssi might be an exemplary model of how the success of a given film can be dependent on its stylised subject and the particular circumstances in which people come to hear and see it. In the uncertainty of the war years, momentary escape from the pressures of everyday reality were certainly experienced as reliefs. Moreover, the film itself distanced the temporal structure of actions from the present to the past by situating the story in the 19th century and in surroundings which were both romantically strange and realistically familiar – mansions, lords, gypsies, frills and lace, circus companies, music and dance, suspense and exoticism. The carefree vagabond's life symbolised the dream for freedom. The dream of love, on the other hand, was embodied by the ultimate star couple of Finnish cinema, Tauno Palo and Ansa Ikonen, or just 'Ansa and Tauno' as they were and are known. Typically both love and freedom gained their expression across class boundaries. This time the mutual mating rites between a logroller and a country girl took place between a vagabond and a noblewoman. And in the end, of course, the vagabond turns out to be a disguised count, a nobleman as well. In both cases, however, the man was more strongly connected to the myths of freedom, whereas the woman was linked with the myths of love.

From this viewpoint, it is easy to divide Finnish films into two main groups – the films that end well (dreams of the both protagonists come true), and the ones that do not end well (dreams of either one or both of the protagonists fail). The latter distinctly designates Finnish melodrama, a typical example being Hannu Leminen's *Morsiusseppele* (*The Bridal Garland*, 1954) in which the romance between different social classes leads to the girl's pregnancy and finally to her suicide. For the man these incidents mark the burden of such a guilt from which one can never be liberated. The contrasting elements in a melodramatic conflict are man and woman, city and countryside, upper class and lower class, bourgeoisie and proletariat, war and peace. Again, this dual system acts as the background motif of these narratives: the conditions for the union of the two elements are always dictated by the ones who have both the power and the prosperity. In this way, besides being epic, most of the Finnish cinema actually is melodramatic and/or comic. If a film ends well, it is a comedy and if it does not end well, it is a melodrama.

The pastoral cinematic tradition, rife with images of nature, is rooted in Finnish national literature, especially in the works of Aleksis Kivi, Johannes Linnankoski and F.E. Sillanpää. Kivi's cornerstone of Finnish prose, *Seitsemän veljestä* (*The Seven Brothers, 1939*), a film by Wilho Ilmari, and a 12-episode television production directed by Jouko Turkka in the late 1980s describes the cultural progress from the forest to the village, church and school, through seven different characters as individuals and a group.[7] The memorable incident in the attempt to reach civilisation is the journey the brothers are forced to take during the night before Christmas from the forest of Impivaara to the village of Jukola. They must run miles barefeet and half-naked in the snow after their only shelter (the sauna!) has been destroyed by fire. And the fire started because the brothers were fighting in the sauna about who is the strongest and thereby the leader of the gang.

The film version follows traditional interpretations of the novel according to which the brothers gain their respected place among the community only after they learn to read – a metaphor of the collective step from the Imaginary to the Symbolic. Turkka's television version half a century later interprets this situation somewhat differently: the barbaric brothers are not forced or even tempted to come out from the forests to the village and thereby to become citizens. Instead, the brothers just follow the suggestions of law and order (embodied by the sheriff and the clerk) because they are made to believe that only after entering the realm of language they can be accepted as human beings at all.

Linnankoski's logger story *Laulu tulipunaisesta kukasta* (*The Song of the Scarlet Flower, 1938*) was directed by Teuvo Tulio: it was filmed before 1938 and after this date several times in Sweden by Mauritz Stiller, among others, and remade by Mikko Niskanen in 1971. This constructs a different relationship between the forest and the village, as the logroller Olavi wanders from village to village along the rapids picking up girls here and there. In a way, the romanticism attached to logrolling and the rapids perpetuates the tradition of *Seven Brothers*. In this case the question is about how the Finnish man as the lord of the forest conquers nature as well as women. According to the nationally characteristic version of masculine mythology, the price of this commitment (again, paradoxically) is the loss of freedom.

The works of F.E. Sillanpää are more closely connected with agrarian settings, the world of farms and fields. The several films based on his books describe the life of agrarian communities which have, as it were, fallen asleep and then suddenly jolted awake by actions of both love and death. This kind of duality is reflected on various levels for example in *Elokuu* (*The Harvest Month*, 1956) by Matti Kassila: the month is August which in Finland is considered as the border between summer and autumn; the day is Saturday, likewise the temporal border between work and leisure. The milieu is a canal that links the countryside to the city. In this tradition the landscape is not just a background or a neutral environment. Instead, it creates a certain atmosphere which regulates both the reactions of the characters in the story and the experiences of the audience. In this sense it acts like a third category of characters. The natural (thunder and lightning) elements support the construction of the narrative in representing conflicts between insurmountable social differences. This boundary can be crossed perhaps only momentarily in the hay shed thereby offering fleeting moments of bliss, but as a basic construction, over time it remains immutable.

Rauni Mollberg's *The Earth Is a Sinful Song* (1973) is based on Timo K. Mukka's novel (1964) with the same title, and the story is situated in the remote environs of Lapland. The landscape's rugged features constitute a majestic background for the petty life of a small village community. Its everyday world, represented in the film through various seasonal rituals, drifts along with its own force as though forgotten by technological progress pulsating elsewhere. The harshness of nature is synchronised to emotions of pain and despair. Mollberg's film quickly achieved a large audience which is not surprising since the film deals with most of the familiar themes drawn from the tradition of Finnish cinema. These include a family group consisting of different generations, the life in the hinterlands, the unsuccessful romance across social and ethnic boundaries, premature pregnancy (and as a consequence of this, the drowning of the fiancé), an alcoholised father who hangs himself, religious commitments, economic hardships and of course the brief moments of bliss in the hay shed.

Whereas one segment in Mika Kaurismäki's *Rosso* could be read in relation to *Kulkurin valssi*, the same way another segment in Aki Kaurismäki's film *Ariel* (1988) can be read in relation to *Elokuu*, and maybe even more generally, as the end of the 'shed tradition' of Finnish cinema. After having decided (or been forced?) to leave home (because of his father's suicide) and to drive to the city (Helsinki) in search for a job, the protagonist backs his Cadillac convertible out of a shack in the midst of a wintery landscape. When the car disappears to the road leading towards the yet unknown promises of the South, the camera lingers on the landscape for a moment just to record how the roof of the shed suddenly collapses.

Then again this is an artificial ending as in Veikko Aaltonen's *Isä meidän* (*Pater noster*, 1992) we return, once again, to the hay shed. During the early 1990s, however, this return (reflecting the return of the protagonist to his abandoned home in the countryside) is not a happy revisit either: in the shed he vividly recalls the sexual abuse that has shadowed his relationship to his now demented father, also a World War veteran.

Leaving the wilds, one traces a path along the rapids and other troubled waters towards an agrarian village. From there the path widens towards a town, then a railroad leading south to the streets of the Finnish metropolis, Helsinki, the 'national village'. In this environment only two more escapes exist for departures (rarely for arrivals): the harbour and especially the airport. From the fire of the burning sauna in *The Seven Brothers*, the water in lumberjack films and the earth in agrarian movies such as the Niskavuori-saga, the tale of the forest has finally become into a closer contact with the last remaining element, air.

A modern way of life with its urban milieu was not entirely unknown to Finnish cinema before the 1960s. One of the sub-genres in this 'urban' (in quotation marks because the context, mentally, is still a village rather than a city) tradition was the modern comedy of the 1930s and 1940s. Comic plots, usually based on women's romances, were staged in the midst of Helsinki high society. The *Family Suominen* - films from the 1940s are another example of how the sunnier side of city dwelling was expressed in Finnish cinema. But again, the requirement of its lightness was the focus on urban way of life through a nuclear family. Seen from this viewpoint, the most popular comic figure of the 1950s in Finnish cinema, Pekka Puupää (Pete Blockhead), embodies a many-sided criticism in relation to this social nucleus. Pekka and buddies were also urban dwellers, although the rural accent together with body language and rustic clothing still alluded to clearly agrarian roots. Faithful to its traditions, however, Finnish (melodramatic) cinema tended to see city and street life in contradictory terms: the milieu was either a framework for light comedy or, as in the melodramas, an omnipresent opposite to the pristine countryside. In this respect it was nothing but a slum corrupted by unhealthy filth, carnal sin and homicide.

Cities and Children

Whereas Niskanen and Mollberg interpreted the pastoral and patriotic tradition, another couple of directors – Risto Jarva and Pertti Spede Pasanen – concentrated on the urban and modern in the 1970s. Jarva perpetuates the well-established representation of contemporary urban life with socially critical but also comical implications. Pasanen adheres to the comic urban tradition along the lines of the modern comedies and Pete Blockhead movies with an inclination of social criticism. Jarva and Pasanen present an interesting dichotomy: Jarva has been praised by the Finnish critics but not well received by the movie-going public while the reverse is true of Pasanen's films.

In terms of this kind of reception one could refer to *Työmiehen päiväkirja* (*A Worker's Diary*) directed by Jarva in 1968. This film has been selected by a group of critics as the best Finnish film of the 1960s. Thematically the film rides the country-city-factory continuum assisted by new wave styles of editing and visualisation. The plot entails a marriage across class boundaries. Layered over these basic plot and story lines are the recurrent consequences – difficulties at work, financial problems, conflicts between the generations and social classes, the burden of the wars as part of the national past, the international political situation. The marriage of the middle-class Ritva and working-class Juhani is strained not only by the different social backgrounds, but also by the economic, political and historical realities of the society in general – worries about money and work, international politics, and the shadow of war.

The success at the Finnish box office between 1973 and 1993 overwhelmingly belongs to Uuno Turhapuro, the comic character created by Pasanen & Co.[8] Uuno, 'Numbskull Emptybrook,' was developed from a few TV gags in the early 1970s. The first feature film entitled simply *Uuno Turhapuro* came out in 1973. Since then Finnish audiences have continued to enjoy Uuno's adventures in nearly 20 films so far, the latest being *UunoTurhapuro, pisnismies* (*Uuno Turhapuro, The Business Man*, 1998).

Uuno's world is constructed according to a very familiar model: his roots are in the country, from where he moved to Helsinki and married a city woman who comes from a much wealthier family. Instead of describing this setting as an unresolvable contradiction with melodramatic overtones, Pasanen uses it from film to film to create situations of humorous conflicts and misunderstandings. In this sense, the tall tale of these Turhapuro films is constituted very simply in the attempts of Uuno's father-in-law to force his daughter to get a divorce from the worthless son-in-law. Uuno, in turn, tries to undermine these attempts because he expects to get the supposedly huge inheritance.

Pasanen criticises, with deft comic procedures, the urbanised and technocratic society (embodied by Uuno's father-in-law) in which organised production and consumption are central to the official world view. In order to maintain control this society tends to repress even the most natural forms of bodily pleasure such as sleeping and eating. Food only means nutrition and sleep is only a way to prepare oneself for tomorrow's productive work. In these terms Uuno seems to be absolutely shameless: his existence is based on unproductive loitering and meaningless consumption which is verified by his favourite pursuits, excessive eating and sleeping. This attitude seems to parody the urban consumer society in which productivity and consumerism are the most important driving forces of the (post)modern world. In Uuno films the familiar fetishes of consumer culture become stripped of their masks of acceptability and social significance. In opposition to Uuno and his optimistic criticism of repressed survival, Finnish cinema of the 1970s and 1980s was otherwise largely pessimistic in trying to describe the feelings of abandonment, departure and nothingness.

A fertile field for Romantic ideas to flourish in their most simple form is the area of children's films. In this sense, children's films can be seen as the innocent and blue-eyed mediators of the basic themes, styles, images, values and scapes characteristic to a national cinema. As one of the central channels of storytelling targetted at child audiences, children's films have proceeded from an idea according to which the child exists as an address: ergo, addressing 'it' must be simple. In the background there is a Romantic or rousseauistic idea of childhood as a genuinely mythical phase.[9] According to this conception, the child exists, as it were, before culture, in a natural state. The child does not need language, because she can communicate with the environment directly by using the secret language of God's Nature which is not (any more) within the reach of adults. Communication in the adult world, however, is dictated by written and spoken languages. Therefore the most important element in moving from natural phase to cultural state, from the world of the object to the world of the sign, is language and learning to use it. One of the central and traditional characteristics of children's films is to guide the child from nature to culture, from image to language, from childhood to adulthood.

The image of thought here is a linear continuum consisting of consequent but separate transferences: nature and culture do not belong together; image and language do not enrich one another; child and adult are not equal human beings; the landscape of the countryside is fundamentally different from the landscape of the urban environments. The logistics are based on the model of cause and effect. From the perspective of the growing individual, language and family are the basic contexts. The entire storyworld of Finnish children's films and I would argue, Finnish cinema in general, is centered around these two frameworks. The basic model in the children's films is a temporarily, partly or entirely orphaned child on his/her journey towards the social prototype, the more or less nuclear family. Ultimately this is a metaphor emphasising the difference between the misery of a divergent and not yet adopted (and domesticated) child and the happiness of a child who finally finds his/her family. Many of these films end with pathetic scenes at the moment in which the lost child-protagonist re-locates his/her mother (rarely the father); the family becomes reunited, reassured, and restored. In viewing this kind of transportation as necessary, the films simultaneously idolise the presupposed, free and natural state of existence characteristic to the image of child thereby cherished.

One of the contradictory characteristics of these films has been the way of understanding child as a neutrally sexless being, as if elements of sex and gender would also belong to the adult world exclusively. At the same time, however, there exists a clear-cut division of roles concerning the opinions, stereotypes, and presumptions between characteristics defined as male or female. The almost uniform division between father/daughter and mother/son couples already refers to this. The adult perspective has determined the framework for gendered (and thereby also sexual) behaviour. On the edge of this code is the explicit or implicit transformation of the gender-free child into a man or a woman through the holy matrimony. The sexless and therefore incomplete, and unfulfilled child becomes a sexed and more complete human being, that is, an adult by learning the rituals of mating and beginning to establish the family.

The strong adult voice of children's films can be heard also in their images of adults which, likewise, are explicitly dualistic. On the one hand, there are the good adults who stand on the side of the child, and on the other, there are the bad adults, who are against the child. In the films themselves, one can discover the difference easily by the way the adults look and talk. In this world the child becomes squeezed between these contradictory, outer, and opposite forces. These groups, however, are not entirely locked; their regulated dynamics are in the ways in which the child can make a bad adult good, entailing that the adult is not yet totally 'lost'.

In the relationship between the adult and the child, money – for example, in the modes of real estate property or inheritance – has an extremely important meaning: it dictates the framework of the entire ethical, educational, moral, and religious maze in which the adults and children of these films experience their adventures. One could say bluntly that these films construct a ruthless economic and ideological power-struggle in which the child is the victim – again, both on the screen and in the audience. Children's films demarcate willingly the adult-world (culture) as separate from the child-world (nature). The latter is characterised by Romantic features of innocence, immediacy and childlike belief, and the former by dependency on money and power. In this way, children's films – aided by their own integrating and guiding ideology, and already when emphasising the dependency between a child and the family – mask in the same form their will to lead the child into the (adult) world of money and power.

In adopting the guiding role, children's films have departed (at least from their own perspective) from a very humble idea – to help the child in his/her journey from nature to culture, from childhood to adulthood, from image to language. Yet, the values of childhood have been seen in the shadow of the pregiven values of adulthood. Childhood has been seen, willingly, as an eternal and immobile myth, the defining of which the adults, and only the adults, have had their say. The same concerns are raised with the notions of image and nature. Thus, children's film is cursed to crash on two essentially adult myths, which belong to notions of both childhood and cinema. What unifies them is a thought according to which it is film and especially film that has such a recording and representational power that can make it possible for adulthood to reach the original and pure nature of childhood – if not in reality, at least virtually on the silver screen. In this way the prototypical space of Finnish cinema is the space in-between the child and the adult, assumed quintessentially as male.

The 70 years of Finnish cinema, from the early 1920s onwards, go through various stages of the Finnish landscape: from the wilds via the fields into the city thereby corresponding to the general cultural progress. Each environment has its own powerful dualities: the forest is a place of escape and shelter, but it is also a frightening and threatening place that can easily become destroyed by technology. For example, in war films exploding trees often illustrate the cruelty of violent devastation: what happens to the landscape is seen as a metaphor for what is happening in the culture in general. Similarly, the agrarian environment of villages and fields provide plenty of open space in which the flame of romance, even open eroticism, can flicker for a moment. The same milieu, season or an hour of night can also offer a framework for impulsive violence. It may even be the same dream that drives one to actions of love or crime, and correspondingly these may both have the same end result – the loss of freedom.

In the end, more than just being representations of the various opposing and interacting elements, Finnish cinema is filled with stories about moving in the space in-between the two poles – from nature to culture, from forest to village, from childhood to adulthood. The question is not what follows when it finally gets to 'the other side', but rather for how long can it wander in the space between the two.

Notes

1   'Connecting People' is one of NOKIA's major advertising slogans and NOKIA, of course, is the telecommunications company rooted in Finland.

2   This is an almost standard description of the ways in which 'progress' has been narrated in most of what has been included to the so called Finnish national literature.

3   See for example Clive, G., *The Romantic Enlightenment*, New York, Meridian Books 1960.

4   Izenberg, G. N., *Impossible Individuality; Romanticism, Revolution, and the Origins of Modern Selfhood 1787-1802*, Princeton, Princeton University Press 1992, p. 8.

5   This can be proved already by mere statistics: of the thirteen films made in Finland and premiered during the past twelve months, nine have been staged in the national history.

6   The success of particularly Finnish topics, themes and characteristics (as they were recognised for example by the popular press) in the recent films directed by Markku Pölönen (*Onnen Maa*, 1993; *Kivenpyörittäjän kylä*, 1995; *Kuningasjätkä*, 1997) has generated again opinions according to which the international screens can be conquered only by using provincial peculiarities based on the idea of the idyllic, lost, past and agrarian lifestyle, i.e. the national immanence. In these films, the landscape of the Finnish countryside becomes clearly a 'sign of the times'; contemporary nostalgia mixed with an idealistic representation of the past. More on the general history of Finnish cinema see Soila, T., Söderbergh Widding, A. & Iversen, G., *Nordic National Cinemas*, London, Routledge 1998, pp. 31-95.

7   It has been noted that *The Unknown Soldier* is just another metamorphosis of a similar group of men in the context of war.

8   More on Uuno films and the phenomenon in general in Dyer, R. & Ginette Vincendeau, G. (eds), *Popular European Cinema*, London, Routledge 1993.

9   I have studied more thoroughly the nature of Finnish children's films (through 15 examples from the 1920s till the mid-1980s) in my book, *Kuviteltuja lapsia; suomalaisen lastenelokuvan lapsikuvasta*, Painatuskeskus, Helsinki, 1987 (Imaginary Children: On the image of child in Finnish children's films). More on the 'rousseauistic' worldview in Rose, J., *The Case of Peter Pan Or the Impossibility of Children's Fiction*, London, Macmillan 1984, pp. 42-65.

East meets West: Mapping the New Europe in Yury Mamin's *A Window to Paris*

Graham Roberts

Is Russia a Western, or an Eastern country? Are Russians, as Slavs, ethnically and spiritually closer to Europe, or to Asia? This is an issue that has preoccupied generations of politicians and intellectuals, regardless of their political affiliations, in this diverse country that has a border both with Finland and with China. The debate quickly became polarised around two schools of thought that survive to this day. The first, represented by the 'Westernisers', holds that Russia is culturally part of mainstream Europe. This view is countered by the 'Slavophiles', who maintain that Russia is a *sui generis* nation-state whose spiritual roots lie in the East.[1] Since the collapse of Communism and the old Soviet Union, the argument has moved into a new and unpredictable phase, with the generally pro-Western stance of President Yeltsin and his right-hand men Boris Nemtsov and Anatoly Chubais, directly opposed by the nationalist rhetoric of Aleksandr Solzhenitsyn and Vladimir Zhirinovsky amongst others.

One of the most ardent 'Westernisers' was Peter the Great (1672–1725), the reforming tsar who realised that in order to modernise, Russia would first have to adopt Western European ideas. It was partly in a desire to do so that he moved Russia's capital geographically closer to Europe, from Moscow to St. Petersburg, the city which he founded in 1702, and which was to serve as his 'window on the West' as he himself put it. The title of the film *A Window to Paris* (*Okno v Parizh*, 1993) by St. Petersburg director Yury Mamin is a deliberate allusion to Peter's project.[2] As such, it announces Mamin's intention to contribute to the debate which the great tsar helped to initiate, as does Mamin's decision to set the action in Peter's city, still at this point named Leningrad (even throughout Soviet history Russians colloquially referred to the city as 'Peter').[3] In effect, as a summary of the plot will make clear, this film depicts a series of what are literally encounters between East and West in order to explore both Russia's place within mainstream Europe, and Russians' relationship with their homeland.

The film's main character, Nikolay Nikolaevich Chyzhov, is a music, dance and literature teacher in a St. Petersburg secondary school specialising in business studies (Mamin satirises the new capitalist mentality in Russia by lining the school's corridor with the slogan 'Time is Money' in various languages, and by the huge framed foreign bank notes hanging on the wall of the school director's office). When we meet Chyzhov he is homeless and is obliged to sleep in the school gymnasium. Before long, however, he is allotted a flat until recently occupied by an old woman who has gone missing, and is presumed dead. During the impromptu drinking binge which his new neighbours host in his honour, he discovers that one of the flat's windows leads magically out onto a rooftop in the heart of Paris. Intrigued and excited, Nikolay and his neighbours make numerous excursions through the window. They have various adventures in the French capital, while marvelling at the wonders of Western consumer culture (one of them even manages to purchase a 2CV, which is the cause of great joy!). Nikolay eventually meets a Frenchwoman, an artist (played by well-known French actress Agnès Sorel), with whom, after a series of misunderstandings and disputes, he enjoys a brief love affair.[4] Meanwhile, since his teaching methods and ideas are increasingly an anachronism in the business school where he works, Nikolay is sacked. His students win their fight to have him reinstated, however, and as a reward he takes them with him through the window to a place, as he puts it, 'where you've never been and where you're hardly likely to go'. Once there they lead a somewhat 'fairy-tale' existence, enjoying themselves at a fair-ground and busking energetically in front of the Sacré Coeur basilica on Montmartre (even though they claim not to have eaten for five days!). The film's denouement is precipitated when the window eventually closes up, as the old woman who had previously occupied Nikolay's flat and who turns up again unexpectedly, had predicted it would. The children decide to remain in Paris, optimistically telling Nikolay that they will find work (one of the girls even hints that she might turn to prostitution, since as she puts it, 'beauty is appreciated everywhere'). Nikolay's attempts to appeal to their sense of patriotism prove unsuccessful, until he takes out his piccolo and entices them, in the manner of the Pied Piper of Hamlin, to hi-jack a plane back to St. Petersburg. The film ends with them all safely back home, but still torn between their homeland and the West.

The polemic which sets Westerniser against Slavophile in Russia is essentially a debate about space, the geopolitical space which Russia occupies as it straddles two continents – Europe and Asia. So it is ironic (although perhaps not surprising) that the main structural device which Mamin uses in *A Window to Paris* to contribute to this debate is space. First, he literalises Peter the Great's spatial metaphor of St. Petersburg as 'a window on the West'. Second, he contrasts images of spaciousness, openness and freedom with those suggesting absence of space, closure and confinement, and he does so in order to draw a distinction between Russia and the West. I shall deal with each of these areas in turn.

As far as the window itself is concerned, perhaps its most striking feature is the ease with which Nikolay and his neighbours are able to pass through it. They in fact stumble on the window by sheer accident, experiencing its magical powers for the first time while still under the effects of alcohol from Nikolay's flat-warming party. They are suddenly woken from their drunken slumbers by the flat's former occupant, who appears as if from nowhere looking for her cat. When she finds the animal she disappears back through the window. Following her, Nikolay and the others suddenly find themselves in the French capital, and wander round for a while as if in a trance. The next day one of Nikolay's neighbours realises that their journey was not a dream, but reality, a fact which in true community spirit he loses no time sharing with Nikolay. Passing through the window, as he demonstrates, is perfectly simple, even if one's body and voice become temporarily distorted in the process. Throughout the rest of the film, the window is used so frequently to pass from one city to the other by all manner of people that Mamin doesn't even bother showing it again. As viewers, we are invited to become as blasé about the window and its magical properties as Mamin's characters.

The apparent effortlessness with which these characters are able to pass through the window from St. Petersburg to Paris and back again no doubt alludes to the fact that it is so much easier now for citizens of post-Soviet Russia and indeed all the former Warsaw Pact countries to travel not just to Western Europe but to anywhere in the world (provided, of course, they can pay). Physical contiguity also underlines the relative geographical proximity of St. Petersburg and Paris (and thereby of the countries for which they stand metonymically). Furthermore, the fact that these cities are so close is buttressed by all sorts of other details which they appear to share, such as taxis, bars, a metro, prostitution, and even out-of-tune pianos (among his various talents, Nikolay is an obsessive piano tuner). Yet it soon becomes clear that such resemblances as there are between these two places are purely superficial, and do not amount to similarity in any meaningful sense. The ease of travel through the window serves in fact as an ironic comment on just how different these two cultures, these two spaces, really are.

The gulf which separates Paris and St. Petersburg becomes obvious the very first time Nikolay and his neighbours venture through the window. In a short but deeply satirical scene, they stumble into a bar in what they still believe to be St. Petersburg, only to find themselves confronted by a rather taciturn barman who refuses to accept their rouble notes, however many they offer him. Surmising, as well they might, that they are in one of the many hard-currency bars for which Soviet Russia was so renowned, they become somewhat exasperated, until the French barman takes a liking to the image of Lenin on their rouble coins. Taking the coins, presumably as a souvenir of his first ever Russian customers, the barman finally serves them. Nikolay and his friends slake their thirst on what they describe as the best beer they've ever had, before toppling out of the bar, none the wiser as to their actual whereabouts. This dialogue of the deaf speaks volumes for the inability of Russians and Westernisers to understand each other, despite apparent social and cultural similarities.

Throughout the film, Mamin emphasises how easy it is to pass through the window precisely in order to underline how radically different these cultures are. Perhaps the best example of this occurs when Nikolay catches up with an old school friend. The friend, who emigrated to the West several years ago, now plays the violin in a chic Parisian restaurant. His method of playing, by running the violin over a bow positioned firmly between his thighs, is hardly conventional, however, and smacks more of the circus ring than of music (it is also visually very funny). He pre-empts Nikolay's criticism by reiterating the stereotypical Russian view of the French, to the effect that they are an uncultured lot, who are interested only in the pleasures of the table (an opinion with which Nikolay finds himself unable to agree). As they walk through the Paris streets that same night, the violinist stops in front of a travel agent's window. He points out that although all his material needs are satisfied by his life in Paris, and since emigrating he has been able to travel all over the world, nevertheless he is deeply unhappy. He misses Russia intensely and would give anything, as he tells Nikolay, to be able to return to his old communal flat in St. Petersburg, if only just for a few minutes. When Nikolay assures him that he can be there within half an hour, his friend dismisses this idea as ridiculous. The camera cuts immediately to the two men in a taxi hurtling through the Petersburg streets, with the violinist blindfolded, still thinking he is in Paris. They eventually get out in front of one of St. Petersburg's most famous landmarks, the statue of Lenin in the Pribaltiskaya area of the city. Realising where he is, the violinist does not thank Nikolay, but instead gets down on his knees and begs to be taken back to Paris, evidently missing the good life in the French capital far more than his old life in Russia (the Russian emigre's ambivalent attitude towards the homeland is one of many targets for Mamin's satire). Just as Mamin chooses to collapse space (and time) by eliding over the journey to St. Petersburg, so we are not shown the return trip to Paris.

In this and so many other scenes, Mamin's camera cuts seamlessly between the two cities, with an effortlessness akin to the ease with which the characters pass through the window itself. This is in direct contrast to, and underscores in an ironic way, the almost total lack of comprehension which exists, both between West and East, and between Russians who have emigrated and those who choose to stay at home. The disappearance of all space, of any physical barrier between the two cities serves only to accentuate the existence of so many other barriers – cultural, spiritual and economic.[5] These are reinforced by the language barrier on which the characters stumble at so many times during the film. Nikolay's attempts at French are comically poor, while all that the Frenchwoman whom he falls in love with manages to reproduce in Russian is a string of the coarsest invective, directed against her new 'neighbours' who slowly invade her private space (Mamin seems here to be making the point that it is their inability to comprehend the concept of 'private space', more than anything else, which sets these Russians apart from their French 'hosts').

The window is important not just for the ease with which one passes through it, however, but also in its own terms, for what it represents as metaphor. The window is in fact a rich image suggestive of openness and space (Nikolay's neighbour describes the window as 'otkrytie veka', which means 'the discovery of the century', but could also be interpreted as 'the opening of the century', from the verb 'otkryt', meaning both 'to discover', and 'to open').

In *A Window to Paris*, the window is a central part of the dichotomy which Mamin establishes between openness and confinement, an opposition which serves further to underscore the distinction between East and West. Mamin paints a utopian vision of a West to which every Russian is striving,[6] and manipulates images of space in order to bolster that vision. How exactly does Mamin use space to this end?

Despite what might be termed the film's 'magical realism' (buttressed by the allusion to Pushkin's anti-realist story 'The Queen of Spades'), at the heart of *A Window to Paris* lies a simple opposition, one which rests upon a distinction between two spatial paradigms. St. Petersburg (and by extension Russia) is characterised by images of closure and confinement, while Paris (and by implication the West) is distinguished by a sense of openness and freedom.

At this juncture it might be appropriate to say something about the history of St. Petersburg as a city and about the way the city has been represented in Russian culture. St. Petersburg occupies in fact a very special place at the heart of Russian culture and indeed the Russian psyche, essentially because it did not evolve naturally but arose virtually overnight, the product of its founder's imagination. In much nineteenth-century Russian literature it was portrayed as an unreal, magical place, where all manner of strange things might happen, where the spirit of a dead countess might haunt a young card-sharp (as in Pushkin's 'The Queen of Spades'), a bronze statue of Peter the Great might pursue a man through the city streets (Pushkin's 'Mednyi vsadnik' ['The Bronze Horseman', 1825]), or a civil servant might wake up one day to find that his nose has disappeared, as in Nikolay Gogol's 'Nos' ('The Nose', 1835). The idea that a St. Petersburg flat might be equipped with a window affording direct access to a foreign country in a manner contrary to the laws of physics is perfectly consistent with this tradition. However, at the same time – and this is a crucial point – Mamin's association of the city with physical entrapment runs entirely counter to this same tradition, which generally represented the city as endless (if controlled) space, with its perfectly geometric streets stretching out as if into infinity.[7]

Right from the opening shots of *A Window to Paris*, the city of St. Petersburg is associated with *enclosed* spaces, creating a sense of entrapment (hardly consonant with Peter the Great's original vision of the city as a 'window'). The film begins with the close-up of a policeman's face, peering through the keyhole of the old woman's flat, trying to ascertain whether she is inside. The camera then cuts to the woman's anxious neighbours huddled together on the landing, framing them very closely so as to suggest a lack of space (Mamin's use of the camera and framing throughout the film plays an important role in accentuating confinement or openness). When he finally breaks into the flat, the policeman looks for its inhabitant *in confined spaces*, namely in the wardrobe and under a table (despite the fact that she is highly unlikely to be in either location). The only sense of openness in this scene comes, not coincidentally, when the camera focuses on paintings of Paris hanging on the old woman's wall.[8]

Similarly, the first time we see Nikolay he is living in an extremely confined space; he wakes up in what appears to be a bedroom, but is then revealed to be an alcove at one end of the gymnasium in the school where he teaches. When Nikolay moves into his new flat, his lack of space is once again emphasised; on his arrival he explains that he's been allotted an 'eighteen square meter flat', and then his friends arrive carrying assorted pieces of furniture, many of which have to be stored in the corridor. Given this repeated emphasis on the lack of space, it is both supremely ironic and extremely fitting that the window which leads out of Nikolay's new flat and into Paris is located behind a wardrobe, a piece of furniture designed specifically to confine.

What is particularly interesting about Mamin's depiction of St. Petersburg in these opening scenes is that he refuses to show us external shots of the city at all.[9] In fact, virtually the first time we see anything of the outside world of St. Petersburg is when the Agnès Sorel character ends up there, accomplishing Nikolay's journey in reverse (this occurs two-thirds of the way into the film). Pursuing one of the Russians, who has stolen a stuffed parrot from her studio, she follows him unsuspectingly back through the window into St. Petersburg. After a struggle she finds herself locked out of the communal flat, stranded on the landing in just a bath robe. Unaware that she is now in St. Petersburg, she makes her way out onto the street in search of help. However, instead of a long, busy street stretching far into the distance (such as the famous Nevsky Prospect, so often the metonymic image of the city itself, as in Gogol's story of the same name), she finds herself in an empty courtyard. This is not just the enclosed urban space *par excellence*, but is both alien to her as a Parisian who speaks no Russian, and potentially threatening to her as a woman (one dressed in nothing but a bath robe, into the bargain). This last fact, the gendered nature of space, is alluded to by the graffiti she walks past ('khui', which means 'cock', or prick'), and also by the two men urinating against a wall whom she unknowingly asks for help (Mamin here seems ignorant of the fact that this is a particularly frequent habit amongst Gallic males too).[10] This sense of enclosure and entrapment is accentuated here by the fact that we are not allowed by Mamin's camera to see the sky, or even the tops of buildings. When some rubbish thrown out of a window lands just in front of her, the woman looks up to see where it came from, but crucially the camera does not follow her gaze. When she finally emerges, by now very frightened, onto a street (through a low archway), the camera follows her either at eye level, or from just above her. This makes her appear small, and therefore vulnerable in this alien space, a fact reinforced subsequently when we see her in a market square full of people, whose bodies press against hers, and whose faces fill the screen. This sense of oppression and imprisonment is complete a short while later when, following an altercation with two Russian policemen, she finds herself in a St. Petersburg police cell (this is a cue for Mamin to satirise Russian policeman as both stupid and corrupt; Nikolay frees her by pretending that they are Edith Piaf and Elvis Presley, and by offering the officers bribes).

The sense of St. Petersburg as enclosed and oppressive urban space, so central to this entire scene, is supported by other images elsewhere in the film. For example, there is the telephone booth on the St. Petersburg street which a youth suddenly smashes up, as if in response to a desire to break free of the booth's confining glass walls. In another scene two Frenchmen who have wandered through the window and have been arrested as vagrants are shown on Russian television, which is another transparent box, and serves as a further, succinct image of entrapment. We are, in fact, shown very little of the city itself as external space with virtually all of the St. Petersburg scenes occurring either in Nikolay's flat or in the school where he teaches (classroom, gym, corridor or director's office). When we do see the city's streets, this is generally at night (as in the taxi ride to Lenin's statue or the escape by Nikolay and his French accomplice from the police station), and the absence of light only accentuates the impression of confinement.

All of this is in stark contrast to the way in which Mamin depicts Paris, which he represents as a city of vast open space. Most obviously, the window itself leads from the confinement of Nikolay's St. Petersburg flat out onto the open rooftop of a Parisian apartment, which affords panoramic views over the whole of the city (Mamin wastes no opportunity to show us familiar Parisian landmarks such as the Eiffel Tower and Notre Dame). The presence on the roof of a large TV satellite dish serves to underscore this impression of openness to the world until, that is, one of Nikolay's neighbours steals it. There is a particularly marked contrast between on the one hand Nikolay's flat, which is dark, cramped and at times crammed full of people (to say nothing of the 2CV!), and on the other hand the Frenchwoman's apartment, which is spacious enough to serve as her artist's studio, and is very bright, thanks, not insignificantly, to its glass ceiling through which its occupant can contemplate the Paris sky.[11] The artist's flat soon becomes an open thoroughfare for the Russians, who traipse through it time and time again, as if it were a public space, rather than a private apartment. And while enclosed courtyards feature prominently in Mamin's St. Petersburg, the director here shows us plenty of Parisian boulevards, mostly from up above. In this way the viewer has the impression that s/he is floating freely above the city as in a dream, in contrast to the nightmare world of St. Petersburg.

Ironically, while St. Petersburg is in reality the city of 'white nights', in Mamin's film it is in Paris that the distinction between day and night becomes blurred, in a way which reinforces the impression of the city as open space. As Nikolay paddles in the Seine, the screen is suddenly filled with the lights of a passing *bateau mouche* sailing down the river. In another scene, Nikolay looks out from a rooftop to the Eiffel Tower, framed against the dawn sky. Indeed, in stark contrast to the way in which St. Petersburg is depicted, in Paris we are constantly shown shots of rooftops and of the sky. The height of the city's buildings is repeatedly emphasised. It is perhaps no coincidence that just before Nikolay and the children return to Russia, they find themselves at Montmartre, in front of the Sacré Coeur basilica, on what is probably the highest point in all Paris. Even as they all march triumphantly through Paris Charles de Gaulle airport, the terminal building, with its steel and glass moving walkways, is represented as spacious and bright (and is shot from ground level up, thereby adding to the impression of openness). There is very much a sense here that Nikolay is taking the children back to the prison where their destiny belongs, a feeling which undercuts the tone of magical realism with which this whole scene is infused.

It is Paris, not St. Petersburg, that is represented as a 'magical' space – hence the boulevard that suddenly transforms itself into a ballroom at one point in the film. And it is Paris, not St. Petersburg, which is depicted as a city of almost infinite space; indeed, three of Nikolay's neighbours spend almost the entire film travelling around the French capital in a taxi, and in a sharply satirical scene they pretend to be a delegation of Russian Communists, turning up at an international political gathering to plead, 'in the name of Communism, pay our taxi fare'.[12] In recent Russian culture, as N. Sirvilya has pointed out (1993, p. 20), the cities of Paris and New York:

> function essentially as symbols of that other-worldly reality where solutions can be found to all those problems which torment us and to which we have no answer, where man has

already built a free, comfortable and safe society commensurate to his needs, a society which in every respect is the opposite of that chaos, discomfort, lack of freedom and total danger which oppresses us.

As we have tried to show, one of the most important ways in which Mamin posits Paris as this 'other-worldly reality' is his manipulation of space, and specifically his radically different representation of space in Paris and St. Petersburg respectively.

This contrast between St. Petersburg confinement and Parisian openness is used by Mamin to bolster what is in many respects, as N. Sirivlya observes, a utopian vision of Western consumer culture. The viewer is invited to marvel at, for example, the 40 types of ham on sale at a Paris market stall, the French beer which apparently tastes so much better than the Russian equivalent, the powerful motor bikes parked in a Paris side street, the row upon row of television sets in an electrical store, or the splendid church with its ornate glass window, into which Nikolay peers while standing in the porchway. Even the fish one catches are much bigger in the Seine than in the Neva (the river on which St. Petersburg stands), as one of Nikolay's neighbours discovers when he too travels through the window to Paris.[13] The three buskers whom at one point we see happily dancing in front of the Sacré Coeur are also a highly sanitised version of Parisian reality.

Ultimately, however, Mamin pulls up short of an entirely pro-Western, anti-Russian film. As Sirvilya astutely observes, Mamin offers a deeply ambivalent vision of Western Europe in *A Window to Paris*. For example, Nikolay and his neighbours take every opportunity to point out the contradictions of this society. One of them wanders about the point of having so many different types of ham if nobody is buying anything. As the same character remarks, alluding to the spiritual gulf which every Russian knows exists between East and West, 'they [in the West] built such churches and yet they don't believe in God'. Mamin reinforces this notion of spiritual emptiness here through his visual depiction of the church as space; as the camera focuses on Nikolay, standing in the entrance, so the inside of the building remains underexposed, a black hole of nothingness. Western society emerges as aesthetically as well as spiritually dead. The Agnès Sorel character spends much of her time producing kitsch, her artistic talent directed towards such activities as stuffing the dead pets of the Parisian bourgeoisie. Mamin also hints at social inequality. In two dreams which Nikolay has, we are presented with an alternative vision of Paris, where beggars sleep in the middle of the street under piles of rubbish and forage for frogs(!), while children dressed in rags wander through the streets of Pigalle at the mercy of pimps and prostitutes. It is significant that in order to reinforce this sense of oppression, Mamin chooses to leave the camera at street level in these two dream sequences, thereby creating a sense of confinement and enclosure hitherto associated not with Paris but rather with St. Petersburg. The real problem is not intrinsically with the West, however. Rather it is the fact that Russians find it so difficult to adapt to this alien culture. This is made perfectly clear when Nikolay's friend and compatriot the violinist finds him a job as a concert pianist. When Nikolay turns up for his debut performance, it emerges that the orchestra he has joined is in fact a naturist association; none of the musicians is wearing any trousers, and no-one in the audience is wearing any clothes at all!

The film's ultimate message, spelled out unambiguously to the children by Nikolay as he stands (anti-)heroically against the Paris skyline, is that 'you may not like Russia, but it is your country, and it is up to you to save it'.[14] Once this has been articulated, and they have all returned to Russia, Mamin's depiction of the city of St. Petersburg changes radically as if in order to chime in with this 'happy ending'. Now for the first time, we actually see the St. Petersburg sky, in which fireworks explode as if in celebration of the children's return. Even here, however, Mamin's use of space is tinged with ambivalence; the patch of sky we see is over the St. Peter and Paul Fortress, not just one of the city's most famous landmarks, but a place of very real imprisonment and confinement. Mamin's ambivalence towards St. Petersburg as urban space is evident in the film's closing sequence, which follows shortly after the fireworks. Nikolay sees the old woman's cat go through a hole in a wall, but when he tries to follow it, the hole disappears. He and his neighbours are then seen chipping away at the wall which, while obviously very solid, is also very high, dwarfing the men as the camera moves progressively back. Confinement and spaciousness come together in this, the very final image of the film, held while the closing credits roll. The suggestion here is surely that although the Berlin Wall has come down, there are still much higher walls in people's imagination preventing a true encounter between East and West.[15]

To conclude, Mamin uses a variety of images of urban space (window, apartment, courtyard, boulevard, rooftop, sky), in order to establish a dichotomy between enclosure and openness, the private and the public, confinement and freedom. He does so in an attempt to draw a distinction between Russia and the West (a distinction which he nevertheless subverts in order to achieve a hollow, deeply ambivalent 'happy ending'). This is not to say that Mamin is either a 'Slavophile' or a 'Westerniser'; most of the Russian characters in this film are vulgar and unsophisticated, while the French are mainly soulless snobs.[16] What Mamin does in *A Window to Paris* is simply draw these two cultures as close as possible together in a way which underlines that they remain worlds apart.[17] In doing so, Mamin satirises his compatriots' starry-eyed love of the West, and all things western. At the same time, however, he articulates the current dilemma facing not just Russians but all Eastern Europeans – that their newly-acquired freedom has brought with it new responsibilities, at the price of the old certainties.[18] Whether Russians, Poles and others can use that freedom to map a genuine space for themselves in the New European Order remains to be seen.

Notes

1. For an excellent account of this issue, see Taylor (1996).
2. For short accounts of Mamin's film career before 1993, see Horton and Brashinsky (1991), pp. 201-7, and Lawton (1992), pp. 216-21. Amongst Western and Russian scholars alike Mamin enjoys a reputation as 'one of the brightest satirical lights on the Soviet horizon of the late 1980s and early 1990s' (Horton and Brashinsky, 1991, p. 201).
3. For the sake of simplicity I will refer throughout this paper to the city as 'St. Petersburg'.
4. One of the curious features of *A Window to Paris* is that Nikolay is the only character to be named. As

well as adding to the film's 'magical realist' properties, this poses not a little difficulty for the critic attempting to write about the film.

5. This clash of opposites is also a feature *within post-Soviet Russia itself*, where two cultures, one traditionally Russian, the other Western and capitalist, now conflict. A perfect example of this is provided in Mamin's film when one of Nikolay's literature lessons, during which he reads the children Aleksandr Pushkin's fantastic story 'The Queen of Spades' ('Pikovaya dama', 1833) is unceremoniously disrupted by men installing computers in the classroom.

6. A similar point is made in the generally negative review of the film by Sirvilya (1993).

7. See, for example, Nikolay Gogol''s St. Petersburg stories, especially 'Nevsky Prospect' ('Nevsky Prospekt', 1835) and 'The Overcoat' ('Shinel'', 1843), and also Andrey Bely's Symbolist novel *Petersburg* (*Peterburg*; 1912).

8. In a similar sense, the framed giant-sized bank notes hanging on the wall in the school director's office can be interpreted as 'windows' onto the capitalist world (they serve as 'icons' to capitalism, rather as, in the Russian Orthodox faith, icons function literally as 'windows' to God).

9. This general absence of external space is reminiscent of what may be regarded as the last text of the St. Petersburg literary tradition, namely Daniil Kharms's 1939 novella, 'The Old Woman' ('Starukha'), in which the main character is also confronted with an old woman in his flat. On this story, and its place within the St. Petersburg literary tradition, see Carrick (1995).

10. It may be appropriate to point out here that in Russian popular mythology, the city of St. Petersburg has always been regarded as 'male' (by analogy with its founder), while Moscow, on the other hand, has tended to be viewed as 'female'. It should also be noted that there is a tendency in Russian culture, as in many others, to define interior and domestic space as female, and exterior, public space as male. The scene in the courtyard is fully consonant with this trend. For a discussion of how contemporary Russian women writers are engaging with and subverting this tradition, see Goscilo (1996).

11. One is reminded by the relative opulence of the French artist's flat of Dave Kehr's comment on Krzysztof Kieslowski's *Three Colours: Blue* (*Trois Couleurs: Bleu*, 1993), to the effect that '*Blue* takes place in a Paris that could only be imagined by an Eastern outsider' (Kehr, 1994, p. 16).

12. The particular neighbour who gives the speech looks and sounds not unlike Mikhail Gorbachev, in what is clearly a jibe at the clichéed, humourless mannerisms of Russian Communists, past and present.

13. While articulating these Russian clichés of the West, Mamin pokes fun at Western clichJs of Russia. In one scene, he shows Russian women dressed in folk costume walking through a market selling Russian dolls entitled 'glasnost' and 'perestroika'. At another moment, Nikolay's neighbour plays a well-known tune from Tchaikovsky's *Swan Lake* on his barrel organ.

14. In an interview given shortly before *A Window to Paris*, Mamim claimed: 'My next film will be about the problem of staying or leaving the Soviet Union [sic]. I feel that leaving it because of the current troubles is a tragedy' (quoted in Horton, 1993, p. 155).

15. As reviewers have pointed out, *A Window to Paris* depicts a meeting not so much between East and West, as between clichés about East and West. To quote Bob Thompson, writing in *The Toronto Sun*: 'East-West culture clashes, greed and the pretence of politics are given the once-over in the most predictable of ways' (Thompson, 1997).

16. Sergei Lavrentiev (1994, p. 136) has read Mamin's films as warnings against the dangers of Russian nationalism.

17. By the way in which it explores the cultural relationship between East and West, Mamin's film is typical of a recent trend in East European cinema. One thinks, for example, of Krzysztof Kieslowski's *Three*

Colours: White (*Trois Couleurs: Blanc*, 1994), in which a Pole returns from Paris to his homeland smuggled inside a compatriot's suitcase. On this film, see Coates (1996-1997), and Roberts (1999). One Russian film which comes to mind here is Petr Todorovsky's *Intergirl* (*Interdevochka*, 1988), whose heroine, Tanya, is a hard-currency prostitute working in Leningrad who marries a Swedish businessman and goes to live with him in Sweden, with disastrous consequences. On *Intergirl*, see Lawton (1992, pp. 211-13,) and Attwood (ed., 1993, pp. 118-19).

18. This dilemma between freedom and security is nothing new in Russia culture. It is explored in a number of works of nineteenth- and twentieth-century Russian literature, such as Dostoevsky's *The Brothers Karamazov* (*Brat'ya Karamazovy*, 1880), and Yevgeny Zamyatin's *We* (*My*, 1921), the latter of which served as a blueprint for George Orwell's *1984*.

Bibliography

Attwood, L. (ed.), *Red Women on the Silver Screen: Soviet Women and Cinema from the Beginning to the End of the Communist Era*, London, Pandora, 1993.

Carrick, N., 'A Familiar Story: Insurgent Narratives and Generic Refugees in Daniil Kharms's *The Old Woman*', *Modern Language Review*, 90, 1995, pp. 707-21.

Coates, P., 'The Sense of an Ending: Reflections on Kieslowski's Trilogy', *Film Quarterly*, 50:2, 1996-1997, pp. 19-26.

Goscilo, H., 'Women's Space and Women's Place in Contemporary Russian Fiction', in Marsh, R. (ed.), *Gender and Russian Literature: New Perspectives* (Cambridge, Cambridge University Press, 1996), pp. 326-47.

Horton, A. (ed.), *Inside Soviet Film Satire: Laughter with a Lash*, Cambridge, Cambridge University Press, 1993.

Horton, A. & Brashinsky, M., *The Zero Hour: Glasnost and Soviet Cinema in Transition*, Princeton, NJ, Princeton University Press, 1991.

Kehr, D., 'To Save the World: Kieslowski's THREE COLORS Trilogy', *Film Comment*, Nov-Dec, 1994, pp. 10-20.

Lavrentiev, S., 'Taxi Blues, Taxi Fares, and Film Viewers', in Brashinsky, M. & Horton, A. (eds.), *Russian Critics on the Cinema of Glasnost* (Cambridge, Cambridge University Press, 1994), pp. 135-7.

Lawton, A., *Kinoglasnost. Soviet Cinema in Our Time*, Cambridge, Cambridge University Press, 1992.)

Roberts, G., 'Double Lives: Europe and Identity in the Later Films of Krzysztof Kieslowski', in Andrew, J., Crook, M., Holmes, D. and Kolinsky, E. (eds.), *Why Europe? Problems of Culture and Identity*, vol. 2: Media, Film, Gender, Youth & Education (Basingstoke – London, Macmillan, 1999).

Sirvilya, N., 'Opyat' khochu v Parizh!', *Iskusstvo kino*, No. 7, 1993, pp. 19-23.

Taylor, R., 'The Double-Headed Eagle: Russia – East or West?', in Bideleux, R. and Taylor, R. (eds.), *European Integration and Disintegration: East and West* (London – New York, Routledge, 1996), pp. 252-80.

Thompson, B., [review of *A Window to Paris* in *The Toronto Sun*, 1997] (http:www.canoe.ca/JamMovieReviewsW/windowparis.html)